NORMAN HALL'S

CORRECTIONS OFFICER

EXAM
PREPARATION BOOK

Also by Norman Hall

Norman Hall's Firefighter's Exam Preparation Book
Norman Hall's Police Exam Preparation Book
Norman Hall's Postal Exam Preparation Book
Norman Hall's State Trooper & Highway Patrol Exam Preparation Book

NORMAN HALL'S
CORRECTIONS OFFICER
EXAM PREPARATION BOOK

by Norman Hall

Adams Media Corporation
Avon, Massachusetts

Published by
Adams Media, an F+W Publications Company
57 Littlefield Street, Avon, MA 02322. U.S.A.
www.adamsmedia.com

ISBN 10: 1-59337-389-9
ISBN 13: 978-1-59337-389-4
Printed in Canada.

J I H G F E D C B

Hall, Norman
The corrections officer exam preparation book / by Norman, Hall.
p.   cm.

1. Correctional personnel — United States — Examinations, questions, etc.
2. Corrections — Vocational guidance — United States.
3. Employment tests — United States. I. Title.
HV9470.H35 1997
365'.076 — dc21   97-22916
CIP

This publication is designed to provide accurate and authoritative information with regard to the subject matter covered. It is sold with the understanding that the publisher is not engaged in rendering legal, accounting, or other professional advice. If legal advice or other expert assistance is required, the services of a competent professional person should be sought.

— From a *Declaration of Principles* jointly adopted by a Committee of the American Bar Association and a Committee of Publishers and Associations

The names used in this book (of suspects and victims) are fictional.
Any similarities to real people are unintentional.

Illustrators: Mark Divico, Kevin Millette, and Marnie Swenson

This book is available at quantity discounts for bulk purchases.
For information, call 1-800-289-0963.

Contents

Preface

Congratulations on your selective choice of exam preparation material. By purchasing this study guide you now have it within your means to give yourself a competitive edge over others. Those who possess such an advantage are typically the successful candidates that get hired.

Competition for Corrections Officer jobs was only moderate, at best, in years past. However, with the advent of private industry downsizing and closures, overseas job exportation, and automation, job security is becoming a major concern for many. Corrections Officer positions offer not only job security, but now have excellent wage and benefit packages, too. It is not hard to understand why competition for these jobs has recently become much more intense.

Since a high test score is the key to getting hired, thorough preparation for the exam offers the means to achieve this goal. By using this study guide, you will, without question, gain a competitive edge over other applicants. At the completion of your studies, you will know exactly what to expect on the exam, how to manage your time during the test, how to best handle the most difficult test sections, and how to avoid common mistakes and pitfalls. You can be certain that you will be able to approach the exam with complete confidence and a sense of ease.

Furthermore, we offer **Guaranteed Test Results**. If, after using this manual, you do not score 80 percent or better on your Corrections Officer exam, you can return this study guide to the publisher for a complete refund (see the back page for details). No other publication offers anything comparable, which should indicate to you how serious I am about helping you with your Department of Corrections job endeavors. I have a personal stake in your success and, as such, I will provide you with the most current, up-to-date material available. Before you begin your study, I would like to wish you the best. Once you are hired by Corrections, the rewards and job satisfaction are great and the service you provide to the community is invaluable.

—*Norman S. Hall*

Chapter 1

Becoming a Corrections Officer

The employment outlook for Corrections Officer positions is, without doubt, the best it has ever been. There are over three thousand federal, state, and municipal correctional facilities nationwide. Statistics provided by the Bureau of Justice show that prisoner populations have more than doubled to over 1.3 million just during the past ten years. That same trend can be expected to continue, too, largely due to the general public's growing intolerance of crime. As a direct consequence of a higher incarceration rate, record amounts of tax dollars have been dedicated to the development of new prisons and the hiring of new Corrections Officers to staff those facilities.

Additionally, there is the ever-present need to fill positions vacated through normal employee turnover. This can be attributed to promotions, transfers, disabilities, retirement, or people just leaving the profession for unspecified personal reasons. Whatever the case, employee turnover rates can vary between 5–25 percent of an existing work force, depending on the locality in question.

For these reasons it is important that the Department of Corrections maintain an active register of qualified people to hire from as vacancies arise. The frequency of exams given to screen prospective applicants can vary. Typically, exams are given once a year; however, some departments examine two or three times annually, depending on the personnel needs of a given jurisdiction. Public test announcements are made several weeks in advance of the exam in the local media — newspaper, radio, and even television — specifying when and where people can apply for the test. Another means of keeping abreast of exam dates is to submit a completed job application form to the Civil Service personnel office. Then when exam dates are determined, you will be promptly notified by mail. This option circumvents the possibility of overlooking a public test announcement.

There are some basic minimum requirements that job applicants must meet for employment eligibility. You must:

- be a U.S. citizen at the time of appointment.

- be at least twenty-one years old and not over forty (minimum and maximum age may vary).

- provide proof of high school graduation or satisfactory completion of the GED test.

- possess a valid state driver's license.

- not have any felony convictions or a dishonorable discharge from military service.

- not use illegal drugs (i.e., pass a drug-screening test).

- have normal color vision and better than 20/100 vision in both eyes, corrected to 20/20 in the better eye and 20/30 in the lesser eye (vision requirements may vary).

- meet minimum medical and psychological standards as prescribed by the Civil Service.

- satisfy residency requirements by the date of hire, if necessary.

Other desirable accomplishments or abilities that would better qualify an applicant would include:

- an associate's degree or course work relating to law enforcement/criminal justice from an accredited college.

- good communication skills, both oral and written. Bilingual applicants are especially sought after by corrections personnel, particularly if the non-English language known is used by local jail populations.

- ability to work under stressful conditions, and to maintain a collective sense of direction.

- ability to work with others as a unit and follow instructions from supervisors.

- some knowledge of first aid and emergency medical care.

THE SELECTION PROCESS

Entry-level Corrections Officer candidates have a wide range of responsibilities. In general, inmate processing and security at a correctional facility or work-release unit is the primary focus. However, that can entail anything from instructing inmates on procedures and regulations to responding to emergency situations requiring physical restraint. (Further details pertaining to essential job functions will be given in the job description section of this study guide.) Not only can the workload be as diverse as it is challenging, it must be accomplished in a professional manner apart from prejudice, manipulation, or favoritism. This requires the candidate to be of sound character, emotionally stable, reliable, and able to act independently within established guidelines. Consequently, it is easy to understand why departments have to thoroughly screen job applicants. The steps that most departments follow in their selection process include the written exam, physical abilities test, oral review board, and background, psychological, and medical evaluations. There may be exceptions to either the order or contents of this screening process, but by and large this accurately reflects what can be expected by a prospective applicant. A brief description of each step involved is given here; elaborations appear in sections throughout this book.

THE WRITTEN EXAM

The Corrections Officer exam is a general aptitude test normally comprising from 75 to 125 multiple-choice questions. Essay-type questions pertaining to report writing and correct grammar usage have been seen on past exams, but only on rare occasions. You are generally given from 1 1/2 to 3 1/2 hours to complete the test. In most cases there are fees ranging from $5 to $25 to cover the cost of submitting these exams; however, applicants who currently receive public assistance or supplemental social security may be exempted (though documentation to that effect will be necessary for a waiver).

The test questions themselves will concern such areas as:

- memory
- reading comprehension
- situational judgment and reasoning
- coding interpretation
- report writing
- grammar, vocabulary, and spelling
- basic mathematics

Although most questions relate to law enforcement/criminal justice, you are not expected to have the same knowledge as an experienced Corrections Officer. Instead, your grasp of general concepts, logic, and reasoning are the main focus of the exam. A passing score consists of 70 percent or better, but to have a realistic chance at employment in most jurisdictions you should place in the top 20 percent. Do not let this aspect be the cause of any undue apprehension. The fact that you have chosen to do the advance preparation using this study guide will most likely give you a top ranking score. Ill-prepared applicants, on the other hand, have a legitimate concern.

Note to military service veterans: Veterans from any branch of the military service may qualify to have additional preference points added to their test scores. If you served in Vietnam between August 5, 1964, and May 7, 1975, or have received the Armed Forces Expeditionary Medal or the Marine Corps or Navy Expeditionary Medal for opposed action on foreign soil (e.g., Iran, Southeast Asia, Grenada, or Lebanon) or the Service Medal for Operation Desert Storm and received an honorable discharge, you may qualify for five additional points.

If you are an honorably discharged veteran who served in active duty in the armed forces at any time and have a service-connected disability for which you may or may not receive compensation, have been awarded the Purple Heart, or are a spouse, widow, or mother of a deceased or disabled veteran, you may qualify for ten additional points. A copy of your DD Form 214 will be required to substantiate the claim. Further specifics are available upon request by contacting the office of personnel of the department to which you intend to apply.

In some instances, when you are notified via mail as to the time and place of the written exam, sample test material will be enclosed. By all means study every page made available. There is an excellent chance that the very material or a comparable facsimile may be incorporated into the actual exam. For this reason, do not take any of this information for granted.

There should also be a map and/or set of directions provided on how to get to the examination site. Review these as well, allowing yourself plenty of time to get there. Thirty minutes to one hour early is desirable. Traffic congestion or unforeseen road construction, particularly in metropolitan areas, have prevented a fair share of applicants from taking the exam. Once the exam has started, latecomers *are not permitted to take the test.* Rescheduled makeup exams are rarely given unless there are extenuating circumstances, and even then it may be submitted at a much later date. The bottom line is not to miss an exam in the first place due to poor planning.

Prior to being admitted to the exam room, you will need to furnish a current picture identification card, which can either be a driver's license or military ID card. Additionally, the validated test application form that was mailed to you earlier will need to be furnished as well. An applicant lacking any of this documentation will not be permitted in the exam room. Do not bring a briefcase, a purse, notepaper, a calculator, a spell checker/dictionary, or a thesaurus with you to the exam; none of these items are permissible. Only a couple of No. 2 pencils will be acceptable. All other materials needed for the exam will be provided by those submitting the exam.

When the examiner gives any kind of instruction, pay close attention. The examiner will explain how to properly fill in personal information that will be used to identify your exam results, and how and when to proceed on the exam. Do not deviate in any manner from established test procedure. If you do, you may disqualify yourself altogether.

A real bonus about multiple-choice exams is that you know that one of the choices has to be the correct selection. Even if the right answer is not immediately apparent, some choices can be eliminated on their own merit, thus further increasing your chances of selecting the correct answer. Another advantage to this form of exam is that if the time remaining to complete the test becomes a crucial factor, you can still mark answers at random (i.e., guess) and still have a 25 percent chance (A, B, C, or D) of picking the correct choice. You are not penalized for incorrect choices unless otherwise stipulated by the examiner. Therefore, it behooves you not to leave any questions unanswered, if possible.

You will be provided an answer sheet, which is usually separate from the test booklet, and a blank sheet of paper for mathematical calculations, notes, or general figuring. It is imperative not to make extraneous marks on an answer sheet; the machine that scores your exam can misconstrue such a marking as an incorrect answer. What follows is an example of an answer blank demonstrating how to mark an answer properly.

The following examples are answer blanks that have been improperly marked, leading to a poor test score.

If you change your mind about any answer, be certain to erase the original answer completely. If two answers for the same question are marked, the question will be scored as incorrect. This holds true even if one of the selections was indeed correct. And invariably, a few applicants make the very costly mistake of marking answers that do not correspond to the question they are working on. A simple oversight like this can be devastating as far as test results are concerned. Check every ten questions or so to make sure you are marking an answer for the corresponding question at hand.

When you look over test questions, be sure to read them carefully and completely. It is easy to fall prey to reading the first or second choice and selecting one of them as the correct answer without bothering to examine the remaining options. Read the entire passage thoroughly and then mark your answer sheet accordingly. Pay close attention to conjunctions such as *and*, *but*, *or*, *when*, *if*, *because*, *though*, *whereas*, and *besides*; these key words can completely alter the meaning of a question. If you overlook one of these words, there is a good chance that you will select the wrong answer. It cannot be emphasized enough to read the entire passage closely before even thinking about the answer sheet.

Do not spend too much time on a question that you are unsure about. Either make an educated guess or skip that question and return to it when you have finished with the rest of the exam. As a time-saver, you can cross out the options in the test booklet that you know are wrong. When you return to that question, you can quickly focus on the remaining selections. If you do elect to skip a question, be sure to skip the corresponding answer blank as well.

A note worth mentioning here is that, statistically speaking, your first choice of an answer is usually correct. Answers that are changed are typically wrong. All too frequently applicants will read too much into a question and obscure the proper choice. Mark the first answer that seems apparent and leave it as it is, unless you can make a strong case for one of the remaining options.

Usually within two to three weeks following the written exam, a scoring key will be posted by the department. Details pertaining to the when and where aspects of the posting are normally included in the preliminary instructions given by the examiner in charge. If you disagree on any particular answer given, there are forms made available to challenge given questions. An appeals process of this nature normally takes thirty to sixty days before a final score is rendered.

Appeals aside, test results are mailed to applicants usually within thirty days. Applicants are ranked according to test results on employment registers kept by the Corrections Department office of personnel. Those who scored highest will be given priority in a subsequent screening.

THE PHYSICAL ABILITY TEST

All correctional facilities want employees to be in top physical condition. While most duties inherent to this job are sedentary in nature, there can be instances that place significant demands on one's overall stamina. Consequently, various physical ability exercises are set up to test an applicant's flexibility, muscular strength, endurance, and aerobic conditioning. These can either be administered as part of the initial selection process or relegated to academy training. If the former holds true, some departments will offer practice trials in advance of the actual test. It is highly recommended you attend such events, as you can become familiar with the drills that will be expected of you. Unfortunately, there is not a standardization of physical fitness exams. One department may run a test that favors muscular strength and endurance, while another department will submit a test that has an obvious bias toward flexibility or aerobic conditioning. Evidence of this variety of events as seen on past exams has included:

- running an obstacle course involving short-distance sprints, weaving around traffic cones, pushing weighted objects a predetermined distance, and use of the balance beam.

- a 125–165-pound dummy drag (simulating victim carry).

- trunk flexion (determining flexibility and extent of reach).

- sit-up, push-up, and pull-up repetitions.

- distance running (e.g., 1/4, 1/2, or 1 mile) and climbing over a 6 foot 8 inch wall or chain-link fence.

- stair climbing (specifically designed to measure pulse rate)

- bench-pressing, curling, and squatting with various weights, using either barbells or variable-resistance weight-training equipment

Despite the differences involved, most if not all applicants are rated on a PASS/FAIL basis. An applicant must pass (i.e., meet the department's prescribed minimum standards) to advance to the next stage of screening.

ORAL BOARD

Traditionally, if a vacancy in the department arises, candidates with the highest test scores are requested to appear before an oral board. This interview is conducted by a panel composed of two to five people, who serve as staff officers or are involved in Corrections personnel management. Typical questions asked of applicants are "How do you think you are better qualified than other applicants? What do you feel are your strong points and weak points? Could you use lethal force against another person?" These kinds of questions give panelists a means of gauging your personal characteristics, oral communication skills, and ability to respond decisively and effectively to situations. Board approval is a prerequisite for further employment considerations.

Note: Discussions relating to how to prepare for both the physical abilities test and the oral board are given at the back of this study guide. Guidelines, as well as hypothetical test questions for the oral board, are provided to give you the best possible insight into what to expect once you have reached this level in the screening process. After studying these questions, you should feel better prepared and subsequently more relaxed during an oral interview. Well-thought-out answers to anticipated questions not only make you appear more confident, but give a favorable first impression to those conducting the interview.

PSYCHOLOGICAL EVALUATION

Beyond probation, Corrections Officers will spend a significant share of their scheduled time working independently within designated areas. It is imperative that he or she be mentally fit to respond appropriately to any incident under such circumstances. The profile of a professional officer not only encompasses a thorough knowledge of operational procedures, it also involves sound judgment.

When a Corrections Officer is the first to respond to a potential disturbance, altercation, accident, or criminal incident, his or her decisions and actions can dramatically affect the outcome. Frequently, there is not enough time to second-guess an initial response. Decisions must be made quickly and in the best interests of those involved. This is particularly relevant when a weapon is present. Sound judgment, good sense, and basic instinct are essential elements in a competent officer. However, these can be undermined by prejudices or biases. If an officer is handicapped by either, it will be impossible for that officer to live up to the professional standards expected.

Psychological evaluations are conducted with the sole purpose of ferreting out such shortcomings. This kind of exam can come in the form of either a one-on-one interview with a qualified psychologist or psychiatrist, or a written exam called a personality test. Either way, the applicant is asked questions that can effectively discern both the sincerity of the candidate and the likelihood of behavior unbecoming a professional Corrections Officer.

Psychological evaluations are not impossible to prepare for. In fact, many of the questions seen on these exams are somewhat similar to what may have been asked in the oral board. Like the oral board, passing the psychological exam is a prerequisite for further employment consideration.

BACKGROUND INVESTIGATION

The information you provide on your job application form concerning personal history is subject to intense scrutiny. Typically, a detective or other qualified staff member is assigned to conduct a thorough investigation into your past. Such areas as your education, employment history, past residences, military career, driving record, personal references, and health status will be reviewed for validity and completeness. It is extremely important that you furnish accurate and complete information about your background. Leaving portions of a personal history statement blank and/or providing information that does not reconcile with a background check is a mistake that has disqualified many candidates in the past. If a discrepancy is discovered, it will be difficult for you to continue in the screening process as a viable contender. It cannot be emphasized enough to be truthful and forthright about your past. If some past indiscretion resulted in your arrest, not only provide complete documentation of the details involved, but point out that a lesson was learned and that you have come a long way from that point in your life. Denying there was a problem or placing the blame on someone else is a sure way to discredit yourself.

There are, however, certain background criteria that will preclude any chance of being hired. A felony conviction and a dishonorable discharge from military service are two circumstances that have already been mentioned in the introduction of this study guide. Multiple convictions for misdemeanor charges demonstrate a pattern of willful disregard for the law. Unpaid traffic tickets or other outstanding warrants fall under this same category. Either of these situations warrants disqualification from employment consideration. If a candidate has demonstrated a past propensity for domestic violence or job-related disturbances that inevitably led to being fired, these, too, would be grounds for dismissal from further screening.

Besides the personal history being examined in detail, candidates will also be subjected to fingerprint screening. A criminal-records search will be conducted, usually at the expense of the applicant. Fees will vary, but they are normally between $15 and $20 for the service. Any applicant who refuses to submit to mandatory fingerprint screening will be disqualified from further consideration.

The confidentiality of your background investigation is strictly controlled. Only top level administrative personnel taking part in the hiring decisions for the department have legal access to such information. Consequently, all information in your file is closed to all outside organizations and/or agencies, as well as to yourself with regard to any recommendations made. This can be unfortunate if a problem surfaces at this stage; unlike the other steps of the screening process, it may be difficult for an applicant to find out why he or she did not receive a hiring recommendation. This can be particularly frustrating to those who have made it this far in the screening process. Filing a formal appeal at this point will be of no avail.

Therefore, the best advice here is to be honest and forthright about your past, and to demonstrate a positive attitude toward any past mistakes. Bear in mind, corrections personnel recognize the fact that no one is perfect. However, a person who shows sincerity, integrity, and honesty is more likely to receive a recommendation than is one who tends to have a sketchy or questionable background.

MEDICAL EVALUATION

Medical guidelines followed by departments can and do change over the years and vary among departments. What may be acceptable to one department may not be acceptable to another (e.g., height and weight requirements or visual acuity standards). Thus, it is recommended that you pick up a medical standards form and medical history questionnaire from the department you intend to apply to. Going about it in this manner, you will know exactly what is required by that department. Be truthful in filling out the medical questionnaire; this is one more element subject to being cross-checked during a background investigation. False information on these forms is bound to be discovered during the course of a thorough medical exam, so be honest about any medical conditions you may have. If you have a borderline condition such as diabetes, hernia, or the like, consult your regular physician to see what, if any, steps can be taken to alleviate the problem. Any medical condition that may potentially prevent or impair the ability of an applicant to perform the duties of Corrections Officer will be grounds for disqualification. At issue, of course, are the obvious concerns of safety for the officer and the welfare of inmates under his or her supervision.

You should be made aware, too, that medical evaluations are required not only prior to hiring but periodically throughout one's career. This holds true for drug screening as well. A clean bill of health is mandated for both the aspiring and the veteran Corrections Officer.

GENERAL JOB DESCRIPTION

Once a candidate is appointed as a Corrections Officer, an extensive amount of training is required prior to receiving the first assignment. This formal training usually occurs at a basic Corrections Officer academy and can entail intensive study that lasts anywhere from several weeks to several months. Areas of study include a complete overview of the criminal justice system; civil rights and constitutional law; federal, state, and local laws; security management; booking/intake procedural guidelines; classification and processing of inmates; observation and communication skills; first aid; firearm training; cultural awareness/ethics and professionalism. In tandem, a candidate must go through fairly rigorous physical training. Physical fitness programs can include running one to two miles, basic calisthenics such as push-ups, pull-ups, and sit-ups, and various stretching exercises, all of which enhance cardiovascular endurance, muscular strength, and flexibility. Mastering the prescribed studies and meeting minimum physical standards are both required to successfully complete academy training.

Once a recruit gets to this stage, he or she will receive on-the-job training under the close supervision of a field training officer. Every aspect of a recruit's performance will be subject to periodic evaluation during a six-to-eighteen-month probation. If the recruit's performance measures up to departmental standards, he or she will be assigned to a correctional facility for full duty and have full entitlement to civil service benefits. This would include a comprehensive medical and dental plan, life insurance, paid vacation and sick leave, vested pension plans, uniform allowances, and the potential for promotion as determined by written exams and/or on-the-job performance. Average beginning salaries for entry-level Corrections Officers can range anywhere from $22,000 to $37,000 and can also include cost-of-living adjustments. Corrections Officers who have attained the rank of sergeant, lieutenant, or captain can earn anywhere from $24,000 to

$52,000 per year. Chief administrative positions such as assistant warden, chief of security, or warden/super-intendent can earn salary packages ranging from $55,000 to $142,000. Top-paying administrative salaries are typically correspondent with larger jurisdictions.

Layoffs within Corrections are relatively rare, and most cuts that have to be made because of budgetary con-straints can be handled through early retirements and/or hiring freezes. The simple truth of the matter is that cor-rectional security is an around-the-clock commitment of personnel and resources; it is subject to neither seasonal adjustments nor any significant downsizing due to tighter fiscal management. Whether government budget planners like it or not, money must be appropriated for adequate security maintenance in area facilities. If cutbacks in civil service become imperative, they usually will come at the expense of other departments.

Besides the budgetary aspects, you have to realize, too, that Corrections has a significant investment in your training to become a qualified officer. Departments are not about to sacrifice such positions unnecessarily.

The working conditions encountered by Corrections Officers can be diverse as well as challenging. Normally, shift assignments are eight hours a day, forty hours a week, on rotating tours (i.e., day, evening, and graveyard). Weekends and holiday work may be mandated periodically, for which an employee will receive premium compensation. Any work beyond an eight-hour-per-day work schedule is considered over-time and paid time and a half. Employees working evening or graveyard shifts or designated to hazardous areas are given additional compensation as well.

Job functions during a shift can include:

- custodial receiving of inmates

- inputting personal data on required computer logs and files

- signing off pertinent warrants and conducting inmate searches

- familiarizing inmates with jail procedures and regulations

- enforcing security guidelines in observance of standard operational procedures

- safeguarding facility equipment and supplies

- documenting inmate infractions of jail regulations

- inmate escort and transportation

- requesting medical attention for inmates when necessary

- contraband searches of suspected inmates or cells

- control-room oversight via closed-circuit television cameras of all entrances and gates within the facility

- supervising inmate recreational activities and visitations

- perimeter security and canine patrol

- handling inmate commissary requests as is appropriate

- ensuring that inmates make court appearances as scheduled

- reporting potentially dangerous situations to superiors

- using physical restraint on inmates, when necessary, or deadly force within prescribed depart-mental guidelines

- processing and releasing of inmates posting bond or given court-authorized personal recognizance leave.

Corrections personnel are entrusted with a wide range of responsibilities, all of which must be conducted in a professional manner. Officers must be careful not to compromise themselves legally or ethically while carrying out their duties. Additionally, all rules and regulations must be uniformly applied without the elements of bias or vindication. Considering the fact that prison environments can be tense and stressful at times, it can be challenging, to say the least, to maintain such standards. Nevertheless, personnel that dedicate themselves to such principles and strive for self-improvement through training programs and education will become an invaluable asset for the judicial system as a whole.

PREPARATION FOR THE WRITTEN EXAM

As noted earlier, the written exam can basically be divided into seven areas, and each will be discussed later in this study guide, followed by sample test questions and answers. Test strategies and hints will be provided and elaborated upon as they apply to each subject area. It is important to note that there can be significant variations in test content, judging by what has been seen on past exams around the country. Some tests place a stronger emphasis on one or more subject areas while having fewer questions, if any, relating to other topics. To prepare yourself adequately for such a test, all seven areas warrant equal consideration. Then, you will be prepared regardless of what you may encounter on your exam.

STUDY SUGGESTIONS

The Corrections Officer exam is not the kind of exam on which you can hope for a high test score after just cramming the night before. Good study habits can have a significant impact on your performance. If you follow the few simple guidelines, you can approach the exam more relaxed and confident, two essential ingredients for top performance on any exam.

Regular study times should be established and tailored to your comfort. Each person's schedule is different. Some people prefer to study for one or two hours at a time and then take a break, while others prefer several hours of straight study. Regardless of how you study, it is important that you do it regularly; do not rely on a marathon. You will remember the subject matter easier and comprehend it better if you establish regular study habits.

Where you study is important, too. Eliminate any distractions that can disrupt your studies. The television, the telephone, and children can hinder quality study time. I suggest you set aside one room in your home as a study place and use it to isolate yourself from distractions. If you elect to use a bedroom as a study area, avoid lying in bed while you read. Otherwise, you may find yourself more inclined to sleep than to learn. It is important to have a good desk, a comfortable chair, and adequate lighting; anything less can hamper studying. If studying in your home is not feasible, go to your local library or some other place that offers an environment conducive to study.

Again, be sure to get plenty of rest. It is counterproductive to study when you are overly tired, because you will learn slower. It is also important not to skip meals—your level of concentration during the exam can suffer if you lack proper nutrition. Coffee and other stimulants are not recommended.

Chapter 2

Memory Recall

One of the most important skills a Corrections Officer uses in the line of duty is memory recall. If an officer can remember the names and behavioral profiles of those incarcerated, prisoner management can become much more effective with respect to avoiding potential confrontations and unnecessary safety risks. Another prime example of the importance of memory involves directives issued by a superior. It is imperative that such directives be followed quickly, accurately, and completely without having to be repeated. Valuable time can be lost and an emergency call may be handled less effectively if directives are second-guessed, forgotten, or jumbled. Additionally, it will be necessary for an officer to be completely familiar with the facility floor plan and inherent security systems, which can involve a multitude of various codes and procedures. The ramifications of possessing marginal memory skills are pretty obvious.

This memory section has been placed at the beginning of this study guide because memory normally is the first subject encountered on the actual exam. Test examiners prefer to arrange an exam in this manner so that the rest of the exam can be given without any further interruptions. Typically a memory exam booklet, film, video, key, or some other form of diagram is passed out to test applicants, who are allowed limited time to memorize as much of the diagram as possible, and then the material is collected. The question-and-answer sheet for this section may be handled separately, but it is likely to be an integral part of the main exam. In any case, the key or diagram will not be available for reference during the test. All your answers must be arrived at by memory alone.

From what has been encountered on past exams, memory-recall sections follow one of three different formats: the first approach may involve studying a picture or sketch on which any detail is subject to questioning; a second may entail studying a portfolio of various criminals, complete with composite sketches, physical descriptions, personal data, and details pertaining to the crime involved; the third involves descriptive passages. A written passage incorporating any of these three formats is then given and pertains to an incident involving a crime or providing information regarding prison policy. Memory-recall questions are based on what the reading specifically said. This closely parallels reading-comprehension-type questions that will be seen at a later point in this study guide. However, memory-recall questions ask only about specifics or what was stated in the reading, and do not involve making any kind of inference.

Whichever format is seen on your exam, you will be given anywhere from five to fifteen minutes to study the key or passage provided. The memory test may appear simple at first, but in fact may require you to quickly memorize between fifty and seventy-five items. Unless you are gifted with a photographic memory, memorizing such volumes of material in such a short time may seem impossible. Don't despair, because this study guide offers a system that will substantially help those with average memory skills and improve the skills of those who are fairly proficient. The technique employed is called *imagery and association*. Any memory task can be simplified by using this system, because it requires you to form images in your mind relevant to the item to be memorized. Each of those images is then linked together in a specific order by means of association. It may sound complicated, but learning to stretch the boundaries of your imagination can be enjoyable.

A. NAMES

Inmate names may be among the items that need to be committed to memory for the exam. Examine the following inmate list:

Scott	Hawkins
Bloomington	Rainey
Malcolm	Cornell
Vaughn	Hernandez

Most people would approach this exercise by rote memorization or, in other words, repetition of thought until recall can be accomplished, which may well be an acceptable option for some. However, the alternative (i.e., imagery and association) can actually be fun. Now, look at the same inmate names again and see what key-word derivatives have been used and what images we can associate with them.

For example:

Scott — toilet paper	Hawkins — hawk
Bloomington — blossoms	Rainey — rain
Malcolm — malcontent	Cornell — corncob
Vaughn — vault	Hernandez — hernia

Carry the process one step further and place these key words in a bizarre context, story, or situation. Using this process, one hypothetical story would be as follows:

A huge roll of SCOTT toilet paper is clutched in the talons of a HAWK, which is perched precariously on a huge flower BLOSSOM towering over the prison yard. Just before it was to RAIN buckets, it swoops overhead and tepees one of the prisoners from head to toe. The affected prisoner becomes such a MALCONTENT that he attempts to escape by using an extremely long CORNCOB to poleVAULT over the perimeter fence. The attempt fails, of course, resulting in a massive HERNIA for the effort.

Sounds ridiculous, doesn't it? However, because of its strong images, you will not easily forget this kind of story.

Another advantage of the imagery technique is that you can remember items in their respective order by simply reviewing where they fit in relation to the other items in the story.

Look at each of the following names and develop a story using imagery. There are no right or wrong key-word derivatives; what is important is that the images conjure up a clear picture in your mind and then interlink.

Work on each of these columns separately:

Lawson	Mueller	Iverson	Schmitt
Clay	Seaman	Cappucine	Walter
Gardner	Whitcomb	Armstrong	Dirksen
Hertz	Blakemore	Bacon	Kreidler
Martinez	Grossman	Meadows	Farmer
Bruno	Jackson	O'Sullivan	Brooks

Once you have finished this exercise, cover the names and see if you can remember all twenty-four items. If your four stories are bizarre enough, you certainly can have this entire list committed to memory in a short time.

B. NUMBERS

Numbers are another problem in memory recall. For most people, numbers are difficult to memorize because they are intangible. To rectify this problem, numbers can be transposed into letters so that words can be formed and associated accordingly. Here is the format for transposition (remember it as if it were your Social Security number, because on the exam you will draw from it regularly):

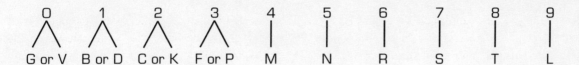

All other letters can be incorporated into words without any significance.

For instance, let's say you are given the number 10603328157. Memorizing this number so well that you can recall it after any length of time would be very difficult. However, by using my memory system, you could use the number to spell out a variety of memorable things. Here is your chance to use your creativity!

After you have had the chance to figure out what words could code such a number, one particular problem should become apparent: the more numbers you try to cram into one word, the harder it is to find a compatible word in the English vocabulary. To simplify matters, there are two alternative ways to form words. The first method is to take two numbers at a time, form a word, and associate it with the next word. Dealing with the same number (10603328157), DOG could be derived from the number 10, RUG from 60, PIPE from 33, CAT from 28, BONE from 15, and S from 7. There are many ways you could imagine and link these words. One possibility would be a DOG lying on a RUG and smoking a PIPE while a CAT prances by carrying a BONE shaped like an S. This is just one way to memorize this long number. Other words and stories could work just as well.

The second alternative, which offers greater flexibility, is using words of any length but making only the first two significant letters of the word applicable to your story. For example, the word DIG-GING could represent 10 in the number 10603328157.

RAV-EN = RUG-BY = REV-OLVER = 60
POP-ULATION = PUP-PY = PEP-PER = 33
CAT-ERPILLAR = CAT-TLE = COT-TON = 28
BIN-OCCULAR = BEAN-S = DIN-NER = 15

By doing this, you have a larger number of words at your disposal to put into stories. With a little originality, it can be fun to see what you can imagine for any given number.

Next are exercises to help you apply this system. The first group of numbers is meant to be used as a transposition exercise. See how many different words you can use to represent each number. The second series is for practice with transposition and story fabrication. This technique may seem difficult at first, but with practice it will enhance your memory capabilities tenfold.

I.			
44	63	86	40
53	97	93	32
61	10	48	26
13	3	60	91
12	57	35	99
8	52	27	16
41	11	21	68

II.	
1352215678	1479532107
7890551236	4485101103
4998803215	8810587310
2011187298	3521797724
1387500921	1928357040

C. PICTURES/SKETCHES

When you are presented with a picture or sketch on your exam, try to mentally walk your way through the diagram and pay particular attention to details. For example, if there are any people, determine their relative position with respect to other landmarks in the scene. Are they initiating some kind of criminal event, being victimized, or just standing idly by serving as potential witnesses to what (if anything) is taking place? Look for location references such as building names, cell block numbers, and institutional signs or logos. If any vehicles are present, what are the license numbers and general descriptions (e.g., two-door, four-door, sedan, van, truck, etc.)? If an emergency is apparent, what exactly is involved? Is a weapon present? If so, how is the perpetrator dressed and what are his/her physical characteristics (e.g., approximate height and weight, color, length of hair, scar or tattoos, etc.)? Are there any time references such as clocks or calendars? Is it day or night? Can the weather be accounted for? Being aware of such things and answering these kinds of questions will definitely sharpen your skills of observation. Now you will need to systematically develop lasting mental images of what was observed and link them into a memorable story. Look at the next example, and try applying this technique to enhance your recollection of the details provided.

Note: You are limited only by your imagination. There really is no one particular story that is correct. To further assist you in this area, one alternative is given immediately following the exercise. It is the intent here to demonstrate the mechanics of imagery and association, and not to convey any absolutes. Chances are you will develop a better story more custom-tailored for your own interpretative abilities than anyone else can develop for you.

Oscar McMannis, the man in the picture attempting to get some sleep, coincidentally looks like an oversized hot dog with facial hair (*Oscar Meyer the Man*). This image is further reinforced by the fact he is "sandwiched" between two bunk beds. Much to Oscar's chagrin, he observes his cellmate, Jack Weaver, the "weaving jackhammer," feverishly hacksawing the bars to their window. About the same moment Weaver becomes aware of his cellmate watching him, the clock above the window falls on his head, causing him to see stars (*night association*). He then tells Oscar to "tend to" his own business and never mind what is going on. *Tend to* are the key words here that refer to the time (*i.e., ten-till-twelve midnight*). The bump on Weaver's head (*shaped like a crescent moon*) was so painful that it took two full rolls of toilet paper to sop up the tears from all of the crying. Weaver was still beside himself because he could swear there was a bat (*i.e., 18*) flying around the cell with a pair of gloves (*09—the month of September*) that glowed (*09th day of the month*) in the dark! Fortunately, the poster to Weaver's right took on animation of its own (*a pair of Nike tennis shoes*) and kicked some sense into Weaver. Exhausted and none closer to actually escaping, Weaver sits down at his desk and fills out a Section 8 report (*military jargon for psychiatric release that, in this case, represents the eight books on the top of the desk*) in triplicate and places a copy in each of the three desk drawers. As Weaver staggers off to bed, he rationalizes that everything that had just happened to him was merely a-bad-nightmare (*A-11-50*).

You can see by the example that a story can become outlandishly crazy. Perhaps it could be said that the crazier the story, the easier it becomes to memorize. More importantly, be sure all concocted images are properly linked together. Otherwise, you will be left with a collage of cute fabrications that can become somewhat meaningless when viewed independently of the main story. You should have a pretty fair idea by now of how to use this memory system to your advantage. Examine the next sketch for five minutes. After the five minutes have elapsed, proceed to the questions and fill in the answers without looking at the diagram again. Check your answers with those provided at the end of the exercise to determine the effectiveness of your storytelling-memorization skills. If you get through only part of your story development before time expires, don't despair. You will find that the more you use this system, the easier it will become to apply it to any memorization task.

SAMPLE SKETCH 1

Study the sketch on the next page for five minutes. *Do not* exceed the time allowed; if you do, you will forfeit the true sense of how an exam is actually conducted. When time is up, turn to the questions without making further reference to the sketch. In the actual exam, the test examiner will collect the sketches when time for studying is up, and then you will be directed to answer the related questions in your test booklet or supplement. You will not be allowed to review the sketch in the course of answering questions.

SAMPLE QUESTIONS, SKETCH 1

1. How many armed guards were depicted in the sketch?
    A. 4
    B. 3
    C. 2
    D. 1

2. The name of the correctional center in question was?
    A. Alcatraz
    B. Peatmont Corrections
    C. Piedmont Corrections
    D. Waverly Corrections

3. The name of the trucking firm that had a vehicle parked at a service entrance was?
    A. Ralston
    B. Purina
    C. Acme
    D. Davis

4. How many prisoners were depicted in the sketch?
    A. 13
    B. 14
    C. 15
    D. 17

5. Of the prisoners shown, how many were smoking?
    A. 5
    B. 3
    C. 2
    D. 1

6. The sketch was primarily a depiction of which of the following facilities?
    A. Gymnasium
    B. Administration buildings
    C. Infirmary
    D. Cafeteria

7. How many Corrections Officers were inside the facility mentioned in the previous question to monitor inmate activities?
    A. None
    B. 1
    C. 2
    D. 3

8. The ID number on the side of the laundry cart being pushed down the hallway by an inmate was?
    A. CP 103
    B. PC 301
    C. PC 103
    D. CP 503

9. How many light fixtures along the perimeter fencing were seen within the sketch?
   A. 2
   B. 3
   C. 4
   D. None of the above

10. How many inmates shown in the sketch were working in the kitchen?
    A. 5
    B. 4
    C. 3
    D. 2

11. Excluding the kitchen and main entrance doors, how many windows to the facility were evident in the sketch?
    A. 3
    B. 5
    C. 6
    D. 7

12. According to the directional postings on the hallway walls, where was cell block D in relation to the facility shown in the sketch?
    A. East
    B. North
    C. South
    D. West

13. According to the clock seen in the sketch, what time of day was it?
    A. 12:45 P.M.
    B. 1:15 P.M.
    C. 3:30 P.M.
    D. 2:00 P.M.

14. According to the directional postings on the hallway wall, where was cell block A in relation to the facility shown in the sketch?
    A. North
    B. South
    C. East
    D. West

15. The fire hydrant shown in the picture can most accurately be described as being located where?
    A. Northeast of cell block D
    B. West of the perimeter fencing
    C. Next to the service entrance
    D. Southwest corner of the cafeteria building

ANSWER SHEET FOR SAMPLE SKETCH 1

1. Ⓐ Ⓑ Ⓒ Ⓓ   6. Ⓐ Ⓑ Ⓒ Ⓓ   11. Ⓐ Ⓑ Ⓒ Ⓓ

2. Ⓐ Ⓑ Ⓒ Ⓓ   7. Ⓐ Ⓑ Ⓒ Ⓓ   12. Ⓐ Ⓑ Ⓒ Ⓓ

3. Ⓐ Ⓑ Ⓒ Ⓓ   8. Ⓐ Ⓑ Ⓒ Ⓓ   13. Ⓐ Ⓑ Ⓒ Ⓓ

4. Ⓐ Ⓑ Ⓒ Ⓓ   9. Ⓐ Ⓑ Ⓒ Ⓓ   14. Ⓐ Ⓑ Ⓒ Ⓓ

5. Ⓐ Ⓑ Ⓒ Ⓓ   10. Ⓐ Ⓑ Ⓒ Ⓓ   15. Ⓐ Ⓑ Ⓒ Ⓓ

Answers can be found on page 56.

Below are sketches of items taken from four people immediately following their arrest and subsequent incarceration. Study the items shown and to whom they belong for a period of ten minutes. Do not exceed the time allowed. When time is up, turn to the questions provided without making further references to the sketches just studied.

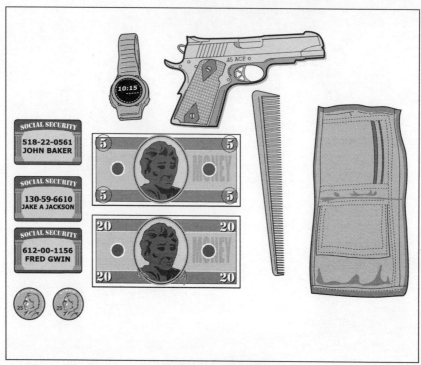

A. DON A. GLEASON

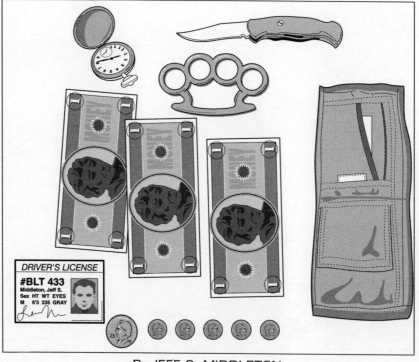

B. JEFF S. MIDDLETON

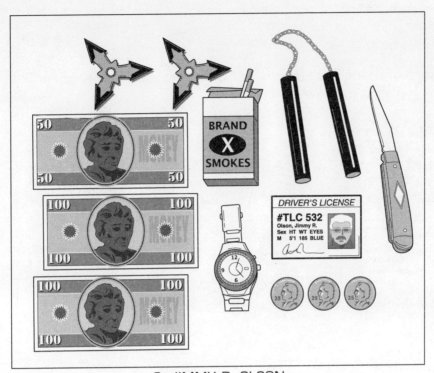

C. JIMMY R. OLSON

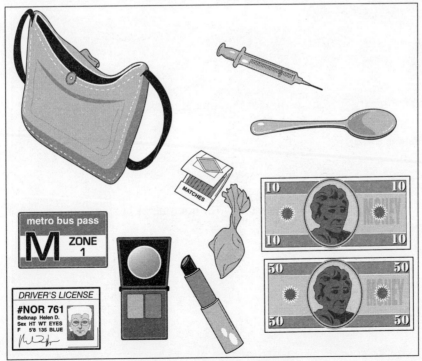

D. HELEN D. BELKNAP

SAMPLE QUESTIONS, SKETCH 2

1. Which of the four suspects carried a firearm at the time of his/her arrest?
   A. Middleton
   B. Belknap
   C. Olson
   D. Gleason

2. Which of the four suspects, judging by what he/she had on his/her person at the time of arrest, presumably had some martial arts training?
   A. Belknap
   B. Olson
   C. Gleason
   D. Middleton

3. Who had the least amount of money at the time of arrest?
   A. Middleton
   B. Olson
   C. Belknap
   D. Gleason

4. Which of the four suspects was obviously tied in to the drug trade?
   A. A
   B. B
   C. C
   D. D

5. BLT 433 represents whose driver's license?
   A. A
   B. B
   C. C
   D. D

6. Who did not have a driver's license at the time of arrest?
   A. Olson
   B. Gleason
   C. Middleton
   D. Belknap

7. How much money did Helen Belknap have at the time of her arrest?
   A. $25.50
   B. $33.75
   C. $60.00
   D. $250.00

8. Mr. Olson's driver's license number was?
   A. NOR 671
   B. BTL 334
   C. TLC 532
   D. DLH 081

9. All of the following numbers represent fake Social Security cards found on Mr. Gleason at the time of his arrest except?
   A. 612-00-1156
   B. 518-22-0561
   C. 530-44-1753
   D. 130-59-6610

10. Who was in possession of brass knuckles at the time of arrest?
    A. Belknap
    B. Gleason
    C. Olson
    D. Middleton

11. Of the four arrested, who among them was an apparent smoker?
    A. A
    B. B
    C. C
    D. D

12. The only Metro Bus Pass inventoried among items confiscated was apparently good for only?
    A. Zone 1
    B. Zone 2
    C. Zone 3
    D. Zone 4

13. All of the following statements are true except?
    A. Middleton was the only individual to be in possession of a knife.
    B. Belknap's apparent drug of choice was heroin.
    C. Gleason was the only person who did not produce a valid driver's license.
    D. Olson wore an expensive Rolex watch.

14. Who among the four suspects arrested did not carry a timepiece?
    A. A
    B. B
    C. C
    D. D

15. All of the following statements are true except?
    A. The only handgun confiscated at the time of arrest was a .45 ACP pistol.
    B. A tube of lipstick, hairbrush, and compact were some of the items found to be in Ms. Belknap's possession at the time of her arrest.
    C. Jimmy Olson's middle initial was R.
    D. Mr. Gleason was the only individual of the four arrested who had possession of a comb.

ANSWER SHEET FOR SAMPLE SKETCH 2

1. (A) (B) (C) (D)　　6. (A) (B) (C) (D)　　11. (A) (B) (C) (D)

2. (A) (B) (C) (D)　　7. (A) (B) (C) (D)　　12. (A) (B) (C) (D)

3. (A) (B) (C) (D)　　8. (A) (B) (C) (D)　　13. (A) (B) (C) (D)

4. (A) (B) (C) (D)　　9. (A) (B) (C) (D)　　14. (A) (B) (C) (D)

5. (A) (B) (C) (D)　　10. (A) (B) (C) (D)　　15. (A) (B) (C) (D)

Answers can be found on page 56.

As mentioned earlier in the discussion of memory recall, another format seen on exams utilizes various criminal composites that include sketches, physical descriptions, and other information pertinent to the issuance of a warrant. Since there are a lot of numbers to remember, this is where the number transposition system can be very useful.

Study the three sketches and associated personal data below for ten minutes. Do not exceed the time allowed. When time is up, turn to the questions provided without making any further references to the composites just studied.

Note: Study each of the suspects for only three minutes. Use the last minute for a quick review.

SAMPLE COMPOSITE SKETCH/FILE 1

Suspect 1

Name:	Ron James McDonald
Alias:	Ron Allan Vincent
Date of Birth:	October 9, 1971 (Hint: look at this as 10-09-71)
Height:	6'1"
Weight:	190 pounds
Hair:	Black
Eyes:	Hazel
Sex:	Male
Race:	African American/medium complexion
Scars or Marks:	L-shaped scar on left cheek
Social Security No.:	431-57-5555
Wants and Warrants:	Wanted for attempted murder and possession of an unlawful weapon
Criminal Record:	No priors

Suspect 2

Name:	David McNeil
Alias:	None
Date of Birth:	January 17, 1969
Height:	5'11"
Weight:	175 pounds
Hair:	Blond
Eyes:	Blue
Sex:	Male
Race:	Caucasian
Scars or Marks:	None known
Social Security No.:	795-00-7311
Wants and Warrants:	Wanted for conspiring to manufacture and distribute a controlled substance
Criminal Record:	Possession of methamphetamine

NCIC (National Crime Information Center) file number: 71-95

Suspect 3

Name: Kathy Jean Tisdale

Alias: Audrey Joan Crawford

Date of Birth: May 7, 1973

Height: 5'5"

Weight: 120 pounds

Hair: Blonde (Sandy)

Eyes: Brown

Sex: Female

Race: Caucasian

Scars or Marks: Rose tattoo on right forearm

Social Security No.: 370-69-1520

Wants and Warrants: Wanted for first-degree kidnapping and second-degree assault

Considered armed and dangerous

Criminal Record: First-degree malicious mischief

CLETS file number: 30-17

SAMPLE QUESTIONS, COMPOSITE SKETCH/FILE 1

1. Ron James McDonald used which one of the names given below as an alias?
   A. James Allen Tisdale
   B. Ron Vincent Crawford
   C. Ron Allan Vincent
   D. None of the above

2. Which of the three suspects had CLETS file number 30-17 assigned to his/her criminal record?
   A. Suspect 1
   B. Suspect 2
   C. Suspect 3
   D. No such file was given

3. Which choice below inaccurately describes Suspect 2?
   A. Height: 5'5"
   B. Weight: 175 pounds
   C. Social Security No.: 795-00-7311
   D. Sex: Male

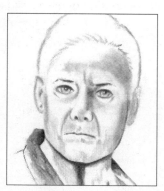

4. The picture shown to the right is a sketch of which suspect?
   A. Ron Vincent Crawford
   B. David McNeil
   C. David Travis
   D. John Allan McDonald

5. According to NCIC file number 71-95, the suspect described was wanted for which of the following crimes?
   A. Second-degree malicious mischief and possession of methamphetamines
   B. Attempted murder and bank robbery
   C. Second-degree kidnapping
   D. Conspiring to manufacture and distribute a controlled substance

6. Which of the three suspects was described as being an African American with a medium complexion?
   A. James Allan McNeil
   B. Ron James McDonald
   C. Audrey Joan Crawford
   D. None of the suspects' files mentioned complexion

7. Which of the three suspects was born on May 7, 1973?
   A. Suspect 1
   B. Suspect 2
   C. Suspect 3
   D. No such DOB (i.e., date of birth) was given

8. Suspect 3 was described as having which of the following scars or marks?
   A. Rose tattoo on the right forearm
   B. Rose tattoo on the left forearm
   C. L-shaped scar on the right forearm
   D. Suspect 3 did not have any scars or marks on record

9. According to the case files provided, who was wanted for attempted murder and possession of an unlawful weapon?
   A. Ron James McNeil
   B. Ron Allan Vincent
   C. Kathy Jean Crawford
   D. David McNeil

10. Which of the three suspects weighed 175 pounds?
    A. Suspect 1
    B. Suspect 2
    C. Suspect 3
    D. None were shown to weigh 175 pounds

11. Who did not have any prior convictions according to the information provided?
    A. Ron James McDonald
    B. Kathy Jean Tisdale
    C. David McNeil
    D. All three suspects were shown to have prior convictions on their criminal records.

12. Which of the following Social Security numbers identifies Ms. Crawford?
    A. 790-50-7311
    B. 478-62-5178
    C. 431-57-5555
    D. 370-69-1520

13. Suspect 1's race, according to the information provided, was?
    A. Indian American
    B. African American
    C. Caucasian
    D. None of the above

14. Which of the three suspects is considered armed and dangerous?
    A. Both Suspects 1 and 2
    B. Only Suspect 2
    C. Only Suspect 3
    D. Both Suspects 1 and 3

15. All of the following statements are true except?
    A. Kathy Jean Tisdale utilized the alias Audrey Joan Crawford.
    B. Suspect 2 was born 5-17-69.
    C. Ron James McDonald has hazel colored eyes and black hair.
    D. Suspect 3 is described as having sandy blonde hair and brown eyes.

ANSWER SHEET FOR SAMPLE COMPOSITE SKETCH/FILE 1

1. Ⓐ Ⓑ Ⓒ Ⓓ   6. Ⓐ Ⓑ Ⓒ Ⓓ   11. Ⓐ Ⓑ Ⓒ Ⓓ

2. Ⓐ Ⓑ Ⓒ Ⓓ   7. Ⓐ Ⓑ Ⓒ Ⓓ   12. Ⓐ Ⓑ Ⓒ Ⓓ

3. Ⓐ Ⓑ Ⓒ Ⓓ   8. Ⓐ Ⓑ Ⓒ Ⓓ   13. Ⓐ Ⓑ Ⓒ Ⓓ

4. Ⓐ Ⓑ Ⓒ Ⓓ   9. Ⓐ Ⓑ Ⓒ Ⓓ   14. Ⓐ Ⓑ Ⓒ Ⓓ

5. Ⓐ Ⓑ Ⓒ Ⓓ   10. Ⓐ Ⓑ Ⓒ Ⓓ   15. Ⓐ Ⓑ Ⓒ Ⓓ

Answers can be found on page 56.

If you are like most people, you may have felt a little rushed completing this last exercise. Since the informational format (name of suspect, DOB, height, weight, etc.) is standard on wants and warrants, a fair amount of test time can be saved by becoming thoroughly familiar with the format. Thus, your number transposition and associated stories will not have to include that information. Awareness of your stories' chronological order will enable you to correctly interpret what information is pertinent to the question at hand. You may even wish to remember this information format in a different order and plug in the facts as they are given. However, don't vacillate between different format orders, because doing so can lead to some confusion.

Once you are comfortable with a certain conformation of the facts, commit them to your long-term memory. You will find this technique to be particularly time saving when you run across such test questions.

Study the three sketches and associated personal data below for ten minutes. Do not exceed the time allowed. When time is up, turn to the questions provided without making any further reference to the composites just studied.

SAMPLE COMPOSITE SKETCH/FILE 2

Suspect 1

Name:	Mark Jason Kluth
Date of Birth:	November 22, 1977
Height:	6'4"
Weight:	205 pounds
Hair:	Brown
Eyes:	Brown
Sex:	Male
Race:	Caucasian
Scars or marks:	Entire palm of right hand has scar tissue from burns suffered as a juvenile.
Social Security Nos.:	432-55-9941, 832-40-5111
Wants and Warrants:	Wanted for storage and concealment of stolen explosives and for unlawful possession of false identification documents
Criminal record:	Possession with intent to distribute counterfeit Social Security cards
	NCIC file number: 19-69

Suspect 2

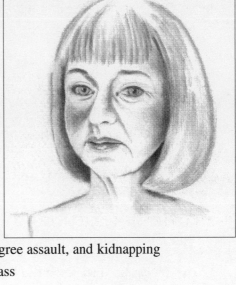

Name: Charlene Kim Olson

Alias: Shelly Elizabeth Hutchins

Date of Birth: July 3, 1952

Height: 5'3"

Weight: 105 pounds

Hair: Gray

Eyes: Blue

Sex: Female

Race: Caucasian

Scars or marks: None known

Social Security No.: 990-30-5432

Wants and Warrants: Wanted for interstate flight, second-degree assault, and kidnapping

Criminal record: First-degree assault and criminal trespass

NCIC file number: 91-15

Suspect 3

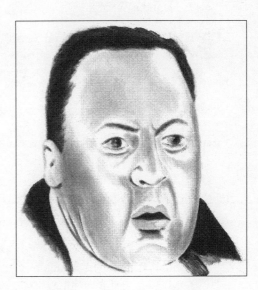

Name: Brian Robert Stowell

Alias: Michael Jason Landon, Brent Hendricks, and Kenneth Warren

Date of Birth: March 12, 1967

Height: 5'10"

Weight: 220 pounds

Hair: Black

Eyes: Hazel

Sex: Male

Race: Caucasian

Scars or marks: Heart-shaped tattoo on left forearm

Social Security No.: 890-55-6000

Wants and Warrants: Wanted for first-degree murder and interstate flight

Considered armed and dangerous

SAMPLE QUESTIONS, COMPOSITE SKETCH/FILE 2

1. Which of the three suspects did not have an assigned National Crime Information Center (NCIC) file number?
   A. Suspect 1
   B. Suspect 2
   C. Suspect 3
   D. All three suspects had NCIC file numbers.

2. 6'4" and 205 pounds are the respective height and weight figure for whom?
   A. Mr. Kluth
   B. Mr. Stowell
   C. Mr. Landon
   D. None of the above

3. Which of the three suspects was born on 7-3-52?
   A. Brent Hendricks
   B. Charlene Olson
   C. Mark Kluth
   D. Kenneth Warren

4. Who utilized multiple Social Security numbers in the commission of criminal activity?
   A. Shelley Hutchins
   B. Kenneth Warren
   C. Charlene Kim Olson
   D. Mark Jason Kluth

5. Which of the three suspects has multiple aliases on record?
   A. Suspect 1
   B. Suspects 1 and 2
   C. Suspects 1 and 3
   D. Suspect 3

6. Who is wanted for interstate flight, second-degree assault, and kidnapping?
   A. Shelley Elizabeth Hutchins
   B. Michael Jason Landon
   C. Tom Howard
   D. Kenneth Robert Stowell

7. NCIC file number 19-96 is the case number assigned to whom?
   A. Mark Jason Kluth
   B. Brian Robert Stowell
   C. Charlene Kim Olson
   D. None of the above

8. What kind of criminal record did Shelley Elizabeth Hutchins have?
   A. No prior convictions
   B. First-degree assault and criminal trespass
   C. Second-degree assault and unlawful possession of false identification documents
   D. Storage and concealment of stolen explosives

9. The picture to the right is a sketch of which suspect?

   A. Tom Howard
   B. Brian Robert Stowell
   C. Mark Jason Kluth
   D. None of the above

10. What crime had Mark Jason Kluth been convicted of?
   A. Second-degree assault and interstate flight
   B. First-degree murder
   C. Possession with intent to distribute counterfeit Social Security cards
   D. Criminal trespass and interstate flight

11. What is Suspect 2's Social Security number?
   A. 832-40-9941
   B. 432-55-9941
   C. 990-30-5432
   D. 890-55-6000

12. According to the files provided, all of the following statements are true of
    the suspect shown to the right except?

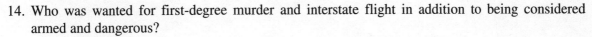

   A. Has a heart-shaped tattoo on right forearm
   B. Was born on 3-12-67
   C. Has hazel eyes and black hair
   D. All of the above statements are correct

13. What physical peculiarity sets Suspect 1 apart from the other
    two?
   A. Palm of right hand has scars from burns.
   B. Heart-shaped tattoo on the back of right hand
   C. Small C-shaped scar on left wrist
   D. No discernible differences were made apparent by the file
      information provided.

14. Who was wanted for first-degree murder and interstate flight in addition to being considered
    armed and dangerous?
   A. Suspect 1
   B. Suspects 2 and 3
   C. Suspect 3
   D. Suspects 1 and 3

15. All of the following are the various aliases used by Suspect 3 except?
   A. Brent Hendricks
   B. Michael Jason Landon
   C. Kenneth Warren
   D. Michael Jason Kluth

ANSWER SHEET FOR SAMPLE COMPOSITE SKETCH/FILE 2

1. Ⓐ Ⓑ Ⓒ Ⓓ   6. Ⓐ Ⓑ Ⓒ Ⓓ   11. Ⓐ Ⓑ Ⓒ Ⓓ

2. Ⓐ Ⓑ Ⓒ Ⓓ   7. Ⓐ Ⓑ Ⓒ Ⓓ   12. Ⓐ Ⓑ Ⓒ Ⓓ

3. Ⓐ Ⓑ Ⓒ Ⓓ   8. Ⓐ Ⓑ Ⓒ Ⓓ   13. Ⓐ Ⓑ Ⓒ Ⓓ

4. Ⓐ Ⓑ Ⓒ Ⓓ   9. Ⓐ Ⓑ Ⓒ Ⓓ   14. Ⓐ Ⓑ Ⓒ Ⓓ

5. Ⓐ Ⓑ Ⓒ Ⓓ   10. Ⓐ Ⓑ Ⓒ Ⓓ   15. Ⓐ Ⓑ Ⓒ Ⓓ

Answers can be found on page 56.

D. DESCRIPTIVE PASSAGES

The third form of memory exercises seen on past exams involves descriptive passages, designed to test an applicant's ability to remember literal details from what one reads. Normally, you will be given a reading that pertains to either a crime or emergency scene, or to some kind of technical or procedural issue. This kind of test differs from reading-comprehension exams in that you are not required to make deductions; rather, you are to memorize the facts only as they appear in the passage. Trivial items become just as important as main concepts.

The best advice here is to become a part of the passage instead of just reading it. If the passage details how a crime scene or other emergency unfolds, think of it as if you were witnessing the events as they occur. It can be helpful to incorporate some bizarre or funny aspects into the story to facilitate better memory of the passage.

Regardless of the passage's length and content, you will be given only a specified amount of time to read. When your time is up for studying the article, the test examiner will collect the readings and then direct you to answer related questions in your test booklet or supplement. You will not be allowed to review what was read while answering the questions provided.

SAMPLE DESCRIPTIVE PASSAGE 1

Study the passage given below for ten minutes. When your time is up, answer the questions that follow without further reference to the passage.

Phillip "Curly" McGregor (inmate L5-0178) was serving 25 years to life in Fayetteville State Penitentiary for armed robbery and second-degree murder. He was convicted of both counts in Westchester Superior Court on May 12, 1975, and he only had 5 years left before being eligible for parole consideration. However, on September 10, 1996, McGregor had set up an appointment, with the approval of Fayetteville authorities, to see Dr. Howard Stevens, an oncologist associated with Good Samaritan Hospital on 7th Avenue and Bristol Parkway. The hospital was 35 miles from the prison. Corrections Officers Jim Melborne (badge number 150) and Helen Bailey (badge number 113) were assigned to transport McGregor to the hospital for his examination. McGregor was placed in restraints prior to transportation in accordance with prison policy. En route to their destination, the prison van had to stop and wait for a light to change at the intersection of 4th Avenue and Montgomery Place, which is only 2 blocks from the hospital. It was at this location that a man emerged from behind a parked pickup truck, jerked open the driver's-side door to the van, and pointed a 9mm pistol in the face of driver Jim Melborne. Both Corrections Officers were immediately disarmed, ordered to get out of the van after releasing McGregor, and told to lie face down in the street and not move. About 2 or 3 minutes after their escape, Officer Bailey radioed CenCom 911 to report the incident. The call was received at 1:17 P.M. Police Officers Gordon Dunmire (badge number 973) and Jack Heston (badge number 151) were the first 2 of 8 police officers to respond. Both Corrections Officers were unable to provide useful descriptions of the suspect because of the speed with which the event unfolded. However, one witness, Mary Creston, who lives just across the street at 1740 Montgomery Place, was able to provide information that was helpful to the investigation. She described the lone suspect who assisted in McGregor's escape as being a white male, approximately 30–35 years of age, 6 foot, 175 pounds, long curly brown hair, brown eyes, and having a mustache. At the time he was wearing acid-washed denim jeans and jacket, white tennis shoes, and a red baseball cap. She also watched the two suspects run to a light green, 2-door sedan parked about a half block away. They were both last seen driving north on Montgomery Place.

It was later determined that McGregor's accomplice was Matt Strong, who just two weeks earlier escaped from a minimum-security work detail at Lincoln Park Corrections. Strong (inmate number T6-5733) was serving a three-year sentence for forgery and unlawful possession of a firearm. As of October 15, 1996, both suspects remain at large and are considered armed and dangerous.

SAMPLE QUESTIONS, DESCRIPTIVE PASSAGE 1

1. Phillip McGregor was serving time in Fayetteville State Penitentiary for which of the following crimes?
   A. Rape and first-degree murder
   B. Forgery and criminal trespass
   C. Robbery and second-degree murder
   D. Unlawful possession of a firearm

2. Which of the following inmate numbers identifies Phillip McGregor?
   A. L1-5780
   B. L5-0178
   C. T6-5377
   D. 6T-5733

3. Who within the story was able to provide a detailed eyewitness account of McGregor's escape?
   A. Jim Melborne
   B. Dr. Howard Stevens
   C. Gordon Dunmire
   D. Mary Creston

4. Which of the following is the home address of the witness described in the previous question?
   A. 1470 Bristol Place
   B. 4th Avenue and Montgomery Place
   C. 1740 Montgomery Place
   D. 7th Avenue and Bristol Parkway

5. What kind of weapon was used by McGregor's accomplice to effect his escape?
   A. 9mm pistol
   B. .45 pistol
   C. 7mm rifle
   D. Switchblade knife

6. What time did CenCom 911 receive the call regarding McGregor's escape?
   A. 1:17 A.M.
   B. 1:17 P.M.
   C. 1:27 P.M.
   D. 1:07 P.M.

7. McGregor's accomplice was later identified as whom?
   A. Jim Melborne (inmate number T6-5377)
   B. Jack Heston (inmate number T6-5733)
   C. Gordon Dunmire (inmate number T6-5377)
   D. Matt Strong (inmate number T6-5733)

8. What was the last date specified in the reading that both McGregor and his accomplice were still at large and considered armed and dangerous?
   A. May 15, 1995
   B. October 15, 1996
   C. September 10, 1996
   D. March 5, 1995

9. All of the following describe McGregor's lone accomplice except?
   A. Approximately 30-35 years of age
   B. Long curly blond hair
   C. 175 pounds
   D. A white male

10. McGregor's nickname is which of the following?
    A. Tiny
    B. Stubs
    C. Curly
    D. A nickname was not given in the passage.

11. How many years did McGregor have left to serve before becoming eligible for parole consideration?
    A. 5 years
    B. 6 years
    C. 10 years
    D. 25 years

12. Which of the following statements about Matt Strong are true according to the passage?
    A. He was serving a 5 year prison term for forgery.
    B. He escaped from a maximum security work detail.
    C. He was convicted of forgery in Westchester Superior Court on May 12, 1975.
    D. None of the above statements are true.

13. According to the reading, the distance between Good Samaritan Hospital and Fayetteville State Penitentiary was?
    A. 2 blocks
    B. 2 miles
    C. 25 miles
    D. 35 miles

14. Who was it in the reading that initially radioed CenCom 911 to report McGregor's escape?
    A. Police Officer Helen Bailey
    B. Corrections Officer Helen Bailey
    C. Police Officer Jim Melborne
    D. Corrections Officer Gordon Dunmire

15. According to eyewitness accounts, both escaped convicts were last seen leaving the area doing which of the following?
    A. Driving a two-toned, two-door sedan north on Montgomery Place
    B. Driving a light green, two-door sedan north on Montgomery Place
    C. Running down an alley between Bristol Parkway and Montgomery Place
    D. Driving a pickup truck north on Montgomery Place

ANSWER SHEET FOR SAMPLE DESCRIPTIVE PASSAGE 1

1. (A) (B) (C) (D)   6. (A) (B) (C) (D)   11. (A) (B) (C) (D)

2. (A) (B) (C) (D)   7. (A) (B) (C) (D)   12. (A) (B) (C) (D)

3. (A) (B) (C) (D)   8. (A) (B) (C) (D)   13. (A) (B) (C) (D)

4. (A) (B) (C) (D)   9. (A) (B) (C) (D)   14. (A) (B) (C) (D)

5. (A) (B) (C) (D)   10. (A) (B) (C) (D)   15. (A) (B) (C) (D)

Answers can be found on page 56.

SAMPLE DESCRIPTIVE PASSAGE 2

Study the passage given below for ten minutes. When your time is up, answer the questions that follow without further reference to what you just read.

On December 15, 1791, Congress ratified the first ten amendments to the U.S. Constitution, known as the Bill of Rights. These and the Fourteenth Amendment, which was ratified in 1868, address specific inalienable rights of an individual in this country. They have had a profound impact on law enforcement and the administration of the criminal justice system. They are as follows:

AMENDMENT I

Congress shall make no law respecting an establishment of religion, or prohibiting the free exercise thereof; or abridging the freedom of speech, or the press; or the right of the people peaceably to assemble; and to petition the Government for a redress of grievances.

AMENDMENT II

A well regulated Militia, being necessary to the security of a free State, the right of the people to keep and bear Arms, shall not be infringed.

AMENDMENT III

No Soldier shall, in time of peace, be quartered in any house, without the consent of the Owner, nor in time of war, but in a manner to be prescribed by law.

AMENDMENT IV

The right of the people to be secure in their persons, houses, papers, and effects, against unreasonable searches and seizures, shall not be violated, and no warrants shall issue, but upon probable cause, supported by Oath or affirmation, and particularly describing the place to be searched, and the persons or things to be seized.

AMENDMENT V

No person shall be held to answer for a capital, or otherwise infamous crime, unless on a presentment or indictment of a Grand Jury, except in cases arising in the land or naval forces, or in the Militia, when in actual service in time of War or public danger; nor shall any person be subject for the same offense to be twice put in jeopardy of life or limb; nor shall he be compelled in any criminal case to be a witness against himself, nor be deprived of life, liberty, or property, without due process of law; nor shall private property be taken for public use, without just compensation.

AMENDMENT VI

In all criminal prosecutions, the accused shall enjoy the right to a speedy and public trial, by an impartial jury of the State and the district wherein the crime shall have been committed, which district shall have been previously ascertained by law, and to be informed of the nature and cause of the accusation; to be confronted with the witnesses against him; to have compulsory process for obtaining witnesses in his favor and to have the assistance of counsel for his defense.

AMENDMENT VII

In suits at common law, where the value in controversy shall exceed twenty dollars, the right of trial by jury shall be preserved, and no fact tried by a jury, shall be otherwise reexamined in any Court of the United States, than according to the rules of the common law.

AMENDMENT VIII

Excessive bail shall not be required, nor excessive fines imposed, nor cruel and unusual punishments inflicted.

AMENDMENT IX

The enumeration in the Constitution, of certain rights, shall not be construed to deny or disparage others retained by the people.

AMENDMENT X

The powers not delegated to the United States by the Constitution, nor prohibited by it to the States, are reserved to the States respectively, or to the people.

AMENDMENT XIV Section 1

All persons born or naturalized in the United States, and subject to the jurisdiction thereof, are citizens of the United States and of the State wherein they reside. No State shall make or enforce any law which shall abridge the privileges or immunities of citizens of the United States; nor shall any State deprive any person of life, liberty, or property, without due process of law; nor deny to any person within its jurisdiction the equal protection of the laws.

SAMPLE QUESTIONS, DESCRIPTIVE PASSAGE 2

1. Which amendment to the Constitution concerns search and seizure?
   A. Amendment II
   B. Amendment III
   C. Amendment IV
   D. Amendment XIV

2. Which amendment concerns the accused being specifically informed of the nature and cause of the accusation and to be confronted by the witnesses against them?
   A. Amendment I
   B. Amendment V
   C. Amendment VI
   D. Amendment X

3. The Bill of Rights was ratified
   A. 11-12-1791
   B. 12-15-1791
   C. 12-15-1868
   D. 12-5-1799

4. Which amendment states, "No State shall make or enforce any law which shall abridge the privileges or immunities of citizens of the United States; nor shall any State deprive any person of life, liberty, or property without due process of law"?
   A. Amendment V
   B. Amendment VII
   C. Amendment X
   D. Amendment XIV

5. Which amendment concerns the right of people to keep and bear arms?
   A. Amendment II
   B. Amendment III
   C. Amendment IV
   D. Amendment V

6. Which amendment concerns the issue of excessive fines and cruel and unusual punishment?
   A. Amendment V
   B. Amendment VII
   C. Amendment VIII
   D. Amendment X

7. The first ten amendments are referred to as:
   A. The Constitution
   B. The Bill of Rights
   C. English Common Law
   D. Civil Rights

8. Which amendment concerns freedom of religion and speech?
   A. Amendment I
   B. Amendment II
   C. Amendment III
   D. Amendment VII

9. "No Soldier shall, in time of peace, be quartered in any house, without the consent of the owner, nor in time of war, but in a manner to be prescribed by law." This quote reflects which of the amendments?
    A. Amendment II
    B. Amendment III
    C. Amendment IV
    D. Amendment V

10. Which amendment concerns the accused's being granted the right to a speedy and public trial?
    A. Amendment I
    B. Amendment IV
    C. Amendment V
    D. Amendment VI

11. Which amendment specifies that the accused cannot face a double jeopardy of life or limb for the same offense, or in other words, be tried again for the same crime if not found guilty the first time?
    A. Amendment XIV
    B. Amendment IX
    C. Amendment VI
    D. Amendment V

12. Which amendment specifies that if the value in a controversy exceeds twenty dollars, the right of trial by jury shall be preserved?
    A. Amendment IV
    B. Amendment VII
    C. Amendment VIII
    D. None of the amendments given above contain these specifics.

13. Assistance of counsel for the accused's defense is addressed by which one of the amendments?
    A. Amendment IV
    B. Amendment V
    C. Amendment VI
    D. Both A and B

14. When was the Fourteenth Amendment ratified?
    A. 1868
    B. 1791
    C. 1776
    D. None of the above dates

15. Which amendment grants equal rights to all persons born or naturalized in the United States?
    A. Amendment VIII
    B. Amendment X
    C. Amendment XIV
    D. Amendment XIX

ANSWER SHEET FOR SAMPLE DESCRIPTIVE PASSAGE 2

1. Ⓐ Ⓑ Ⓒ Ⓓ	6. Ⓐ Ⓑ Ⓒ Ⓓ	11. Ⓐ Ⓑ Ⓒ Ⓓ
2. Ⓐ Ⓑ Ⓒ Ⓓ	7. Ⓐ Ⓑ Ⓒ Ⓓ	12. Ⓐ Ⓑ Ⓒ Ⓓ
3. Ⓐ Ⓑ Ⓒ Ⓓ	8. Ⓐ Ⓑ Ⓒ Ⓓ	13. Ⓐ Ⓑ Ⓒ Ⓓ
4. Ⓐ Ⓑ Ⓒ Ⓓ	9. Ⓐ Ⓑ Ⓒ Ⓓ	14. Ⓐ Ⓑ Ⓒ Ⓓ
5. Ⓐ Ⓑ Ⓒ Ⓓ	10. Ⓐ Ⓑ Ⓒ Ⓓ	15. Ⓐ Ⓑ Ⓒ Ⓓ

Answers can be found on page 57.

ANSWERS FOR MEMORY RECALL SAMPLE QUESTIONS

SAMPLE SKETCH 1

1. D	6. D	11. C
2. C	7. C	12. A
3. A	8. C	13. B
4. B	9. A	14. A
5. B	10. D	15. D

SAMPLE SKETCH 2

1. D	6. B	11. C
2. B	7. C	12. A
3. A	8. C	13. A
4. D	9. C	14. D
5. B	10. D	15. B

SAMPLE COMPOSITE SKETCH/FILE 1

1. C	6. B	11. A
2. C	7. C	12. D
3. A	8. A	13. B
4. B	9. B	14. C
5. D	10. B	15. B

SAMPLE COMPOSITE SKETCH/FILE 2

1. C	6. A	11. C
2. A	7. D	12. A
3. B	8. B	13. A
4. D	9. B	14. C
5. D	10. C	15. D

SAMPLE DESCRIPTIVE PASSAGE 1

1. C	6. B	11. A
2. B	7. D	12. D
3. D	8. B	13. D
4. C	9. B	14. B
5. A	10. C	15. B

SAMPLE DESCRIPTIVE PASSAGE 2

1. *C*	6. *C*	11. *D*
2. *C*	7. *B*	12. *B*
3. *B*	8. *A*	13. *C*
4. *D*	9. *B*	14. *A*
5. *A*	10. *D*	15. *C*

Your score for each of the exercises would be as follows:

14–15 correct — Excellent
12–13 correct — Good
10–11 correct — Fair
Less than 10 correct — Poor

Chapter 3

Reading Comprehension

From the start of academy training to the highest rank achieved, a Corrections Officer will have to study and interpret a vast amount of information and apply it to innumerable situations. How efficiently that knowledge is acquired depends largely on the officer's reading comprehension. Some people find it easier than others to comprehend written material. Experts attribute this difference to inherited ability, but, for the most part, it is directly related to the kind of reading habits acquired in elementary school. Of course, if bad habits are acquired, they can impede, rather than enhance, a person's ability to read, and comprehension will suffer as well.

Let's examine a few reading habit facts and fallacies: One misconception is the belief that *subvocalizing*, moving your lips or other parts of your mouth or throat as you read silently, is detrimental to your comprehension. Teachers have even gone to the extent of passing out candy in class to prevent students from subvocalizing. In truth, subvocalizing has been proven in various studies to be beneficial. Students who did subvocalize while reading were shown to have a better understanding of most material studied. This was especially true when difficult or technical information was read.

Another widespread fallacy is that a student should not read word for word. Rather, some people suggest that reading should be done by looking at several words as a unit. Furthermore, these units should provide sufficient insight into the article's content. The idea is that time is saved and reading comprehension is improved, but studies demonstrate that exactly the opposite is true—reading comprehension is improved only when each word is read.

Some teachers also believe that if a student does not fully understand the material presented, it is better to continue on instead of rereading. The line of reasoning here is that if a student does not learn what is read the first time, repetitive reading only proves to be unproductive and a waste of time. Many studies have disproved this theory. In fact, rereading can be a necessity when the material being studied is complicated or abstract. Articles should be reread as many times as necessary to get the full meaning of the text before continuing.

Another misguided belief is that any text can be completely and quickly comprehended if key words are discerned. This very concept has given rise to the speed-reading industry. Speed-reading experts claim that reading at 250 to 300 words per minute is too slow when it is possible to skim at a rate of 3 to 6 times that speed. What they fail to mention is that comprehension is sacrificed for the sake of speed. This raises the question: What is gained if a fair share of information is not fully understood or retained?

The other major shortcoming of skim-reading practices is that key words may be taken out of context and, when viewed cumulatively, may cause the reader to misconstrue the underlying meaning of the article. Verbs and prepositions that link nouns can dramatically alter the tenor of the material being studied. If verbs and prepositions are not given attention as key words, a passage may be read as meaning one thing when skimmed although in fact it means something entirely different. You can be assured that college students studying for the LSAT, VAT, MCAT, or other professional exams do not skim their readings. Subject matter expected to be covered on these exams is closely scrutinized without regard to speed. There is no acceptable substitute for full and accurate reading comprehension.

To better hone your reading skills, practice reading as much material as possible, taking care to avoid the bad habits just discussed. You will find it is easier to do this if the articles you read are on topics of interest.

Nothing will discourage reading more than a dull or boring article. Reading of any kind is beneficial; newspapers, magazines, and fiction and nonfiction books are a few possible sources.

As you read an article, try to discern the underlying meaning of the reading. What is the author trying to say? Are there ideas or other forms of information that support any conclusions? If so, which are the most important? In this respect, certain concepts can be prioritized. You will find that if you follow such an inquiry into all your reading, your comprehension and reading efficiency will improve immensely.

Another way to enhance reading efficiency is to develop a better vocabulary. Quite often, words encountered in your readings may be unfamiliar to you. Don't skip over such words. Use a dictionary to discover the meanings of unfamiliar words and then make a mental note of them. Some people find it easier to write each word on a small card as a reminder. As a challenge, try incorporating that particular word into your everyday language. A continuance of this practice is a viable way of building a strong vocabulary.

If a dictionary is not handy when you encounter an unfamiliar word, it is still possible to discern the meaning of the word. Start by looking at the word and see how it is used within the sentence. This should give you some clue as to its general meaning. For example:

The restaurant patron was extremely *vexed* when the waiter accidentally spilled coffee on his lap. Obviously, the customer would not be happy under such circumstances, so we know the word *vexed* implies a degree of dissatisfaction.

Another method that can be used to further understand or define an unfamiliar term uses basic word derivations or etymology. Word derivations can provide a partial, if not complete, meaning for a term. For example, take a look at the work *injudicious*. The first two letters, *in,* are a prefix that means "not" or "lack of." The root of the word, *judiei,* means "judgment." The last portion of the word, *ous,* is the suffix, and it means "characterized by." Therefore, *injudicious* may be interpreted as a characterization of someone who lacks judgment.

The following etymology table has been provided for your convenience. This, in conjunction with viewing unfamiliar terms in context, will lend the best possible insight without the assistance of a dictionary.

Common Prefixes

Prefix	Meaning	Example
a-	or without	atypical — not typical
ab-	away from	abnormal — deviating from normal
ac-	to or toward	accredit — to attribute to
ad-	to or toward	adduce — to bring forward as evidence
ag-	to or toward	aggravate — to make more severe
an-	nor or without	anarchy — a society with no government
ante-	before or preceding	antenatal — prior to birth
anti-	against or counter	antisocial — against being social
at-	to or toward	attain — to reach to
auto-	self or same	automatic — self-acting
bene-	good or well	benevolence — an act of kindness or goodwill
bi-	two or twice	bisect — to divide into two parts
circum-	around	circumscribe — to draw a line around or encircle
com-	together or with	combine — to join
con-	together or with	conciliate — to unite or draw together
contra-	against or opposite	contradict — to oppose or be against what someone else says
de-	removal from	decongestant — relieves or removes congestion

dec-	ten	decade — a ten-year period
demi-	half	demigod — partly divine and partly human
dis-	apart, negation, or reversal	dishonest — a lack or negation of honesty
dys-	diseased, bad, difficult, faulty	dyslexia — impairment of reading ability
e-, ex-	from or out of	evoke — to draw forth or bring out
extra-	beyond	extraordinary — outside or beyond the usual order
hemi-	half	hemisphere — half of the globe
hyper-	excessive or over	hyperactive — excessively active
hypo-	beneath or under	hypodermic — something introduced under the skin
im-	not	impersonal — not personal
in-	not	inaccessible — not accessible
ir-	not	irrational — not having reason or understanding
inter-	among or between	interdepartmental — between departments
intra-	inside or within	intradepartmental — within departments
kilo-	thousand	kiloton — one thousand tons
mal-	bad or ill	malcontent — dissatisfied
mis-	wrong	misinterpret — to interpret wrongly
mono-	one or single	monochromatic — having only one color
non-	not	nonresident — person who does not live in a particular place
ob-	against or opposed	object — to declare opposition or disapproval
omni-	all	omnivore — an animal that eats all foods, both plant and animal
per-	through or thoroughly	perennial — continuing or lasting through the years
poly-	many or much	polychromy — an artistic combination of different colors
post-	after or later	postglacial — after the glacial period
pre-	before or supporting	presuppose — to suppose beforehand, previous — going before in time or order
pro-	before or supporting	proalliance — supportive of an alliance
re-	again, former state or position	reiterate — to do or say repeatedly
retro-	backward or return	retrogressive — moving backwards
self-	individual or personal	self-defense — the act of defending oneself
semi-	half or part	semifinal — halfway final
sub-	below or under	submarine — something underwater
super-	above or over	superficial — not penetrating the surface
tele-	distance	telegraph — an instrument used for communicating at a distance
trans-	across, over or through	transparent — lets light shine through
ultra-	beyond or excessive	ultraconservative — beyond ordinary conservatism
un-	not	unaccountable — not accountable or responsible

Common Suffixes

Suffix	Meaning	Example
-able, -ible	capacity of being	readable — able to be read, eligible, qualified to be chosen
-ac	like or pertaining to	maniac — like a mad person
-age	function or state of	mileage — distance in miles
-ally	in a manner that relates to	pastorally — in a manner that relates to rural life
-ance	act or fact of	cognizance — knowledge through perception or reason
-ary	doing or pertaining to	subsidiary — serving to assist or supplement
-ant	person or thing	tyrant — a ruler who is unjustly severe
-ar	of the nature or pertaining to	nuclear — pertaining to the nucleus
-ation	action	excavation — act or process of excavating
-cede, -ceed	to go or come	intercede — to go or come between; succeed, to follow
-cide	destroy or kill	homicide — the killing of a person by another
-cy	quality	decency — the state of being decent
-dy	condition or character	shoddy — pretentious condition or something poorly made
-ence, -ery	act or fact of doing or pertaining to	despondence — loss of hope; confectionery — place of making or selling candies or sweets
-er	one who does	lawyer — one who practices law
-ful	abounding or full of	fretful — tending to fret or be irritable
-ic	like or pertaining to	artistic — having a talent in art
-ify	to make	magnify — to make large
-ious	full of	laborious — full of labor or requiring a lot of work
-ise	to make	devise — to create from existing ideas
-ish	like	childish — like a child
-ism	system or belief	capitalism — an economic system that revolves around private ownership
-ist	person or thing	idealist — a person who has ideals
-ize	to make	idolize — to make an idol of
-less	without	penniless — without a penny
-olgy	the study of	archaeology — the study of historical cultures using artifacts of past activities
-ly	in a manner	shapely — well formed
-ment	the act of	achievement — the act of achieving
-ness	state of or quality	pettiness — the state of being petty or small-minded
-or	person who acts	legislator — person who enacts legislation
-ory	place	dormitory — building that provides living quarters
-ship	condition or character	censorship — overseeing or excluding items that may be objectionable to those concerned
-tude	state of or result	solitude — state of being alone or apart from society
-ty	condition or character	levity — lightness in character
-y	quality or result	hefty — moderately heavy or weighty

Common Roots

Root	Meaning	Example
acou	hearing	acoustical — pertaining to sound
acro	farthest or highest point	acrophobia — fear of heights
acu	needle	acupuncture — puncturing of body tissue for relief of pain
aero	air or gas	aeronautics — study of the operation of aircraft
alt	high	altitude — a position or region at height
ambi	both	ambidextrous — capable of using both hands equally well
anter	in front	anterior — toward the front
anthrop	human being	anthropology — science of mankind
aqueo, aqui	water	aquatic — living in water
audio	hearing	audiology — science of hearing
auto	self	autocratic — ruled by a monarch with absolute rule
avi	bird, flight	aviary — large cage for confining birds
bio	life	biography — written history of a person's life
bona	good	bonafide — in good faith
capit	head	capital — involving the forfeiture of the head or life (as in capital punishment)
carb	carbon	carboniferous — containing or producing carbon or coal
carcin	cancer	carcinogen — substance that initiates cancer
carn	flesh	carnivorous — eating flesh
cent	a hundred	centennial — pertaining to 100 years
centro, centri	center	centrifugal — movement away from the center
cepha	head	hydrocephalus — condition caused by excess fluid in the head
chron	time	synchronize — to happen at the same time
citri	fruit	citric acid — an acid found in fruit juices
corpor, corp	body	corporate — combined into one body
crypt	covered or hidden	cryptology — an art of uncovering a hidden or coded message
culp	fault	culprit — criminal
cyclo	circular	cyclone — a storm with strong circular winds
demo	people	democracy — government ruled by the people
doc	teach	doctrine — instruction or teaching
dox	opinion	paradox — self-contradictory statement that has plausibility
duo	two	duologue — conversation involving two people
dyna	power	dynamometer — device for measuring power
eco	environment	ecosystem — community or organisms interacting with the environment

embry	early	embryonic — pertaining to an embryo or the beginning of life
equi	equal	equilibrium — balance
ethn	race, group	ethnology — study of human races or groups
exter	outside of	external — on the outside
flor	flower	florist — dealer in flowers
foli	leafy	defoliate — to strip a plant of its leaves
geo	earth	geophysics — the physics of the earth
geri	old age	geriatrics — medicinal studies pertaining to old age
graphy	write	autograph — a person's own signature
gyro	spiral motion	gyroscope — rotating wheel that can spin on various planes
horti	garden	horticulture — science of cultivating plants
hydro	water	hydroplane — form of boat that glides over water
hygi	health	hygiene — practice of preservation of health
hygro	wet	hygrometer — instrument used to measure moisture in the atmosphere
hypno	sleep	hypnology — science that treats sleep
ideo	idea	ideology — study of ideas
iso	equal	isotonic — having equal tones or tension
jur	swear	jury — body of persons sworn to tell the truth
lac, lacto	milk	lacteal — resembling milk
lamin	divided	laminate — to bond together layers
lingui	tongue	linguistics — study of languages
litho	stone	lithography — art of putting design on stone with a greasy material to produce printed impressions
loco, locus	place	locomotion — act or power of moving from place to place
macro	large	macrocosm — the great world, the universe
man	hand	manual — made or operated by hand
medi	middle	mediocre — average or middle quality
mega	large	megalopolis — urban area comprising several large adjoining cities
mero, meri	part or fraction of	meroblastic — partial or incomplete cleavage
micro	small or petty	microscopic — so small as to be invisible without the aid of a microscope
mini	small	miniature — an image or representation of something on a smaller scale
moto	motion	motive — what moves someone to action
multi	many	multimillionaire — person with several million dollars
navi	ship	navigation — to direct course for a vessel on the sea or in the air
neo	new	neonatal — pertaining to the newborn

noct, nocti	night	nocturnal — occurring in the night
oct, octo, octa	eight	octagonal — having eight sides
olig, oligo	scant or few	oligarchy — government that is controlled by a few people
oo	egg	oology — branch of ornithology dealing with bird eggs
optic	vision or eye	optometry — profession of testing vision and examining eyes for disease
ortho	straight	orthodontics — dentistry dealing with straightening the teeth
pent, penta	five	pentagon — having five sides
phob	panic or fear	arachnophobia — fear of spiders
phon	sound	phonograph — instrument for reproducing sound
pod	foot	podiatry — the study and treatment of foot disorders
pseudo	false	pseudonym — fictitious name
psych	mental	psychiatry — science of treating mental disorders
pyro	fire	pyrotechnics — art of making or using fireworks
quad	four	quadruped — animal having four feet
quint	five	quintuple — having five parts
sect	part or divide	bisect — divide into two equal parts
spiri	coiled	spirochete — spiral-shaped bacteria
stasi	to stand still	hemostatic — serving to stop hemorrhage
techni	skill	technician — skilled person in a particular field
terri	to frighten	terrible — capable of exciting terror
tetra	four	tetrahedron — a shape with four faces
therm	heat	thermostat — device that automatically controls desired temperatures
toxi	poison	toxicology — science concerning the effects, antidotes, and detection of poisonous substances
uni	single	unilateral — involving one person, class, or nation
urb	city	suburb — outlying part of a city
uro	urine	urology — science of studying the urinary tract and its diseases
verb	word	proverb — a name, person, or thing that has become a byword
veri	truthful	verify — to prove to be truthful
vit	life	vitality — liveliness
vitri	glass or glasslike	vitreous — resembling glass
vivi	alive	viviparous — giving birth to living young
vol	wish	volunteer — to enter into or offer oneself freely
zo, zoi, zoo	animal	zoology — science of studying animal life

Vocabulary at one time constituted a major part of the Corrections Officer exam. Now, however, it is fairly common to see vocabulary test questions constitute only 5–10 percent of the entire exam. Additionally, some words not commonly used are incorporated into reading-comprehension questions. Without some understanding of what those terms mean, your comprehension of the passage can be diminished.

Most reading-comprehension test questions encountered on past exams ask questions that concern three things. First, what is the basic underlying theme of the passage, or what would be a suitable title or heading that summarizes the article? In most cases, this is an inferential question. In other words, you have to assimilate all the information given and select one of four possible options that best encompasses the meaning of the article. There will not be a sentence taken directly out of the article to serve as a potential option. These questions require judgment on your part.

Secondly, some questions may concern literal reading comprehension — that is, questions about certain details, ideas, or facts. If the answer is not immediately apparent, it can be determined by simply going back to the applicable part of the reading and picking out the correct answer directly.

The last type of question may concern interpretation. After studying the information in an article, a comparable or hypothetical situation may be posed, and it will be left to you to interpret how what you have read applies to it.

It is ironic, but you may find it easier to read the questions before reading the passage presented. This is somewhat of a backward approach to reading comprehension, but it will alert you to what is considered important and, hence, what to look for in the article, thus saving time.

Sample questions complete with answers and supporting explanations follow. The questions presented are not copies of past exams, but they do represent a good overview of what to expect on the actual exam.

SAMPLE QUESTIONS, READING COMPREHENSION

Passage 1

All crimes, regardless of their nature, leave some degree of evidence behind. How an officer goes about gathering physical evidence can make the difference between offering evidence that is material and relevant in a trial versus that which is bound to be thrown out under cross-examination.

Preservation of the crime scene is the number-one priority before and during the actual investigation. The number of investigators or specialists surveying the crime scene should be kept to an absolute minimum. Unauthorized persons should be removed from the premises until the investigation is complete. Bystanders can inadvertently step on or otherwise destroy or remove valuable evidence. In fact, some people have been known to obstruct justice willfully by destroying evidence in the hope of protecting a friend or relative. For obvious reasons, efforts should also be made to protect evidence from the elements, such as wind, sun, rain, or snow.

Not only is minimizing the potential for evidence contamination very important, but so is the way an officer proceeds with the search for and collection of evidence. The mechanics of the search itself, if conducted in a careful and orderly manner, can preclude duplication (i.e., covering the same area twice) in the investigation. This search and collection needs to be carried out within a reasonable time because certain kinds of evidence are perishable (principally organic compounds such as blood and semen) and begin to deteriorate quickly. In addition to the time element, temperatures above 95° Fahrenheit or below freezing can also have a detrimental effect on such evidence.

In the course of the actual search itself, officers should be on the lookout for any evidence prior to actually entering the crime scene. Normally, searches are begun by scanning the floor and walls, and then proceed to the ceiling. When marking and securing evidence, investigators should be extremely careful not to destroy any of it. Dropping a delicate article or accidentally marking or scratching items are two examples of how evidence can be damaged. All evidence, once located, should be cataloged (recorded), listing a description and relative location where found in the crime scene. This compiling of records essentially provides the chain of evidence prosecutors can use at trial to secure a conviction.

Answer questions 1–5 on the basis of Passage 1.

1. What would be an appropriate title for this passage?

    A. How best to secure criminal convictions through evidence handling

    B. What an officer should not do during the investigation of a crime scene

    C. The intricacies of evidence gathering

    D. Procedural guidelines and cautions for crime-scene investigations

2. What two words would be considered suitable adjectives in summarizing the content of this article?

    A. Prudent and compulsory

    B. Intelligent and inquisitive

    C. Circumspect and expeditious

    D. Attentive and compliant

3. Officer Pat Gregory was quick to respond to a warehouse burglary after receiving an anonymous tip. The burglars were not on the premises when Officer Gregory arrived. However, in their haste to flee they had left a crowbar on the warehouse floor. The warehouse door had obviously been jimmied to allow entry. Officer Gregory, in confirming that belief, picked up the crowbar and carefully placed the prying edge against the impression marks made on the door. The crowbar was placed in its original position on the warehouse floor after Officer Gregory had confirmed his suspicions. Assuming that someone other than Officer Gregory was responsible for the burglary investigation, Officer Gregory's actions were:

    A. Right, because the evidence, even though it had been moved, was placed back to its original position.

    B. Wrong, because he may have left an extra scratch or even traces of paint from the crowbar in the impression on the door.

    C. Right, because his confirmation will save another investigator valuable time.

    D. Wrong, because he should have wrapped the crowbar handle in either plastic or a paper towel prior to picking it up.

4. Which type of evidence given below is most prone to deterioration with time and temperature extremes?

    A. Blood stains

    B. Fired casings and bullets

    C. Hairs and fibers

    D. Dirt and soil particles

5. Which of the following is *not* considered an underlying objective for investigators in sealing off a crime scene?

    A. To prevent willful obstruction of justice by persons close to the investigation

    B. To prevent persons outside of the investigative unit from inadvertently destroying evidence

    C. To illustrate to the public that police know what they are doing

    D. To preserve the crime scene as is

Passage 2

Correctional institutions over the years have become much more discreet over the issue of searches and seizures, largely due to litigation filed by inmates. The Fourth Amendment provides that people and their property, as well as personal effects, have rights against any unreasonable search or seizure. However, these protections have been limited in scope for inmates out of obvious concerns for security maintenance.

Incident to arrest, a police officer is only allowed to search the person and area within proximate reach for a potential weapon. Searches cannot be expanded further unless there is a warrant issued by a magistrate specifying exactly what can be searched. Corrections personnel, on the other hand, are not bound by such rigid standards. If an inmate is suspected of smuggling contraband into the facility and thereby becoming a threat to security, it is within their discretion to conduct cell searches, pat-down searches, or even strip searches if necessary. The courts have ruled on past cases (*Hudson v. Palmer* [1984] and *Block v. Rutherford* [1984]) that prisoners essentially do not have the right to privacy. However, more intrusive searches, such as strip searches or body-cavity searches, might interfere with Fourth Amendment rights. Intrusive searches must be done in a reasonable and professional manner. Every attempt should be made under such circumstances to preserve the dignity and privacy of affected inmates. Searches conducted otherwise are invitations for legal problems.

Answer questions 6–10 on the basis of Passage 2.

6. What would be an appropriate title for this passage?

    A. The legal precedents established by *Hudson v. Palmer* (1984) and *Block v. Rutherford* (1984)

    B. The rights of prison inmates

    C. Search and seizure guidelines and limitations as established by law

    D. The consequences of an unreasonable search or seizure

7. The word "incident" (to arrest) as it is applied in the reading most nearly means?

    A. As a preliminary

    B. Dependent on

    C. In the course of

    D. Preparatory

8. Officer Bill Stanton and Gary Fullerton subjected inmate Carl Vinson to a strip search after a contact visit with a girlfriend who was known to have a criminal record of controlled substance possession. During the search, Officer Fullerton made degrading remarks pertaining to Vinson's "manhood between his legs" and pretty much laughed at him throughout the entire procedure. According to the reading, the search of inmate Vinson was conducted how?

    A. Properly, within the limits stipulated by the Fourth Amendment.

    B. Improperly, because a warrant was not issued by a magistrate specifying that such a search was necessary.

    C. Properly, because reasonable suspicion did exist that inmate Vinson may have come into possession of a controlled substance.

    D. Improperly, because despite the reasonable grounds for a search, it was done unprofessionally, thereby leaving open the future prospect of a legitimate lawsuit.

9. Inmate James Carter had two weeks earlier made some derogatory remarks about Corrections Officer Mark Hanley's wife and family. Consequently, Carter found himself constantly being the subject of pat-down searches conducted by Officer Hanley. This happened in spite of the fact that Carter was under close observation in a high-security unit and had not recently had the opportunity to potentially smuggle contraband into the facility. Based on what was stated in Passage 2, which of the following statements is true?

   A. Officer Hanley's pat-down searches were legitimate and subsequently legal.

   B. Officer Hanley acted improperly because of the lack of a warrant from a superior officer.

   C. Officer Hanley acted improperly due to the lack of probable cause and exercising his authority to get back at inmate Carter.

   D. Officer Hanley acted properly because anyone who makes such remarks to authorities is likely to possess contraband.

10. All of the following are true statements concerning the narrative except?

   A. Cell searches and strip searches fall under the same provisions of the Fourth Amendment.

   B. Strip searches can be conducted when reasonable suspicion exists that an inmate may be concealing contraband.

   C. Random pat-down searches, in the absence of probable cause, are not legitimate institutional procedure and, therefore, are potentially the subject of court intervention.

   D. Courts have established that inmates have a narrow definition of what to expect in terms of privacy while incarcerated.

Passage 3

All correctional institutions have policies pertaining to the use of force against inmates. Corrections Officers have a duty to prescribe established regulations to maintain internal discipline. If an officer finds him- or herself the subject of physical assault or witnesses a third party under similar circumstances, it is an officer's right to use reasonable force to enforce compliance of facility rules. This right does not, however, extend to meting out punishment for rule infractions. Deadly force can only be used if a person convicted of a felony is attempting to escape or if the same party has committed or is committing a felony that poses a physical threat of harm to others. All other situations confronted by Corrections Officers require discretionary force to effect the lawful purposes intended.

Answer questions 11–15 on the basis of Passage 3.

11. Which of the following would be the most appropriate title for this particular passage?

   A. Institutional policy concerning cruel and unusual punishment

   B. Self-defense measures for correctional employees

   C. The use of deadly force and its restrictions

   D. Enforcement of institutional rules and regulations

12. Harvey Craswold had been booked for second-degree reckless endangerment, which, according to statutes, is a misdemeanor. During intake processing, Craswold saw an opportunity to escape and fled without hesitation. Corrections Officer Ann Talbott, who was one of the two Corrections Officers handling his case, promptly drew her firearm and shot Mr. Craswold in the leg. Under the circumstances and according to the narrative . . .

    A. Officer Talbott acted within procedural guidelines to prevent Craswold's escape.

    B. Since Officer Talbott only shot Mr. Craswold in the leg, it can be surmised that she used reasonable force.

    C. Officer Talbott violated the standards set for using deadly force.

    D. Officer Talbott should have waited for Craswold to commit a felony, such as assaulting someone, and then shot him.

13. What single word would best describe what Corrections Officers should show when decisions regarding deadly force must be made?

    A. Constraint

    B. Composure

    C. Expediency

    D. Confidence

14. Inmate John Livingston had just left metal shop when Officer Lyle Simmons noticed a peculiar shaped bulge in the waistband of his prison trousers. Officer Simmons told Livingston to face the wall so that he could do a pat-down search. Instead of complying with the officer's directives, Livingston produced a crude-looking knife and, in a menacing tone, told the officer he was going to regret his decision for not minding his own business. Officer Simmons was unarmed at the time but Sergeant Ray Dixon, who happened to be in close enough proximity to witness what took place, was armed. Dixon drew his firearm and ordered inmate Livingston to drop the knife. Without even acknowledging Dixon's presence, Livingston lunged at Simmons. Officer Dixon shot and killed Livingston before he even made a second step toward Simmons. According to the narrative, Officer Dixon . . .

    A. Acted properly because Livingston refused to have a pat-down search

    B. Acted improperly because Livingston did not acknowledge his orders

    C. Acted properly because Livingston posed a serious threat to Officer Simmons

    D. Acted improperly because he failed to explain to Livingston that he was committing a serious infraction

15. All of the following statements are true with respect to the narrative except?

    A. Rule enforcements should be expedient and disproportionate to any and all infractions committed to demonstrate to prisoners who is in charge.

    B. *Reasonable* is the key word for the amount of force necessary to make inmates comply with institutional rules and regulations.

    C. The perception of physical harm to a third party is a precondition for the use of deadly force by a Corrections Officer.

    D. All of the above statements are true according to the reading.

Passage 4

By and large, correctional institutions perform a balancing act over incoming mail for inmates. While the First Amendment guarantees the freedom of speech, institutional interests such as rehabilitation and security must be maintained. Rejection of any mail (e.g., newsletters, periodicals, personal correspondence, etc.) for whatever reason is essentially censorship. However, various court rulings have upheld that such censorship within correctional environments is permissible, but only to the extent that the material involved espouses violence, serves to inhibit rehabilitation, or inflames racist sentiment. Any censorship beyond those limitations will not be legal.

Typically, most departments have well-established lists of what is and what is not acceptable. However, the decision to return "borderline or grey-area" material is a sensitive legal issue and one that is usually made at the administrative level instead of at the line-staff level. First Amendment rights for inmates have and probably will always remain a controversial issue.

Answer questions 16–20 on the basis of Passage 4.

16. The main focus of the narrative is?

    A. Discretionary censorship of prison mail

    B. Inmate rights in general

    C. Legal ramifications of the First Amendment

    D. Both selections A and C

17. Which of the following situations would most likely warrant legal rejection by a correctional institution?

    A. An inmate receiving a gift subscription to *Playboy* magazine

    B. An inmate getting a newsletter from the National Association of Weightlifters

    C. An inmate receiving religious material from a Muslim cleric

    D. An inmate getting via the mail a book that teaches the martial arts

18. Inmate Wilson was twice convicted for rape and was sentenced to serve ten years. Corrections Officer Squires liked inmate Wilson because he epitomized the model prisoner, so, as a small token of appreciation, he allowed Wilson to receive via the mail a small amount of sexually explicit material. According to the reading, Officer Squires's actions were?

    A. Justifiable in the sense of rewarding Wilson for his exemplary behavior

    B. Justifiable because a small measure of pornography has never hurt anyone before

    C. Contrary to institutional policy because Wilson is a convicted rapist and exposure to sexually explicit material should be considered detrimental to his rehabilitative efforts

    D. Contrary to institutional policy because Squires should have allowed complete access to any and all such mailings

19. The term used in the reading to describe selective screening of incoming mail for inmates was?

    A. Judicial prudence

    B. Censorship

    C. Bias

    D. Reasonable cause

20. According to the reading, the limitation on restricting mail coming to an inmate largely depends upon what?

   A. The moral values of the administrator in charge

   B. Judicial interpretation of the First Amendment and institutional security

   C. Line-staff officers' subjective views of what is in the best interests of inmates

   D. Public perception that inmates have too many rights as it is

ANSWER SHEET FOR READING-COMPREHENSION SAMPLE QUESTIONS

1. Ⓐ Ⓑ Ⓒ Ⓓ
2. Ⓐ Ⓑ Ⓒ Ⓓ
3. Ⓐ Ⓑ Ⓒ Ⓓ
4. Ⓐ Ⓑ Ⓒ Ⓓ
5. Ⓐ Ⓑ Ⓒ Ⓓ
6. Ⓐ Ⓑ Ⓒ Ⓓ
7. Ⓐ Ⓑ Ⓒ Ⓓ

8. Ⓐ Ⓑ Ⓒ Ⓓ
9. Ⓐ Ⓑ Ⓒ Ⓓ
10. Ⓐ Ⓑ Ⓒ Ⓓ
11. Ⓐ Ⓑ Ⓒ Ⓓ
12. Ⓐ Ⓑ Ⓒ Ⓓ
13. Ⓐ Ⓑ Ⓒ Ⓓ
14. Ⓐ Ⓑ Ⓒ Ⓓ

15. Ⓐ Ⓑ Ⓒ Ⓓ
16. Ⓐ Ⓑ Ⓒ Ⓓ
17. Ⓐ Ⓑ Ⓒ Ⓓ
18. Ⓐ Ⓑ Ⓒ Ⓓ
19. Ⓐ Ⓑ Ⓒ Ⓓ
20. Ⓐ Ⓑ Ⓒ Ⓓ

Answers can be found on pages 81–82.

VOCABULARY

The next twenty-five questions will test your vocabulary. Study how the word in the question is used in the context of the sentence. In many cases, the meaning of unfamiliar terms can be discerned. If this method still leaves doubt, attempt to break the word down using the etymology tables provided earlier. Between these two methods, most words seen in entry-level Corrections Officer exams can be determined.

1. Establishing the point at which to arrest someone is an important factor in determining the *admissibility* of evidence. *Admissibility* most nearly means:

    A. Condition

    B. Likelihood of being allowed

    C. Necessity

    D. Interpretation

2. The prospect of imminent danger to either the public or law-enforcement personnel constitutes *exigent* circumstances. *Exigent* most nearly means:

    A. Broad and far-reaching

    B. Extenuating

    C. Requiring immediate action

    D. Unfortunate

3. A *cursory* search of the area was made prior to leaving. *Cursory* most nearly means:

    A. Extensive

    B. Thorough

    C. Superficial

    D. Detailed

4. Lawfully impounded inventory should not be used as a *pretext* to search for evidence. *Pretext* most nearly means:

    A. Precondition

    B. Means

    C. Rule

    D. Excuse

5. The Exclusionary Rule was adopted for the purpose of upholding the *integrity* of the courts. *Integrity* most nearly means:

    A. Moral character

    B. Superiority

    C. Fairness

    D. Improbable

6. The report said that the accused was convinced that the danger of serious harm was *imminent*. *Imminent* most nearly means:

    A. Justifiable

    B. Impending

    C. Remote

    D. Irrelevant

7. The landmark case would serve as a *precedent* for future court rulings. *Precedent* most nearly means:

   A. Source of confusion

   B. Majority view

   C. Visible reminder

   D. None of the above

8. The State of New York could not try Gary Willhouse for kidnapping because it did not have *jurisdiction*. *Jurisdiction* most nearly means:

   A. Justification

   B. Authority

   C. Enough power

   D. Probable cause

9. The theft of professional services and public utilities is still considered theft of property, albeit *intangible* property, whether taken by deception or by failure to pay for such services. *Intangible* most nearly means:

   A. Insignificant

   B. Invaluable

   C. Not corporeal

   D. White-collar

10. The evidence was ruled *immaterial* to the case at hand. *Immaterial* most nearly means:

    A. Not pertinent

    B. Admissible

    C. Substantive

    D. Relevant

11. The fact that Mr. Wilson had been convicted twice for trafficking in narcotics lessened his *credibility* as a star witness. *Credibility* most nearly means:

    A. Trustworthiness

    B. Anxiety

    C. Incredulity

    D. Demure

12. Violence was so common in one neighborhood that residents soon became *indifferent* to the occurrences. *Indifferent* most nearly means:

    A. Attentive

    B. Apathetic

    C. Intolerant

    D. Indignant

13. Cheryl was quite *overt* in her sexual advances toward an undercover officer. *Overt* most nearly means:

    A. Shy

    B. Blunt

    C. Conspicuous

    D. Slow

14. There can be fairly substantial *disparities* in what Corrections Officers earn, depending on where they live and serve. *Disparities* most nearly means:

    A. Penalties

    B. Similarities

    C. Compensations

    D. Differences

15. Detective Peterson was hoping his actions would not be *misconstrued* as aggressive. *Misconstrued* most nearly means:

    A. Misinterpreted

    B. Judged

    C. Criticized

    D. Analyzed

16. Officer Mitchell demonstrated flagrant *incompetence* by not Mirandizing the suspect at the time of the arrest. *Incompetence* most nearly means:

    A. Inability

    B. Inhibition

    C. Incongruity

    D. Disregard

17. It is *imperative* that someone be told at the time of his or her arrest what specifically it is that he or she is being arrested for. *Imperative* most nearly means:

    A. Unimportant

    B. Immaterial

    C. Compulsory

    D. Considerate

18. Officer Miller experienced some degree of *trepidation* every time he had to unholster his handgun in the line of duty. *Trepidation* most nearly means:

    A. Having power

    B. Hesitation

    C. Quandary

    D. Trembling

19. The buildings in the downtown core were pretty *dilapidated*. *Dilapidated* most nearly means:

    A. Modern

    B. Tall

    C. Neglected

    D. New

20. The purpose of investigative detention is to resolve an *ambiguous* circumstance. *Ambiguous* most nearly means:

    A. Infallible

    B. Uncertain

    C. Argumentative

    D. Interesting

21. Officers are instructed not to act *condescendingly* toward citizens in the line of duty. *Condescending* most nearly means:

    A. Discourteous

    B. Harsh

    C. Unprofessional

    D. Patronizing

22. Unconscious intoxicated persons should be transported to a nearby medical facility by an ambulance instead of a patrol car to alleviate potential civil *liability*. *Liability* most nearly means:

    A. Responsibility

    B. Exemption

    C. Scrutiny

    D. Considerations

23. The phone calls were intended to *intimidate* the witness. *Intimidate* most nearly means:

    A. Comfort

    B. Ostracize

    C. Frighten

    D. Relieve

24. Building containment for the two officers was nearly impossible because there were too many means of *egress* for the suspect. *Egress* most nearly means:

    A. Entrance

    B. Exits

    C. Approach

    D. Attack

25. The purpose of traffic control is twofold: to *expedite* traffic and to eliminate potential traffic conflicts. *Expedite* most nearly means:

    A. Deter

    B. Speed the progress of

    C. Prevent congestion

    D. Monitor

ANSWER SHEET FOR VOCABULARY SAMPLE QUESTIONS

1. (A) (B) (C) (D)
2. (A) (B) (C) (D)
3. (A) (B) (C) (D)
4. (A) (B) (C) (D)
5. (A) (B) (C) (D)
6. (A) (B) (C) (D)
7. (A) (B) (C) (D)
8. (A) (B) (C) (D)
9. (A) (B) (C) (D)

10. (A) (B) (C) (D)
11. (A) (B) (C) (D)
12. (A) (B) (C) (D)
13. (A) (B) (C) (D)
14. (A) (B) (C) (D)
15. (A) (B) (C) (D)
16. (A) (B) (C) (D)
17. (A) (B) (C) (D)
18. (A) (B) (C) (D)

19. (A) (B) (C) (D)
20. (A) (B) (C) (D)
21. (A) (B) (C) (D)
22. (A) (B) (C) (D)
23. (A) (B) (C) (D)
24. (A) (B) (C) (D)
25. (A) (B) (C) (D)

Answers can be found on page 82.

ANSWERS TO READING-COMPREHENSION QUESTIONS

1. *D.* Only selection D best describes the scope of the article. Selections A and C are, at best, ambiguous in defining the content of the reading. Selection B was, in fact, mentioned in the passage, but it only addressed what an officer is not to do rather than providing a more complete overview of what is involved in evidence collection, as the passage does.

2. *C.* *Circumspect* and *expeditious* are the correct selections. The article points out that an officer has to look around a crime scene carefully and then be expeditious or prompt in gathering the evidence found in order to avoid potential contamination.

3. *B.* Selection B is correct because the officer may have inadvertently damaged crucial evidence or even created false leads for investigators if, in fact, the crowbar on the floor was not the tool used to gain entry. Selection A may seem correct, but Officer Gregory, no matter how good his intentions may have been, actually moved the evidence from its original position. Selection C is not a viable concern for Officer Gregory. Selection D further exemplifies the potential for contaminating crucial evidence (i.e., misplacement of physical evidence).

4. *A.* Selection A is the correct answer because the article mentioned that organic compounds are more prone to deterioration with time and temperature extremes and cites blood as an example. Hair is considered organic in nature as well, but it does not have the same kind of enzymatic or bacterial breakdown as blood. The remaining selections are inorganic and not subject to the same kind of degradation from the elements.

5. *C.* Only selection C is considered false. The rest of the alternatives provided are, in fact, underlying objectives for authorities in roping off a given crime scene.

6. *C.* Selection A was merely cited as a court-case reference to support the intent of the article. It, by itself, fails to comprehensively define what the article was about. Selections B and D touch only on specifics and do not properly summarize the passage.

7. *B.* Selection B is the correct interpretation of the word *incident* as used in the reading.

8. *D.* Selections A and C are false because the reading dictates a professional code of conduct on behalf of those responsible for such searches. Officer Fullerton's behavior toward inmate Vinson falls well short of those established standards. Selection B confuses the fact that warrants are not necessary for inmate searches and seizures.

9. *C.* Selection C is correct because of the lack of probable cause. Officer Hanley's actions were purely vindictive and outside established guidelines, thereby making selection A false. Selection B is false for the same reason established in the previous question. Selection D is an all-inclusive statement that has little merit.

10. *A.* All statements are true with the exception of selection A. As searches become more intrusive, particular attention must be given to both an inmate's dignity and privacy as mentioned in the reading.

11. *D.* Selections B and C partly touch on what was discussed in the reading, but fail to summarize the intent of the article. Only selection D qualifies in that respect. *Cruel and unusual punishment* was not specifically addressed.

12. *C.* The reading is quite clear with regard to using deadly force. Such circumstances were not the case for Mr. Craswold. He was in for a misdemeanor charge, not a felony charge, and he did not directly pose a threat to anyone in his bid for freedom.

13. *A.* Selections B, C, and D could be considered important factors in making such decisions. However, the word *constraint* best exemplifies control or restraint of using such authority.

14. *C.* Selection C is the basic premise why officer Dixon's actions were justified. Refusing a pat-down search, as stated in selection A, would not be, by itself, justification for the shooting. Failure to acknowledge Dixon's directives or explanation of prison policy, as suggested by choices B and D, are moot points, considering the immediate threat posed to Officer Simmons.

15. *A.* Selections B and C are true according to the reading. Selection A implies the use of physical force beyond what is reasonable — in effect, exacting punishment that was stated in the narrative as impermissible.

16. *D.* Both selections A and C reflect the main theme of the article. Selection B is too vague and fails to accurately describe the intent of the reading.

17. *D.* Selections A through C would neither jeopardize institutional security nor hinder rehabilitation programs for the inmates in question. However, selection D has the most likely proclivity to initiate violence at some level.

18. *C.* Selection C completely details the reason why Officer Squires was wrong for dispensing such material to inmate Wilson.

19. *B.* Censorship

20. *B.* Selection B reflects the legal precedent for inmates receiving mail. As much as it may be tempting for Corrections personnel to exercise their own subjective agendas in an attempt to "clean up" what inmates view (as mentioned in selections A and C), it must be tempered in accordance with judicial views of the First Amendment. Selection D has little merit concerning the issue of mail censorship.

ANSWERS TO VOCABULARY SAMPLE QUESTIONS

Note: The answers have been provided for the vocabulary section without explanation. If further reference is needed, consult a dictionary.

1.	*B*	8.	*B*	14.	*D*	20.	*B*
2.	*C*	9.	*C*	15.	*A*	21.	*D*
3.	*C*	10.	*A*	16.	*A*	22.	*A*
4.	*D*	11.	*A*	17.	*C*	23.	*C*
5.	*A*	12.	*B*	18.	*D*	24.	*B*
6.	*B*	13.	*C*	19.	*C*	25.	*B*
7.	*D*						

Your score for each exercise would be as follows:

For the reading comprehension exercises:

    18–20 correct — Excellent
    16–17 correct — Good
    13–15 correct — Fair
    less than 13 correct — Poor

For the vocabulary exercises:

    23–25 correct — Excellent
    21–22 correct — Good
    19–20 correct — Fair
    less than 19 correct — Poor

Chapter 4

Situational Judgment and Reasoning

Of all the sections in this study guide, this one covers the bulk of questions seen on most exams. The type of questions involving judgment and reasoning are varied, but include such topics as:

- interdepartmental protocol

- public relations

- appropriate use of equipment and related safety practices

- how to best handle emergency situations

- chart and table interpretation

All questions draw upon your ability to think and reason. One type of question involves general institutional policies and procedures. These questions do not necessitate complete familiarity with correctional procedures; that comes with academy training. Instead, enough information is provided within the question to answer it solely on the basis of common sense. Keep in mind that the problem in the question must be identified first. How best to solve that problem within the scope of alternatives provided in the quickest and safest manner should be apparent.

Questions of this nature can be fairly difficult to study for. Common sense or the power of reasoning is not something that can be learned from a study guide. The best advice that can be offered is to read each question carefully and completely. Often words such as *always*, *except*, *not*, *least*, and *first* can entirely change the meaning of the question. Any answers that involve something illegal or contradictory or something that poses a threat to the public or Corrections personnel are probably incorrect. Options that demonstrate duplicity or appear self-serving are probably wrong as well. Look at the examples below and determine the correct answer.

An ever-present concern for Corrections Officers is that ordinary items that can easily be taken for granted may serve as potential weapons in the wrong hands. Taking this fact into consideration, which of the following items should warrant the most amount of concern?

A. Plastic comb

B. Notepad with a spiral binder

C. Pencil

D. Tube of lipstick

If you chose C, you are correct. An inmate with enough determination could probably fashion all four selections into potential weapons. However, a pencil would be the most immediate concern due to its sharp point and subsequent similarity to a knife.

Assume that you are a Corrections Officer posted in the prison library. Inmate Nelson approaches you and asks for your opinion regarding a case history he has researched that closely parallels his own. You should:

A. Side with his views to pacify him

B. Not respond to the question

C. Tell him that what he is doing is pointless because he does not have the legal grounds for an appeal

D. Explain to him that it would be inappropriate for you to give an opinion on such matters

If you chose D, you are correct because it is not your position to render legal advice, which would best be served by an attorney retained by him or appointed for him in a court of law. The remainder of selections would only cause unnecessary friction or problems.

A second format of questions involves the interpretations of tables or charts containing specific information. On the basis of what is provided, correlations or relationships need to be extrapolated, or the figures they contain may need to be understood and recognized for their significance. Look at the next sample provided:

Captain Hayworth was reviewing the infraction report for Evergreen Prison's medium security unit.

Date	Day	Infraction Involved	Time Occurred	Location
8/1	Friday	Inciting others to riot	5:50 A.M.	Unit A
8/3	Sunday	Intentional failure to follow safety regulations	9:15 P.M.	Unit B
8/4	Monday	Intentional failure to stand count	4:08 P.M.	Unit F
8/5	Tuesday	Refusal to obey lawful orders	3:45 P.M.	Unit C
8/8	Friday	Inciting others to riot	7:10 A.M.	Unit A
8/9	Saturday	Intentional failure to stand count	3:11 P.M.	Unit E
8/11	Monday	Intentional failure to stand count	11:59 P.M.	Unit F
8/14	Thursday	Refusal to obey lawful orders	6:13 A.M.	Unit B
8/16	Saturday	Unauthorized use of telephone	4:02 P.M.	Unit A
8/19	Tuesday	Refusal to obey lawful orders	8:15 A.M.	Unit C
8/23	Saturday	Intentional failure to stand count	6:49 P.M.	Unit F
8/25	Monday	Theft of food	10:41 A.M.	Unit C
8/26	Tuesday	Refusal to obey lawful orders	12:00 noon	Unit C
8/30	Saturday	Intentional failure to stand count	8:47 P.M.	Unit F
8/31	Sunday	Intentional failure to follow sanitary regulations	12:15 P.M.	Unit C

Shift schedules are as follows:

Tour I   8:00 A.M.–4:00 P.M.
Tour II   4:00 P.M.–Midnight
Tour III Midnight–8:00 A.M.

If Captain Hayworth wanted to add extra security in areas where the worst infractions were committed, which of the following actions would most likely achieve that goal?

    A. Assign additional staff to work Tour III on Fridays in Unit A

    B. Assign additional staff to work Tour I on Saturdays in Unit E

    C. Assign additional staff to work Tour II on Tuesdays in Unit C

    D. Assign additional staff to work Tour I on Fridays in Unit A

This sample is essentially a two-part question. First, it must be established which of the infractions shown can be regarded as the most severe, and then it must be decided how to appropriate additional security in dealing with the specific area of concern. If you answered with selection A, you are correct. Inciting others to riot is the most serious of the various infractions shown, and Tour III in Unit A on Fridays is the shift of concern. Selection D was partially correct; however, Tour III was the affected shift, not Tour I.

If Captain Hayworth wanted to concentrate on the problem of reducing the incidence of inmates refusing to obey lawful orders, he would most likely succeed by assigning additional personnel to:

    A. Tour II on Saturdays in Unit E

    B. Tour III on Saturdays in Unit A

    C. Tour I on Tuesdays in Unit C

    D. Tour I on Tuesdays in Unit A

If you chose C as being the correct answer, you were right once again. The infractions chart clearly illustrates a consistent problem of inmates in Unit C not complying with lawful orders issued on Tuesdays during Tour I.

Assuming, for the question, that all infractions are treated with the same degree of correctional attention (i.e., effort expended to correct the situation), which day of the week poses the least challenge to line staff?

    A. Saturday

    B. Sunday

    C. Monday

    D. Wednesday

If you chose Wednesday, you are correct due to the lack of any infractions reported on that particular weekday throughout the entire month of August.

These few questions were only intended to give you a brief overview of what to expect on the actual exam. The exercise that follows will provide a more comprehensive study opportunity with respect to material seen on past tests. The correct answers and explanations are provided at the end of the exercise for your reference.

SAMPLE QUESTIONS, SITUATIONAL JUDGMENT AND REASONING

1. Corrections Officer Stevens witnesses an altercation break out between two inmates in metal shop. As he approaches closer in an attempt to intercede, one of the men pulls out a shank and stabs the other in the chest. The victim immediately collapses. It is quite obvious to Officer Stevens that the chest wound is bleeding profusely. Secondary to restraining and securing the inmate responsible for the stabbing, which of the options given below would be the next appropriate action to take?

   A. Radio for an ambulance while getting statements from other inmates who witnessed the event

   B. Immediately file an incident report

   C. Seal the immediate area to allow for a proper crime investigation

   D. Attempt to slow the bleeding and summon medical assistance

2. Corrections Officer Kent was assigned to a transportation detail involving an elderly woman who needed to appear for an arraignment hearing. Out of respect for her age and potential for discomfort, Officer Kent elected not to place her in handcuffs while she was in his custody. Officer Kent's actions could be considered as?

   A. Good policy because it demonstrates that Corrections Officers do have some sensitivity when it comes to processing senior citizens.

   B. Good policy because, under the circumstances, Officer Kent has full control of the situation.

   C. Bad policy because Officer Kent is subject to a greater potential risk of assault or escape.

   D. Bad policy because Officer Kent would appear too soft or lacking authority in the way he handled the incident.

3. Good defense posture is absolutely necessary to implement effective defensive tactics. All of the following would be considered good form except?

   A. Keeping your feet moderately spread and staggered

   B. Keeping your legs and back straight

   C. Bending the knees

   D. Lowering the buttocks

4. Inmate Harrison offers Officer Howard a carton of cigarettes as a token of her appreciation for her keeping a watchful eye on an adversarial cellmate. If Officer Howard was to accept such an offer, her actions would be considered?

   A. Acceptable because inmate Harrison's concerns were legitimate.

   B. Unacceptable because accepting any kind of a gift from an inmate, for whatever purpose, may lead to future requests for special favors.

   C. Acceptable because it demonstrates that inmate Harrison is making important strides in her rehabilitation.

   D. Unacceptable because Officer Howard should have received something of greater value for her extra attention to the matter.

5. Inmate Boyle has a well-known medical history of suffering from severe diabetes. If he is either deprived of his regular insulin medication or is subjected to moderate to extreme physical exertion, it potentially places him at high risk for diabetic shock or coma. Assuming Officer Forest is cognizant of inmate Boyle's condition, he would best handle this situation by:

   A. Assigning him work details that would not adversely place him at risk

   B. Excusing him from any and all physical activities

   C. Bending over backward to accommodate his every wish

   D. Telling other prisoners that he will be receiving preferential treatment

Answer questions 6–7 on the basis of the following line graph.

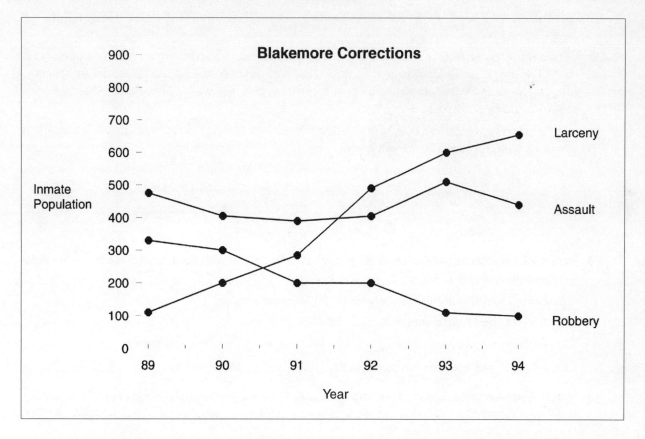

6. According to the statistics provided in the line graph, which of the following statements would be considered correct?

   A. For the five-year period between 1988 and 1994, there was a steady increase of inmates serving time for the crime of larceny.

   B. While the number of inmates serving time for the crime of assault pretty much remained the same, there was a noticeable decline in the number of inmates serving time for robbery.

   C. For the five-year period beginning in 1989, there was a steady decrease of inmates serving time for the crime of assault.

   D. While the number of inmates serving time for the crime of robbery pretty much remained the same, there was a significant decrease in the number of inmates serving time for the crime of assault.

7. All of the following statements are true except?

    A. In 1992, there were more inmates serving time for larceny convictions than for assault convictions.

    B. In 1990, there were three hundred inmates incarcerated for the crime of robbery.

    C. There were fewer inmates serving time for the crime of assault in 1990 than in 1993.

    D. There was no change in inmate population with regard to robbery convictions between the years of 1990 and 1991.

Answer questions 8–9 on the basis of the following pie chart.

1996 FISCAL BUDGET APPROPRIATIONS FOR WESTHAMPTON CORRECTIONS

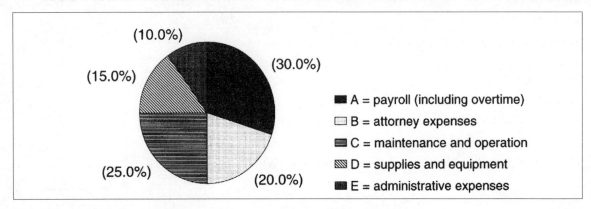

8. Which of the following statements would be considered true with respect to Westhampton's budgetary appropriations?

    A. Both A and B represent the largest outlay of expense.

    B. Both D and E represent the largest outlay of expense.

    C. Both payroll and maintenance and operation represent the largest outlay of expense.

    D. Supplies and equipment represents the smallest of financial outlays.

9. All of the following statements are false except?

    A. Attorney expenses are shown to be greater than either payroll or administrative expenses.

    B. Among D, E, and B, D would be considered the largest expense of the three.

    C. Maintenance and operation is the second largest budget appropriation shown.

    D. All of the above statements are false.

10. A Corrections Officer had just dropped off two prisoners for intake and booking when he noticed that a $100 bill had been inadvertently left on the back seat of the car. What is the most appropriate action this officer should take?

    A. Give the money to an immediate supervisor and request that it be sent to the Corrections Officer Guild

    B. Keep the money and make no mention of its existence

    C. Ask both of the prisoners if they lost the money

    D. Submit a formal written report on the matter and turn it in for evidence/property storage

11. Which of the following is the most important reason for a Corrections Officer to wear a badge while on duty?

    A. It serves as a means of identification.

    B. It is meant to convey authority.

    C. It serves to intimidate inmates.

    D. It represents an effort to maintain a professional appearance.

Study the infractions and associated codes listed in the following table. Answer questions 12–20 on the basis of this reference.

	Infraction	Statute Code Violation	Penalty Level
1.	Unauthorized use of machinery or equipment	RA-571	I
2.	Refusal to attend scheduled work detail	RA-695	II
3.	Counterfeiting or forging an article of identification or legal document	RA-981	III
4.	Unauthorized possession of money totaling $25 or less	BT-05	I
5.	Unauthorized possession of money totaling more than $25	BT-06	II
6.	Gambling	RA-72	II
7.	Refusal to submit to medically supervised drug screening	RA-702	III
8.	Possession of unauthorized drugs or controlled substances	RA-132	III
9.	Reckless destruction of official property; estimated damages not exceeding $50	BT-07	I
10.	Reckless destruction of official property; estimated damages greater than $50 but not exceeding $100	BT-07A	II
11.	Reckless destruction of official property; estimated damages exceeding $100	BT-07B	III
12.	Possession of a weapon	RA-609	III
13.	Material thrown at staff or visitors	RA-409	I
14.	Provoking prohibited gatherings or demonstrations	RW-695	III

Established penalty guidelines are as follows:

Penalty Level I: Curtailment of specified privileges for five days for first offense or fifteen days for second offense. Additional offenses of this level warrant an upgrade to the next higher level of penalty.

Penalty Level II: Confinement to cell for a period of five days for first offense or ten days for second offense. Additional offenses of this level warrant an upgrade to the next higher level.

Penalty Level III: Twenty days in isolation for first offense or thirty days in isolation for second offense. Additional offenses warrant permanent transfer to a maximum-security unit.

Note: If multiple infractions are committed by the same inmate and the infractions in question carry different penalty levels, the penalty assessment is to be based on the more serious of the two (e.g., a Level I and a Level II offense committed by an inmate would be assessed as two Level II offenses, etc.).

12. Corrections Officer Powers had reasonable suspicion that inmate Beck was responsible for a bottle of Tylenol 3 that turned up missing in the medical ward. Inmate Beck's scheduled medical appointment coincided with the time that health-care workers noticed the item in question was missing. Pursuant to a cell search of Beck's belongings, the bottle of Tylenol 3 was recovered. Under the circumstances, inmate Beck should be charged with which of the following statute code violations?

   A. RA-695

   B. RA-132

   C. RA-702

   D. BT-07B

13. Referring to the previous question, if this incident was inmate Beck's second violation involving unauthorized possession of drugs, he became eligible for what kind of penalty?

   A. Ten days of confinement to his cell

   B. Fifteen days of revoked privileges

   C. Thirty days in an isolation unit

   D. Permanent transfer to a maximum-security unit

14. Inmate Fontaine was cited by Corrections Officer Blakemore for having been caught at gambling while playing cards with fellow cellmates and, in addition, had $28.00 on his person beyond what was authorized according to prison regulations. Under such conditions, inmate Fontaine violated which of the statutes provided below?

   A. RA-702 and BT-05

   B. RA-72 and BT-06

   C. RA-132 and BT-05

   D. Only RA-72

15. Referring to the previous question, the consequences for inmate Fontaine's actions, according to established penalty guidelines, would be?

   A. Five days of revoked privileges

   B. Five days of confinement to his cell

   C. Ten days of revoked privileges

   D. Ten days of confinement to his cell

16. Corrections Officer Michaels has reason to believe that inmate Justin may be on some sort of controlled substance. He subsequently orders inmate Justin to accompany him to the men's restroom, where they can, under his direct supervision, get a urine sample for analysis. Inmate Justin, however, refuses, in no uncertain terms, Officer Michael's request. According to the situation, inmate Justin would be in willful violation of which of the following statute codes?

   A. RA-695

   B. RA-702

   C. RA-132

   D. None of the above

17. Inmate Sorenson, a staunch union activist, attempts to form a prohibited collective bargaining unit for inmates on his cell block. Despite an earlier citation for such activity, inmate Sorenson persisted in his efforts and, as a result, received a second citation. The penalty prescribed for Sorenson's tenacity would be which of the following?

    A. Thirty days in an isolation unit

    B. Twenty-five days in an isolation unit

    C. Thirty days of revoked privileges

    D. Fifteen days of confinement to his cell

18. Referring to the previous question, inmate Sorenson's offense would merit which of the following penalty levels?

    A. I

    B. II

    C. III

    D. None of the above

19. Which of the following statements is true with regard to statute code violations?

    A. RA-609, RA-702, RA-132, and RA-72 all qualify as Penalty Level III infractions.

    B. BT-05, RA-571, BT-07, and RA-409 all qualify as Penalty Level I infractions.

    C. BT-06, BT-07A, BT-07B, and RA-695 all qualify as Penalty Level II infractions.

    D. BT-07, RW-695, RA-72, and RA-981 all qualify as Penalty Level III infractions.

20. In an unprovoked fit of rage, inmate Daniels throws his serving tray against the cafeteria wall and inadvertently damages a prison wall clock valued at $55.00. Prior to his forced removal from the premises, he also manages to hit Officer Belmont in the chest with a wad of mashed potatoes from another inmate's plate. Assuming inmate Daniels is cited for any and all infractions appropriate to such an outburst, what kind of discipline can be expected?

    A. Five days of revoked privileges

    B. Ten days of confinement to his cell

    C. Five days of confinement to his cell

    D. Twenty days in an isolation unit

21. Corrections Officers are told not to appear at places within their patrol jurisdiction at regular intervals. What is the most likely reason for such a policy?

    A. A regular routine inspires complacency.

    B. It is within their means to handle larger assignments.

    C. An officer can more thoroughly patrol his or her assigned areas.

    D. Established patterns of patrol make it easier for the criminal element to go about its business with less of a threat of getting caught.

22. Officer Easton is in charge of supervising an in-house work detail of fifteen inmates. Around lunchtime, he decides to conduct an informal count and, after two attempts, becomes relatively assured that someone is missing. Officer Easton's next best action would be?

    A. Order a formal "stand for count" to confirm his suspicion

    B. Sound a general alarm to notify all prison personnel that an escape attempt was in progress

    C. Wait until his shift's end to report the discrepancy

    D. Inform his immediate supervisor of the situation

23. Inmate Rogers, a convicted felon serving three years for attempted robbery, tells Officer Clark the real reason for his being there in the first place was his ill-fated attempt to support a wife and three kids. Recently, his family suffered another financial setback, and he was getting extremely frustrated that he could not provide any help, considering his present circumstances. Officer Clark would best handle this situation by doing which of the following?

    A. Show some degree of sympathy by loaning Rogers some money

    B. Tell him that, as a prisoner, he should not be concerned with things outside of his control

    C. Refer the matter to a department employee who handles social concerns for inmates

    D. File an infraction report detailing Rogers's propensity for violence

24. During a routine patrol of the prison exercise yard, Officer Kay Wentworth notices a downed power line on the basketball court. No arcing or burning is apparent. The most appropriate way for Officer Wentworth to handle such a situation would be which of the following?

    A. Pick up the wire and move it off the basketball court where it would no longer pose a hazard to inmates

    B. Secure the area immediately and call the electric utility repair department

    C. File a report on the matter, and then resume patrol

    D. Attempt to move the wire out of harm's way using her baton to avoid direct contact

25. Corrections Officer Claymore felt that fellow officer Larson failed in several respects to serve as adequate backup during an inmate scuffle that occurred earlier. The best means for Claymore to address such concerns would be which of the following?

    A. Wait until the time comes when he needs backup and, in retaliation, refuse to provide it

    B. Confront the officer directly and discuss the problem

    C. Report to an immediate supervisor Larson's inability to perform his duty

    D. File a written request for a more competent partner

26. Procedural guidelines call for the use of handcuffs as a temporary measure to restrain an inmate from fighting or causing harm to him- or herself. With such a policy in effect, which of the following conditions would warrant such action?

    A. An inmate who yells infrequent obscenities from his cell

    B. An inmate who refuses to improve his personal hygiene

    C. An inmate who constantly berates Corrections Officers

    D. An inmate who keeps slugging his fists against the bars to his cell

27. Corrections Officers are instructed to always be on the watch for certain behavioral signs that indicate growing tension among inmates; such changes may be a prelude to area disturbances or even riots. Which of the following situations would least likely be an indicator of such a development?

    A. A noticeable increase in inmate sick calls

    B. An increase in voluntary lockups

    C. A decrease in the number of transfer requests

    D. Attendance declines at movies or other functions that are typically popular among inmates

28. Officer Bentley witnesses inmate Tyler, a reputed gang leader, commit a minor infraction while associating with a small group of inmates suspected of having similar affiliations. Considering the circumstances, which of the following actions taken by Officer Bentley would be prudent?

    A. Make an example of Tyler before his peers by disciplining him on the spot

    B. Ignore the infraction altogether because of his gang affiliation

    C. Ignore the infraction because it was only minor

    D. Explain to Tyler, apart from the group, that he committed a minor infraction and that repetition of such violations would not be tolerated

29. Corrections Officer Rosenthal noticed a significant change of behavior by inmate Snyder after receiving some personal correspondence through the mail. Snyder looked extremely tired from an obvious lack of sleep, ate very little, and became very withdrawn. During a routine inspection of Snyder's cell, Snyder tells Officer Rosenthal that "death is a better alternative than to continue living in this hole." Officer Rosenthal's worst possible response to this situation would be which of the following?

    A. Remove all potential sharp objects from the cell or items that he could potentially hang himself with

    B. Report the incident to his immediate supervisor and do a frequent visual check of the prisoner in question

    C. Stress to inmate Snyder how his suicide would impact his family

    D. Be sympathetic and nonjudgmental toward Snyder

30. Inmate Powell informs Corrections Officer Collier that inmate Stevens stole a carton of cigarettes from him earlier in the week. Officer Collier would best handle this situation by doing which of the following actions?

    A. Get the specific details pertaining to the incident from the complainant (i.e., inmate Powell)

    B. Immediately cite inmate Stevens for the infraction of theft

    C. Ask other inmates about Powell's allegations and whether it has credibility

    D. Inform the shift supervisor of the purported theft

31. Which of the following steps would have the least effect in curtailing drug contraband from being smuggled into a prison?

    A. Log all prescription drugs as well as over-the-counter medication given

    B. Search public use and visiting areas once a week

    C. Ensure that inmates take their prescribed medication

    D. Monitor all deliveries made, including the regular search of mail and packages

Answer questions 32–33 on the basis of the supervisory directive provided next.

Corrections Officers are trained to instruct nonresistive inmates in the following ways:

- refer to the inmate by his or her first name

- issue clear or specific directives with regard to any task that needs to be performed

- state any time limitations that are applicable

- ask if there are any appropriate questions or anything that needs to be reclarified

If the inmate in question becomes resistive:

- again refer to the inmate by his or her first name

- restate the same directives

- explain the consequences of failing to obey the directive

- and then answer any appropriate questions before leaving

32. Officer Smith finds inmate Kyle in the cafeteria playing cards with two other inmates. Officer Smith tells the group to sweep and mop the kitchen floor before inspection at 7:30 P.M. The inmates agreed it would get taken care of before resuming their card game. Without further questions, Officer Smith leaves to attend other duties. According to the supervisory directive, Officer Smith's actions would be considered which of the following?

    A. Correct, because the inmates in question were not resistive to the idea of having to clean the kitchen floor.

    B. Incorrect, because Officer Smith should have elicited some questions from the inmates prior to leaving.

    C. Incorrect, because Officer Smith failed to identify by name the person(s) directly responsible for carrying out his orders.

    D. Incorrect, because Officer Smith failed to spell out the consequences for not acting on his request.

33. Officer Larry Moss, during his routine patrol, notices inmate Joseph Powers's cell to be in filthy disarray. Officer Moss tells inmate Powers directly that he was to have his cell cleaned up and ready for inspection at 5:30 P.M. When asked if he had any questions, inmate Powers asked Officer Moss, "What the hell business is it to you that my cell looks the way it does?" Officer Moss reiterates to inmate Powers that he was to have his cell cleaned up and ready for an inspection by 5:30 P.M. and that failure to comply would result in a two-day revocation of special privileges. When asked if he had any further questions, inmate Powers inquired if Officer Moss was "that hard" on his old lady. Officer Moss responded prior to leaving, "My wife would never allow for such behavior in the first place." According to the supervisory directive, Officer Moss's action would be considered which of the following?

    A. Correct, because Officer Moss followed protocol to the letter.

    B. Incorrect, because Officer Moss should have cited him an infraction without having to repeat instructions.

    C. Incorrect, because Officer Moss remained indifferent toward inmate Powers's belligerence.

    D. Incorrect, because Officer Moss responded to an inappropriate question asked by Powers prior to leaving.

34. All correctional institutions constantly struggle to discover and eliminate contraband, which would comprise articles that are not authorized for inmate use or that potentially pose a threat to staff, visitors, or the general security of the institution. Contraband can be categorized as either being dangerous or a nuisance. From the items given below, which comes closest to the latter of the two descriptions?

    A. A handheld electronic video game

    B. A loose plumbing fixture

    C. Shop tools

    D. A wire

Following are hypothetical codes established by a statute law committee to represent various infractions committed by inmates for which time is being served. On the basis of this information, answer questions 35–37.

CARSTON CORRECTIONS MEDIUM-SECURITY UNIT

Infraction Involved	Applied Code	No. of Inmates Affected
First-degree murder	CRW 8A.32.513	18
Second-degree murder	CRW 8A.35.213	23
Involuntary manslaughter	CRW 9B.67.125	17
First-degree rape	CRW 9C.67.215	33
Second-degree rape	CRW 9C.76.215	34
Third-degree rape	CRW 9B.76.512	12
First-degree extortion	CRW 6A.52.761	3
Bribery	CRW 5D.67.761	5
First-degree rendering criminal assistance	CRW 5E.89.900	6
First-degree child molestation	CRW 9C.06.125	31
Second-degree child molestation	CRW 9C.07.215	32
Unlawful imprisonment	CRW 5B.52.761	4

35. The fewest number of inmates serving time for any one particular infraction would be represented by which of the following codes?

    A. CRW 6A.52.761

    B. CRW 5B.52.761

    C. CRW 9C.76.215

    D. CWR 9C.67.215

36. The code CWR 5E.89.900 represents what kind of infraction and the number of affected inmates, respectively?

    A. First-degree rendering of criminal assistance / 6

    B. First-degree rape / 33

    C. Bribery / 5

    D. None of the above

37. Which of the following statements is false with regard to the statistics provided?

    A. There are fewer inmates serving time for CRW 9C.07.215 code infractions than there are inmates serving time for first-degree rape convictions.

    B. The three most numerous crimes for which inmates are serving time for, in descending order, are CRW 9C.76.215, CRW 9C.67.215, and CRW 9C.07.215.

    C. Based on the inmate numbers provided, CRW 5D.67.761 represents the fourth lowest kind of conviction served when taking all crimes into consideration.

    D. First-degree extortion, unlawful imprisonment, and involuntary manslaughter are represented by infraction code numbers CRW 6A.52.761, CRW 5B.52.761, and CRW 9B.67.125, respectively.

38. A general rule of thumb for Corrections Officers to follow is to assume that all inmates have the potential to carry communicable diseases. Consequently, special care should be exercised to avoid coming into direct contact with an inmate's blood or other bodily fluids. On the basis of this information, which of the following situations would most likely be an inadvertent cause for violating such an important rule?

    A. Wearing protective latex gloves where exposure to blood is likely

    B. Sealing sharp instruments such as razor blades, syringes, etc., in a plastic Baggie

    C. Disposing of contaminated trash in a thick-gauge, leakproof plastic sack

    D. Marking and handling contaminated clothing with gloves on at all times

39. All of the following would be a good means to effectively communicate with most inmates except?

    A. Utilize consistent conversational volume

    B. Exercise an extensive vocabulary

    C. Control the rate of speech

    D. Temper the tone of voice

Answer questions 40–42 on the basis of the following information.

There are three levels of security that dictate what an inmate can possess in his or her cell. Apart from this, all other items are to be considered unauthorized. Study the lists provided and then decide which of the illustrations that follow would be considered unauthorized.

Security Level 1 (Standard)	Security Level 2 (Revocation of privileges)	Security Level 3 (Cell confinement)
toothpaste	plastic comb	plastic cup
washcloth	newspapers	broom
towel	blankets	washcloth
reading lamp	notepads	plastic comb
blankets	soap	blankets
notepads	pens	towel
portable radio	plastic cup	toothbrush
broom	towel	pillows
plastic comb	toothpaste	soap
pens	toothbrush	dustpan
		toothpaste

soap

newspapers

fan

pillows

portable television

dust pan

plastic cup

toothbrush

paperback books

washcloth

dustpan

portable radio

broom

pillows

40. Inmate Dawson was a recent Security Level 1 transfer from another correctional unit. However, due to his refusal to comply with a lawful order shortly after his arrival, inmate Dawson was bumped up to Security Level 2 status. Which of the following items found in inmate Dawson's cell pursuant to a cell search could be considered unauthorized?

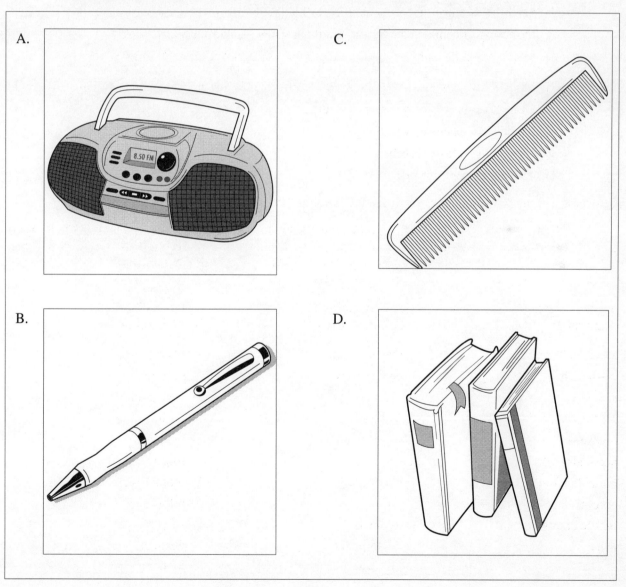

A.

B.

C.

D.

41. Inmate Ballard was considered a model prisoner. However, pursuant to a standard inspection, the four items illustrated below were found to be in Mr. Ballard's possession. Which of these articles would be considered unauthorized?

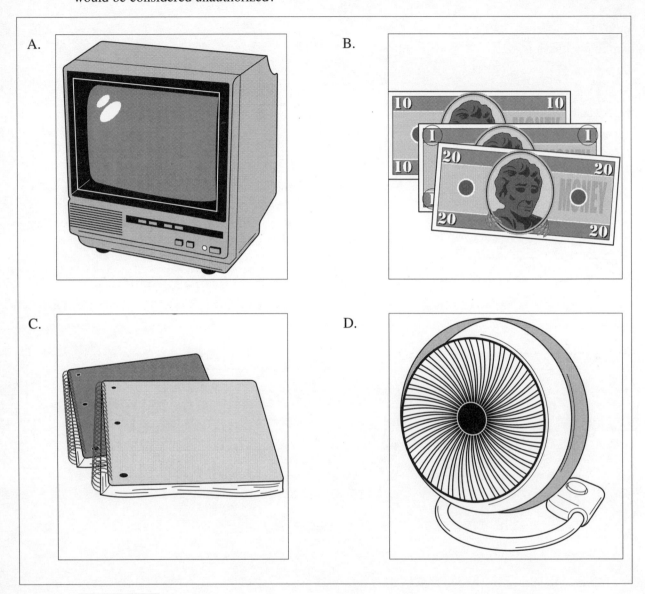

A.

B.

C.

D.

42. Inmate Ford was confined to his cell for a period of twenty days for being caught in possession of a manufactured weapon. If inmate Ford had possession of the four items listed below, which of the articles would be considered unauthorized under the circumstances?

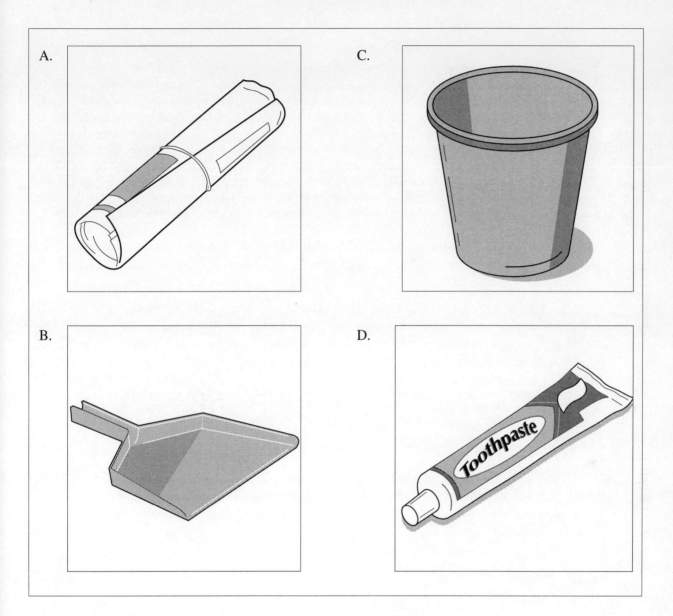

A.

B.

C.

D.

43. As a Corrections Officer, you can expect, without exception, to encounter one of many ploys of resistance used by inmates, albeit some avenues are more subtle than others. Which of the following actions would least likely be such an intent?

    A. Excessive smoke breaks taken

    B. Making excuses or rationalizations for noncompliance of requests

    C. Regularly bring up new issues to talk about

    D. Demonstrating confusion over orders issued for the first time

When prisoners are classified for security risks, administrative personnel consider various criteria for making such decisions. The type of offense committed and criminal background are, of course, the major factors taken into consideration. Personality traits, age, and physical condition are considered as well. Inmates who demonstrate a tangible major risk to an institution—such as those who have committed capital offenses (i.e., crimes that warrant the death penalty) or violent offenses—or who have escape histories typically receive maximum-security classification. Inmates who are sixty or older, regardless of the offense involved, demonstrate a propensity for nonviolence, or are just serving exceptionally long sentences are usually granted medium-security classification. Inmates who have little time left to serve or who demonstrate a propensity for nonviolence in addition to having a record of good behavior while incarcerated typically receive minimum-security status. On the basis of this information, classify the prisoners described in the next two questions.

44. Harry Ashton, inmate 12–750, is seventy-two years of age and serving twenty-five years to life for bank robbery and attempted kidnapping in 1975. For time already served, he only has five years left before being considered eligible for parole. Under the present circumstances, inmate Ashton would most likely receive which of the following risk classifications?

    A. Maximum security

    B. Medium security

    C. Minimum security

    D. Cannot determine from the information provided

45. Bernard Wiley, inmate number 12–751, is thirty-three years of age and serving three to five years for larceny (i.e., robbery without the aspect of force involved) and has three major infractions on record since being incarcerated. Under the present circumstances, inmate Wiley would most likely receive which of the following risk classifications?

    A. Maximum security

    B. Medium security

    C. Minimum security

    D. Cannot be determined from the information provided

ANSWER SHEET FOR SAMPLE QUESTIONS ON SITUATIONAL JUDGMENT AND REASONING

1.	Ⓐ Ⓑ Ⓒ Ⓓ	16.	Ⓐ Ⓑ Ⓒ Ⓓ	31.	Ⓐ Ⓑ Ⓒ Ⓓ
2.	Ⓐ Ⓑ Ⓒ Ⓓ	17.	Ⓐ Ⓑ Ⓒ Ⓓ	32.	Ⓐ Ⓑ Ⓒ Ⓓ
3.	Ⓐ Ⓑ Ⓒ Ⓓ	18.	Ⓐ Ⓑ Ⓒ Ⓓ	33.	Ⓐ Ⓑ Ⓒ Ⓓ
4.	Ⓐ Ⓑ Ⓒ Ⓓ	19.	Ⓐ Ⓑ Ⓒ Ⓓ	34.	Ⓐ Ⓑ Ⓒ Ⓓ
5.	Ⓐ Ⓑ Ⓒ Ⓓ	20.	Ⓐ Ⓑ Ⓒ Ⓓ	35.	Ⓐ Ⓑ Ⓒ Ⓓ
6.	Ⓐ Ⓑ Ⓒ Ⓓ	21.	Ⓐ Ⓑ Ⓒ Ⓓ	36.	Ⓐ Ⓑ Ⓒ Ⓓ
7.	Ⓐ Ⓑ Ⓒ Ⓓ	22.	Ⓐ Ⓑ Ⓒ Ⓓ	37.	Ⓐ Ⓑ Ⓒ Ⓓ
8.	Ⓐ Ⓑ Ⓒ Ⓓ	23.	Ⓐ Ⓑ Ⓒ Ⓓ	38.	Ⓐ Ⓑ Ⓒ Ⓓ
9.	Ⓐ Ⓑ Ⓒ Ⓓ	24.	Ⓐ Ⓑ Ⓒ Ⓓ	39.	Ⓐ Ⓑ Ⓒ Ⓓ
10.	Ⓐ Ⓑ Ⓒ Ⓓ	25.	Ⓐ Ⓑ Ⓒ Ⓓ	40.	Ⓐ Ⓑ Ⓒ Ⓓ
11.	Ⓐ Ⓑ Ⓒ Ⓓ	26.	Ⓐ Ⓑ Ⓒ Ⓓ	41.	Ⓐ Ⓑ Ⓒ Ⓓ
12.	Ⓐ Ⓑ Ⓒ Ⓓ	27.	Ⓐ Ⓑ Ⓒ Ⓓ	42.	Ⓐ Ⓑ Ⓒ Ⓓ
13.	Ⓐ Ⓑ Ⓒ Ⓓ	28.	Ⓐ Ⓑ Ⓒ Ⓓ	43.	Ⓐ Ⓑ Ⓒ Ⓓ
14.	Ⓐ Ⓑ Ⓒ Ⓓ	29.	Ⓐ Ⓑ Ⓒ Ⓓ	44.	Ⓐ Ⓑ Ⓒ Ⓓ
15.	Ⓐ Ⓑ Ⓒ Ⓓ	30.	Ⓐ Ⓑ Ⓒ Ⓓ	45.	Ⓐ Ⓑ Ⓒ Ⓓ

Answers can be found on pages 103–106.

ANSWERS TO SAMPLE QUESTIONS ON SITUATIONAL JUDGMENT AND REASONING

1. *D*   Since it was obvious to Officer Stevens that the victim of the stabbing was bleeding severely, it is imperative that he attempt to stop or at least slow the bleeding by applying pressure to the wound. Someone under such circumstances can bleed to death in just minutes. A person's life takes precedence over all other matters.

2. *C*   When suspects are handcuffed, the officer gains better protection from potential assault as well as discouraging an attempt to escape. While the reading did not specify the nature of the charges for which the suspect was appearing in court, elderly ladies are just as capable as others of committing murder, assault, etc.

3. *B*   Choices A, C, and D all contribute to lowering the center of gravity of a Corrections Officer. Officers in this stance are more difficult to move or be knocked off balance. On the other hand, an officer doing what is prescribed in B would have a high center of gravity and a very narrow base of support. Consequently, a person in this stance is moved fairly easily. Balance and a low center of gravity are keys to a good defense posture.

4. *B*   Inmate Harrison may have a realistic concern for her safety as stated in selection A, but it is within Officer Howard's accepted responsibilities to keep abreast of such situations and act accordingly; performing such duties belies express favoritism. However, if Officer Howard were to accept some sort of gift for merely doing her job, it would, in a sense, obligate her to act on future requests on behalf of the inmate(s) involved. Choices C and D can both be considered pointless options.

5. *A*   Inmate Boyle should not be given any "special" treatment beyond what his medical condition prescribes. Both choices B and C would be illustrative of disparate treatment or favoritism. Selection D would only serve to inflame discontent among fellow prisoners.

6. *B*   Selection A is incorrect because the five-year reference period begins in 1989, not 1988.

7. *D*   There was a noticeable decrease of inmates serving time for robbery convictions between the years 1990 and 1991.

8. *C*   Selection C (i.e., payroll and maintenance/operation or A and C in the chart) account for the two largest shares (30% + 25%) of the total budget as opposed to either selection A (30% + 20%) or selection B (15% + 10%). Selection D is false because administrative expenses actually represent the smallest financial outlay.

9. *C*   Payroll is the largest expense shown (30%) followed by maintenance and operation (25%).

10. *D*   Choice D is the best way a Corrections Officer can protect him- or herself from false claims of theft. Giving the money to an officer's guild or outright keeping the money would be wrong, illegal, and contrary to the ethics expected of a Corrections Officer. Selection C is incorrect because witnesses should be questioned by an investigator assigned to the case. The money could serve as important evidence to further incriminate the prisoners for the crimes committed.

11. *A*   Selection D is true to some extent; however, the badge more importantly serves as a means to identify the Corrections Officer. Both choices B and C are false on their own merit.

12. *B*   Inmate Beck came into unauthorized possession of a drug, which constitutes statute code violation RA-132.

13. *C*   A second offense for a Penalty Level III infraction carries thirty days in an isolation unit.

14. *B*   Selection B accounts for both of the infractions committed by inmate Fontaine.

15. *D*   Since inmate Fontaine committed two infractions, both of which happen to be Penalty Level II, established penalty guidelines have it that he should be confined to his cell for a period of ten days.

16. *D*   Selection B would have been the correct choice had Officer Michaels ordered a "medically" supervised drug screening instead of taking on the duty himself. Consequently, inmate Justin cannot be cited for his refusal to go along with such a test.

17. *A*   A second infraction of RW-695 carried thirty days in an isolation unit since it is a Penalty Level III offense.

18. *C*   Penalty Level III offense

19. *B*   Only selection B can be recognized as being true.

20. *B*   The event qualifies inmate Daniels as having violated statute codes RA-409 and BT-07A with respective penalty levels of I and II. Since BT-07A is the worse of the two infractions (i.e., Level II as opposed to Level I), it should be treated as though he committed two Level II offenses. Confinement to a cell for ten days is the discipline warranted.

21. *D*   If inmates know in advance when to expect any kind of search or inspection, it would become relatively easy to hide or move contraband to avoid discovery. There is some truth to selection A, but choices B and C are not the reason for such a policy.

22. *A*   It would be prudent for Officer Easton to verify his beliefs by conducting a formal count first. It would be a portrayal of incompetence to leap to any conclusions concerning an escape without first confirming the fact.

23. *C*   Under no circumstances should an officer loan money to prisoners. For as much as Officer Clark is aware, this may be just a ruse concocted by Rogers in an attempt to get money. Infraction reports are only meant to document actual violations, not serve as psychological evaluations. Selection B would only serve to inflame the situation.

24. *B*   All downed power lines, cables, etc., should be treated as if they are "hot." The absence of arcing or burning does not necessarily indicate that the line is de-energized. Selections A and D can both result in the officer being electrocuted. Selection C is incorrect even though an incident report is filed. If the officer leaves the area to continue her patrol, the situation remains a potential threat to inmate safety. The area should be secured until utility repair crews have restored the service.

25. *B*   Selection B would be the most appropriate approach to handle an incident of this nature. If the question had implied that this was a recurrent problem, then selection C would have been an appropriate response. Retaliation or "getting even" is an attitude unbecoming of a professional Corrections Officer. Inadequate backup can result in an officer being seriously injured or killed. Selection D is of the same order as selection C. It should be considered only after the officer has been addressed directly and the problem continues to persist.

26. *D*   Selection D is the only choice that involves justifiable restraint with the use of handcuffs. To act similarly in the remaining situations given would only constitute an improper means of discipline.

27. *C*   Selections A, B, and D demonstrate different means of maintaining a low profile in an attempt to avoid potential threats. Choice C does not reflect this kind of pattern. Rather, there would be an increase in transfer requests seen as inmates attempt to remove themselves from the situation entirely.

28. *D* Selection A has the potential for a minor issue to escalate into something much more serious. Additionally, any form of discipline should be kept private as much as possible. Ignoring the infractions, for whatever reason, would only set the stage for future manipulation or, worse, a complete lack of respect for authority.

29. *C* Selections A, B, and D are all actions that would have a deterrent effect on a potential suicide. However, selection C may be the very reason for inmate Snyder's behavior in the first place. Making such statements may only serve to deepen his resolve to kill himself.

30. *A* Selection A best describes what is necessary. Acting on the promise that a theft had occurred without the benefit of finding out the facts first, as demonstrated by choices B and D, is an exercise of poor judgment. Selection C would be a poor way to conduct any kind of investigation unless one of those questioned was an actual witness to what took place.

31. *B* Selections A, C, and D all involve a high degree of accountability and supervision. Selection B falls short in this regard.

32. *C* According to the supervisory directive, Officer Smith should have stated on a first-name basis those chosen for kitchen cleanup duty. Failure to act on such a request under those circumstances makes it easier to effectively discipline those responsible. Selection B is wrong because the directive did not stipulate a mandatory question-and-answer period. Choice D is incorrect because the prisoners appeared to be compliant or nonresistive to Officer Smith's request. The mention of disciplinary action is only warranted for resistive inmates.

33. *D* Officer Moss was wrong to respond to such an inappropriate question. Selection B is incorrect because directions must be repeated under such circumstances before any disciplinary action can be taken. Remaining indifferent toward Powell's behavior, as prescribed in selection C, would be a proper response. Arguing or debating with an inmate accomplishes nothing, except possibly insubordination.

34. *A* Video games have the potential of becoming a nuisance to other inmates. The other selections provided can all potentially serve as weapons.

35. *A* First-degree extortion would qualify since there are only three inmates affected.

36. *D* CRW 5E.89.900 represents the infraction of first-degree rendering of criminal assistance. CWR 5E.89.900 is a code not provided within the context of the chart. Letter transposition errors of this nature are quite easily overlooked.

37. *C* First-degree extortion is the lowest with three. Unlawful imprisonment is the second lowest with four. Bribery, which is represented in this selection, is the third lowest with five. First-degree rendering criminal assistance or CRW 5E.89.900 correctly represents the fourth lowest kind of conviction for which time is being served.

38. *B* Sharp objects would be better handled by placing them in a puncture-proof container. A plastic bag offers very little, if any, protection from an accidental cut or needle stick.

39. *B* Selections C and D both contribute in conveying confidence and tend to have a calming effect. However, selection B would result in an inmate feeling as though he or she were being "talked down to." An attempt to impress inmates in such a way would more than likely cause the opposite to happen.

40. *D* Paperback books are considered unauthorized for Security Level 2 inmates.

41. *B* Prisoners are not allowed money regardless of security level, according to the list provided.

Note: Pay close attention to selection arrangements. Selection B in question 41 is positioned where selection C is positioned in question 40. An oversight in this kind of change can result in a wrong answer being marked.

42. *A*   Newspapers are unauthorized for Security Level 3 inmates.

43. *D*   Selections A, B, and C are all various means used by inmates to stall or demonstrate passive resistance. Selection D may be wrong for the legitimate purpose of not fully hearing or comprehending an initial order. However, if the behavior persists following a reclarification, there is sufficient reason to believe that the inmate is willfully not complying with the request.

44. *B*   Despite the nature of the crimes Ashton committed, his age is of pivotal importance in determining risk classification. Had he been younger than sixty, he would have been classified a maximum-security risk.

45. *B*   Even though inmate Wiley's crimes constitute the profile of a minimum-security risk, his record of serious infractions while incarcerated would justify medium-security status.

Your score for this exercise would rate as follows:

41–45 correct — Excellent
36–40 correct — Good
31–35 correct — Fair
Less than 31 correct — Poor

Chapter 5

Coding Interpretation

Coding interpretation is somewhat comparable to situational judgment and reasoning. This form of exercise will test your ability to assess various instructions and then accurately discern number-letter transposition. While this kind of test has little relevancy to actual job details performed by Corrections Officers, it is imperative that prospective employees be able to respond correctly to instructions issued, whether number-letter coding or procedural policy.

Typical question formats will involve a number-letter key of some variety and provide various codes that represent either correct or incorrect interpretations. However the question is worded, you may either have to select the correct/incorrect codes involved or determine the number of coding errors made. These questions may on the surface seem simplistic enough, but if you rush through the exercise, it becomes very easy to inadvertently misconstrue interpretations. Therefore, take your time and cross out all incorrect codes before deciding which is the correct answer. By observing that basic rule, the risk of making an error is substantially minimized.

Below is a cross section of sample questions to provide you with a sense of what can be expected. Study these and you should be able to work your way through the practice exercises without much difficulty.

SAMPLE 1

Key	1	2	3	4	5
Code	A	B	C	D	E

According to the number-letter key presented, which of the following codes is considered inaccurate?

    A. 341   CDA
    B. 251   BEA
    C. 423   DBC
    D. 134   ADC

Selection D is the correct answer because, according to the key, the number 134 should be represented by the letters ACD. The latter two letters in this selection are incorrectly reversed.

SAMPLE 2

Key	W	A	X	E	M
Code	6	5	4	3	2

According to the number-letter key presented, which of the following codes represents the word *exam*?

1. 6243
2. 3452
3. 4562
4. 2345

Selection B is the correct answer because, according to the key, the word *exam* translates into the number 3452.

SAMPLE 3

Study the following codes presented in relation to the key provided. There may or may not be coding errors. Select the answer that represents the number of correctly coded sequences given.

Key	A	E	I	O	U	Y	W	Z
Code	0	1	2	3	4	5	6	7

Key	Code
AIUWO	02463
OUIEAZ	342157
YWZUO	56743
IUA	240
WZOUAEI	6734021
EEYZA	11570

A. 2
B. 3
C. 4
D. 6

Selection C is the correct answer. Both codes OUIEAZ and WZOUAEI are in error. Selection A would have been the correct answer had the directions stipulated the number of incorrect coded sequences given.

SAMPLE 4

Key	P	R	I	S	O	N
Alternate	35	7	34	9	10	3
Code	6	42	24	43	15	8
	28	1	2	27	13	12

Study the multiple-number codes that represent a designated letter in the key. Examine the following group coding translations and determine which is in error.

	Key	Code
A.	P, I	6, 2
	R, S, O	42, 9, 13
	O, N, P	10, 8, 6
B.	I, S, S, R	24, 43, 9, 42
	R, P, P, N	7, 6, 28, 3
	P, O, O, R	35, 10, 10, 7
C.	R, R	42, 1
	S, O, P	43, 15, 6
	N, R, P, I	8, 7, 28, 34
D.	S, I, R, P	9, 34, 24, 35
	S, P, O, N	9, 6, 10, 3
	R, N, N, I, R	7, 8, 3, 34, 42

Selection D is the correct answer. Code S, I, R, P could have been represented by any one of the following three choices:

9, 34, <u>7</u>, 35
9, 34, <u>42</u>, 35
9, 34, <u>1</u>, 35

However, 9, 34, 24, 35 represents an entirely different code (S, I, I, P).

These few questions were intended to give you a brief overview of what can be expected in the actual exam. The practice questions that follow should help you increase your proficiency at working coding exercises. The correct answers and a rating scale to gauge your test performance have been provided toward the end of this exercise for your reference.

SAMPLE QUESTIONS FOR CODING INTERPRETATION

Answer questions 1–3 on the basis of the following code format.

Key	A	B	C	D	E
Code	1	2	3	4	5

1. Which of the following selections represents an accurate code interpretation?
   A. BC   23
   B. EA   51
   C. DB   42
   D. All of the above

2. Which of the following selections represents an accurate code interpretation?
   A. 321   CBA
   B. 451   DEB
   C. 532   DCB
   D. 334   BCD

3. Which of the following codes would properly account for the number 513421423?

    A. EACDBADBD

    B. EACEBADBD

    C. EACDBADBC

    D. None of the above

Answer questions 4–6 on the basis of the following code format.

Key	8	6	4	2	0
Code	B	A	R	E	K

4. Which of the following selections represents an accurate code interpretation?

    A. 42   ER

    B. 68   BA

    C. 06   AK

    D. None of the above

5. Which of the following selections represents an inaccurate code interpretation?

    A. 208   EKB

    B. 460   RAK

    C. 802   BKE

    D. 426   RAE

6. Which of the following codes represents the word *baker*?

    A. 86042

    B. 86024

    C. 08642

    D. 68420

Answer questions 7–9 on the basis of the following code format.

Key	N	S	L	I	E	T
Code	8	7	6	5	4	3

7. Which of the following selections represents an inaccurate code interpretation?

    A. 875   NSI

    B. 658   LEN

    C. 465   ELI

    D. None of the above

8. Which of the following codes represents the word *listen*?

    A. 657438

    B. 675438

    C. 657348

    D. 867435

9. Which of the following codes would represent the letters given in their alphabetical order?
   A. 456873
   B. 465837
   C. 548673
   D. None of the above

Answer questions 10–12 on the basis of the following code format.

Key	1	2	3	4	5	6	7	8	9	0
Code	T	L	C	D	R	O	G	F	H	M

10. Which of the following selections represents an inaccurate code interpretation?
    A. DROGFL   456782
    B. HRTLCC   951233
    C. MDLTGH   042170
    D. OTHRLG   619527

11. Which of the following codes represents the word *frog*?
    A. 8507
    B. 8543
    C. 7508
    D. None of the above

12. Which of the following codes would represent the letters given in their alphabetical order?
    A. 1478206539
    B. 3487920651
    C. 3489720651
    D. 3478920651

Answer questions 13–15 on the basis of the following code format.

Key	15	27	13	11	30	26	16
Code	X	Z	Y	P	Q	H	J

13. Study the codes presented below in relation to the key provided. There may or may not be coding errors. Select the answer that represents the number of incorrectly coded sequences given.

    13, 11, 30, 16, 15   Y P Q J X
    27, 15, 27, 13, 30, 11   Z X P Y Q P
    26, 27, 11, 16, 13, 13   H Z J P Y Y
    15, 11, 30, 30, 27, 16, 13   X P Q Q Z J Y
    30, 13, 27, 26, 16, 16   Q Y Z H J J

    A. 1
    B. 2
    C. 3
    D. 4

14. Which of the following codes would accurately represent all of the numbers given in their descending order?

    A. Q Z H J X Y P

    B. Q H Z J X Y P

    C. Q Z P J X Y H

    D. P Y X J H Z Q

15. Which of the following codes would accurately represent all the odd numbers in their ascending order?

    A. P Y X J H Z Q

    B. J H Q

    C. P Y X Z

    D. P X Y Z

Answer questions 16–19 on the basis of the following code format.

Key	1	3	4	6	5	8	10	11
Code	02	05	12	03	08	10	07	01

16. Assuming the bottom row of numbers is representative of the months of the year, determine which of the following codes accurately reflects the months of February, March, and May, respectively.

    A. 11, 1, 6

    B. 11, 6, 3

    C. 1, 6, 3

    D. None of the above

17. With the same assumptions prescribed in the previous question, which of the following codes accurately reflects the months of July, August, and December, respectively?

    A. 10, 4, 5

    B. 7, 8, 12

    C. 3, 8, 12

    D. None of the above

18. Which of the following codes accounts for all odd numbers in the key without regard to any particular order?

    A. 03, 05, 07, 01

    B. 05, 08, 02, 01

    C. 12, 03, 07, 10

    D. None of the above

19. Which of the following codes accounts for all even key numbers in their descending order?

    A. 07, 10, 03, 12

    B. 10, 8, 6, 2

    C. 12, 10, 08, 07

    D. None of the above

Answer questions 20–24 on the basis of the following code format.

Key	05	01	07	13	15	50	10	31	70	51
Code	07	05	13	01	31	10	50	15	51	70

20. Study the following codes in relation to the key provided. There may or may not be coding errors present. Select the answer that accurately accounts for the number of code translations.

Key	Code
05, 01, 07, 13	07, 05, 13, 01
50, 10, 70, 51	10, 50, 51, 70
07, 01, 15, 05	01, 05, 31, 07
15, 07, 01	31, 13, 05

   A. 2

   B. 3

   C. 4

   D. None of the above

21. Which of the following selections represents an incorrect code translation?

Key	Code
A. 01, 07, 15, 05, 70, 51	05, 13, 31, 07, 51, 51
B. 31, 50, 13, 01, 70, 05	15, 10, 01, 05, 51, 01
C. 15, 31, 07, 01, 50, 51, 01	31, 50, 13, 05, 10, 70, 05
D. All of the above	

22. Which of the following codes represents all odd numbers in any given order that are less than fifteen but greater than three?

   A. 05, 31, 01, 13, 07

   B. 31, 01, 07

   C. 07, 01, 13

   D. 01, 07, 05, 31

23. Which of the following selections represents the most accurate of the code translations given?

Key	Code
1. 01, 13, 51, 10, 01	05, 01, 70, 10, 13
2. 70, 31, 07, 05, 15	51, 15, 13, 01, 01
3. 15, 07, 50, 70, 13	31, 13, 10, 51, 31
4. 50, 31, 01, 05, 10	10, 13, 05, 07, 50

   A. 1

   B. 2

   C. 3

   D. 4

24. Which of the following selections represents the least accurate of the code translations given?

Key	Code
1. 15, 50, 31, 07, 01	31, 10, 15, 13, 05
2. 13, 50, 10, 01, 07	01, 50, 15, 05, 13
3. 07, 70, 51, 01, 13	13, 51, 05, 05, 01
4. 01, 05, 70, 07, 01	05, 07, 70, 13, 05

    A. 1

    B. 2

    C. 3

    D. 4

Answer questions 25–30 on the basis of the following multiple code format.

Key	1	2	3	4	5	6	7
Alternate	A	J	F	O	S	G	L
Codes	B	E	H	T	U	P	R
	C	K	N	Q	W	Y	X
	D	M	I	V	Z	E	A

25. Which of the following codes would accurately represent the number 2456?

    A. J T U P

    B. M V W Y

    C. E Q S G

    D. All of the above

26. The code word *lemon* is an accurate translation of which of the following numbers?

    A. 76243

    B. 72243

    C. Both selections A and B

    D. None of the above

27. Which of the following numbers would most accurately reflect the correct spelling of the code word *appeal*?

    A. 766616

    B. 165616

    C. 166247

    D. 766357

28. Which of the following numbers would most accurately reflect the correct spelling of the code word *inmate*?

    A. 332752

    B. 332147

    C. 332132

    D. 336155

29. Which of the following numbers would least accurately reflect the correct spelling of the code word *warden*?

    A. 577123

    B. 517242

    C. 517153

    D. 577177

30. According to the number-letter key provided, which, if any, selections represent a coding error?

    A. 146321   B O Y I M D

    B. 73215621   L N J A S E K C

    C. 3456712   F Q Z G X A M

    D. None of the above

Answer questions 31–35 on the basis of the following multiple code format.

Key	U	V	W	X	Y	Z
Alternate	40	03	16	01	28	08
Codes	32	31	38	02	25	13
	23	30	12	10	24	42
	04	33	09	11	41	07
	15	27	21	20	39	47

31. According to the letter-number key provided, which of the following selections represents a code that is in alphabetical order?

    A. 33, 23, 38, 21, 11, 42

    B. 04, 27, 16, 41, 10, 42

    C. 15, 03, 09, 01, 39, 08

    D. None of the above

32. According to the letter-number key provided, which of the following selections represents a code that is in reverse alphabetical order?

    A. 25, 11, 16, 27, 40

    B. 08, 25, 20, 16, 15, 03

    C. 20, 38, 33, 16

    D. None of the above

33. Study the following codes in relation to the key provided. Select the answer that accounts for the number of coding errors found.

Code	Key
03, 12, 04, 25, 42	V W U Y Z
16, 11, 40, 47, 09	W X U Z X
21, 27, 02, 39	W V X U
33, 13, 01, 23, 30, 21	V Z V U V W
12, 11, 10	W X X
03, 38, 41, 07, 16, 15, 25	V W Y Z W U Y

A. 5 errors

B. 4 errors

C. 3 errors

D. All lines are correctly coded.

34. Study the following codes in relation to the key provided. Select the answer that accounts for the number of correct codes found.

Code	Key
16, 31, 04, 47, 07, 08, 40	W V U Z Z Z U
09, 12, 10, 38, 32, 39	W W Y W U Y
03, 24, 21	V Y W
30, 15, 42, 02, 23, 39, 12	V U Z X U Y W
32, 03, 41, 04, 28, 13	U V Y Z Y Z
01, 07, 23, 39, 10, 24, 47	X Z U Y Y Y Z

A. 5

B. 3

C. 2

D. All lines are correctly coded.

35. Which of the following selections represents the most accurate of the code translations given?

Key	Code
1. 40, 03, 11, 24, 09, 15, 01, 30, 11	U V X Y W U Z V X
2. 20, 47, 30, 04, 38, 02, 07, 32, 27	X Z V V W X Z U V
3. 33, 01, 28, 12, 27, 10, 24, 31, 04	V X Y W V Y X V U
4. 16, 01, 28, 33, 09, 41, 32, 25, 13	W X Y V U Y U Y Z

A. 1

B. 2

C. 3

D. 4

Answer questions 36–40 on the basis of the following code format.

Key	N	M	O	P	Q	R	S
Code	9	8	7	6	5	4	3

36. Which of the following key selections, when translated into numerical code and added together, equals the sum of 21?

    A. N S O Q

    B. M Q S Q

    C. P Q S N

    D. None of the above

37. Which of the following key selections, when translated into numerical code and added together, equals the sum of 28?

    A. P P Q M N

    B. O Q R S P

    C. M M Q R

    D. Q R N O S

38. Which of the following key selections, when translated into numerical code and added together, equals the sum of 32?

    A. M O Q Q P

    B. P S N M Q

    C. N O P O S

    D. None of the above

39. Which of the following key selections, when translated into numerical code and added together, does not equal the sum of 35?

    A. M O Q R M S

    B. P M N N S

    C. Q R S N O O

    D. None of the above

40. Which of the following key selections, when translated into numerical code and added together, does not equal the sum of an even number?

    A. M O Q S N

    B. S R Q P O

    C. N N Q O R

    D. P M N Q P

Answer questions 41–45 on the basis of the following multiple code format.

Key	B	L	M	F	A	K	E	I	R
Alternate	1	10	12	5	13	2	19	20	14
Codes	7	16	6	9	17	4	15	30	26
	3	22	18	11	21	8	23	28	24

41. Which of the following codes would represent the best alphabetical order of the letters given in the key?

    A. 17, 7, 19, 5, 30, 2, 10, 3, 13

    B. 13, 1, 15, 21, 23, 16, 7, 2, 12

    C. 21, 1, 23, 5, 28, 8, 7, 11, 13

    D. 17, 3, 15, 5, 30, 26, 6, 13, 2

42. Which of the following selections would be considered improperly coded?

    A. F R M B A K L 9, 14, 6, 1, 21, 4, 16

    B. E I A M B L K 19, 30, 21, 12, 7, 10, 8

    C. R A I L F I M E 26, 13, 28, 18, 10, 9, 20, 12, 19

    D. All of the above are correctly coded.

43. Which of the following selections translates into an even-numbered code?

    A. B F A K E R L E

    B. M B L K I R A

    C. F R K I L B E B

    D. L I A K B E I K

44. Which of the following key selections, when translated into the smaller numerical codes available and added together, equals the sum of 36?

    A. K B F M I

    B. R M B L F

    C. E A B M

    D. F L F A K B K

45. Which of the following key selections, when translated into the larger numerical codes available and added together, represents the greatest number?

    A. E A M B K R

    B. K R I F L A

    C. I R F M L B

    D. M A A I R R

ANSWER SHEET FOR SAMPLE QUESTIONS ON CODING INTERPRETATION

1.	Ⓐ Ⓑ Ⓒ Ⓓ		16.	Ⓐ Ⓑ Ⓒ Ⓓ		31.	Ⓐ Ⓑ Ⓒ Ⓓ
2.	Ⓐ Ⓑ Ⓒ Ⓓ		17.	Ⓐ Ⓑ Ⓒ Ⓓ		32.	Ⓐ Ⓑ Ⓒ Ⓓ
3.	Ⓐ Ⓑ Ⓒ Ⓓ		18.	Ⓐ Ⓑ Ⓒ Ⓓ		33.	Ⓐ Ⓑ Ⓒ Ⓓ
4.	Ⓐ Ⓑ Ⓒ Ⓓ		19.	Ⓐ Ⓑ Ⓒ Ⓓ		34.	Ⓐ Ⓑ Ⓒ Ⓓ
5.	Ⓐ Ⓑ Ⓒ Ⓓ		20.	Ⓐ Ⓑ Ⓒ Ⓓ		35.	Ⓐ Ⓑ Ⓒ Ⓓ
6.	Ⓐ Ⓑ Ⓒ Ⓓ		21.	Ⓐ Ⓑ Ⓒ Ⓓ		36.	Ⓐ Ⓑ Ⓒ Ⓓ
7.	Ⓐ Ⓑ Ⓒ Ⓓ		22.	Ⓐ Ⓑ Ⓒ Ⓓ		37.	Ⓐ Ⓑ Ⓒ Ⓓ
8.	Ⓐ Ⓑ Ⓒ Ⓓ		23.	Ⓐ Ⓑ Ⓒ Ⓓ		38.	Ⓐ Ⓑ Ⓒ Ⓓ
9.	Ⓐ Ⓑ Ⓒ Ⓓ		24.	Ⓐ Ⓑ Ⓒ Ⓓ		39.	Ⓐ Ⓑ Ⓒ Ⓓ
10.	Ⓐ Ⓑ Ⓒ Ⓓ		25.	Ⓐ Ⓑ Ⓒ Ⓓ		40.	Ⓐ Ⓑ Ⓒ Ⓓ
11.	Ⓐ Ⓑ Ⓒ Ⓓ		26.	Ⓐ Ⓑ Ⓒ Ⓓ		41.	Ⓐ Ⓑ Ⓒ Ⓓ
12.	Ⓐ Ⓑ Ⓒ Ⓓ		27.	Ⓐ Ⓑ Ⓒ Ⓓ		42.	Ⓐ Ⓑ Ⓒ Ⓓ
13.	Ⓐ Ⓑ Ⓒ Ⓓ		28.	Ⓐ Ⓑ Ⓒ Ⓓ		43.	Ⓐ Ⓑ Ⓒ Ⓓ
14.	Ⓐ Ⓑ Ⓒ Ⓓ		29.	Ⓐ Ⓑ Ⓒ Ⓓ		44.	Ⓐ Ⓑ Ⓒ Ⓓ
15.	Ⓐ Ⓑ Ⓒ Ⓓ		30.	Ⓐ Ⓑ Ⓒ Ⓓ		45.	Ⓐ Ⓑ Ⓒ Ⓓ

Answers can be found on pages 121–123.

ANSWERS TO SAMPLE QUESTIONS ON CODING INTERPRETATION

1. *D*   All of the coding selections given are accurate.

2. *A*   321-CBA

3. *C*   E A C D B A D B C

4. *D*   None of the code selections given are accurate. The coding interpretations are reversed in every case.

5. *D*   426-RAE

6. *B*   86024 represents *baker*.

7. *B*   658-LIN would be the correct code.

8. *C*   657348 is the code that represents the word *listen*.

9. *A*   E I L N S T represents the alphabetical order of the letters provided in the key. Therefore, the code that represents this particular order would be 456873.

10. *C*   MDLTGH 042179 is the correct coding instead of what is given.

11. *D*   8567 represents *frog*.

12. *B*   C D F G H L M O R T represents the alphabetical order of the letters provided in the key. Therefore, the code that represents this particular order would be 3487920651.

13. *B*   27, 15, 27, 13, 30, 11 and 26, 27, 11, 16, 13, 13 would be correctly coded as Z, X, Z, Y, Q, P and H, Z, P, J, Y, Y, respectively.

14. *A*   Descending numerical order is 30, 27, 26, 16, 15, 13, which is represented by code Q, Z, H, J, X, Y, P.

15. *C*   Ascending numerical order of odd numbers is 11, 13, 15, and 27, which is represented by code P, Y, X, Z.

16. *C*   02, 03, and 05 (i.e., the months of February, March, and May) are accurately translated in selection C, according to the key.

17. *D*   While selection A is a code that represents the months in question, it does not account for them in their respective order. 10, 5, 4 would, on the other hand, but since it was not an optional selection, choice D is correct.

18. *B*   1, 3, 5, and 11 are the odd numbers in the key, which are represented by codes 02, 05, 08, and 01, respectively. Since code order is not important for the question at hand, selection B would be the correct choice.

19. *A*   10, 8, 6, and 4 are the even numbers in their descending order. Selection A represents an accurate code translation.

20. *B*   Three of the alternatives are correctly coded. 07, 01, 15, 05 would be correctly translated into 13, 05, 31, 07, not 01, 05, 31, 07.

21. *D*   All three selections are miscoded.

22. *C*   Odd key numbers that are less than fifteen but greater than three are 13, 07, and 05, or 01, 13, and 07 when translated into code.

23. *C*   Selection 4 only had the first number properly coded. Both selections 1 and 2 had the first three numbers properly coded. However, selection 3 had the first four numbers properly coded, thus making it the most accurate choice provided.

24. *B*   Selection 1 represents the most accurate coding translation. Both selections 3 and 4 (or choices C and D, whichever way you look at it) have their first two numbers properly coded.

However, selection 2 (i.e., B) only has its first number properly translated, thus making it the least accurate choice provided.

25. *D*   All of the selections given accurately translate into the number 2456.

26. *C*   *Lemon* represents both 72243 and 76243.

27. *A*   The first five numbers of selection A are accurately translated. All other selections have fewer numbers that have been correctly added.

28. *B*   The first five numbers of selection B are accurately coded. All other selections have fewer first numbers that have been correctly coded.

29. *B*   Only the first three numbers of selection B are accurately coded. All other selections have one or more additional numbers that have been correctly coded.

30. *D*   All selections are correctly coded.

31. *C*   Only selection C represents an alphabetical code.

32. *A*   Despite not including the letter Z, selection A is in a reverse alphabetical order.

33. *C*
16, 11, 40, 47, 09	should be	W, X, U, Z, W
21, 27, 02, 39	should be	W, V, X, Y
33, 13, 01, 23, 30, 21	should be	V, Z, X, U, V, W

34. *B*
09, 12, 10, 38, 32, 39	should be	W, W, X, W, U, Y
32, 03, 41, 04, 28, 13	should be	U, V, Y, U, Y, Z
01, 07, 23, 39, 10, 24, 47	should be	X, Z, U, Y, X, Y, Z

35. *A*   Selection A (i.e., 1) has the first six numbers correctly coded. All other selections have fewer first numbers correctly coded.

36. *B*
NSOQ	or	9 + 3 + 7 + 5 = 24
MQSQ	or	8 + 5 + 3 + 5 = 21
PQSN	or	6 + 5 + 3 + 9 = 23

37. *D*
PPQMN	or	6 + 6 + 5 + 8 + 9 = 34
OQRSP	or	7 + 5 + 4 + 3 + 6 = 25
MMQR	or	8 + 8 + 5 + 4 = 25
QRNOS	or	5 + 4 + 9 + 7 + 3 = 28

38. *C*
MOQQP	or	8 + 7 + 5 + 5 + 6 = 31
PSNMQ	or	6 + 3 + 9 + 8 + 5 = 31
NOPOS	or	9 + 7 + 6 + 7 + 3 = 32

39. *D*
MOQRMS	or	8 + 7 + 5 + 4 + 8 + 3 = 35
PMNNS	or	6 + 8 + 9 + 9 + 3 = 35
QRSNOO	or	5 + 4 + 3 + 9 + 7 + 7 = 35

40. *B*
MOQSN	or	8 + 7 + 5 + 3 + 9 = 32
SRQPO	or	3 + 4 + 5 + 6 + 7 = 25
NNQOR	or	9 + 9 + 5 + 7 + 4 = 34
PMNQP	or	6 + 8 + 9 + 5 + 6 = 34

41. *A*   Selection A represents the correct order of the first seven letters (i.e., A, B, E, F, I, K, and L), whereas the remaining choices have fewer letters in alphabetical arrangement.

42. *C*   R A I L F I M E is improperly coded. There is not only a wrong translation, but also an extra number.

43. *D*   Since the codes only have to be determined if they are odd or even, the last letter of each code can be scrutinized to make that determination. The letters E, A, and B in the key (the last letters in choices A, B, and C, respectively) all represent odd numbers. However, selection D (i.e., K) represents an even-numbered choice.

44. *B*

K B F M I	or	2 + 1 + 5 + 6 + 20 (i.e., smaller numerical codes available) = 34
R M B L F	or	14 + 6 + 1 + 10 + 5 = 36
E A B M	or	19 + 13 + 1 + 6 = 39
F L F A K B	or	5 + 10 + 5 + 13 + 2 + 1 + 2 = 38

45. *D*

E A M B K R	or	23 + 21 + 18 + 7 + 8 + 26 (i.e., larger numerical codes available) = 103
K R I F L A	or	8 + 26 + 30 + 11 + 22 + 21 = 118
I R F M L B	or	30 + 26 + 11 + 18 + 22 + 7 = 114
M A A I R R	or	18 + 21 + 21 + 30 + 26 + 26 = 142

Your score for this exercise would be as follows:

    41–45 correct — Excellent
    36–40 correct — Good
    31–35 correct — Fair
    Less than 31 correct — Poor

Chapter 6

Report Writing, Grammar, and Spelling

The ability of a Corrections Officer to write authoritative investigative reports is important for several reasons. Probably one of the most significant is that such reports serve as official, permanent records that detail circumstances surrounding criminal justice activity. Additionally, these same recorded facts may be used as potential leads by people outside of the Department of Corrections (e.g., the FBI, DEA, GPS, etc.) to further an investigation. Reports can also be used within the Corrections system to decide what forms of disciplinary action should be taken for unlawful behavior exhibited by inmates. In the more serious cases, reports can additionally have direct implications on penalty assessments made by a parole hearing board or in trial court.

From an administrative view, reports serve to enhance vital communication between staff (such as resolving any shift problems or delegating manpower in the most effective manner possible to handle problem areas), as well as play a key role in determining promotions and budget recommendations. The ramifications of good report writing are considerable.

During the exam, you will not be expected to write an actual report. However, the test questions will follow one of two different formats. One form involves reading a narrative. A blank report form of some kind is furnished in conjunction with the reading. You will then be required to find information within the reading pertinent to various sections of the report.

The second format is essentially the opposite of the first. You are provided with a report that has already been filled out. From it you will need to extract information appropriate to the question asked. This exercise is not difficult, but a little care should be used in determining the who, what, when, where, why, and how factors of any particular incident. The reason for such caution is that there may be several facts in an incident that could go in one part of a report.

For example, there may be several *who's* contained in one report. Who is the complainant (i.e., the victim or reporter of the purported crime)? Who is the perpetrator? Who is the witness, if there is one? Who responded to the incident? Who filed the report? It can be easy to misconstrue information inserted into a report if close attention is not paid to the question at hand. The best advice here is to read either the narrative or prepared report through once to familiarize yourself with what has taken place. Then read each question carefully and go back to the reading to discern what information is being requested. Once you have worked through the exercises provided in this study guide, you should be prepared for comparable questions on the actual exam.

The second part of this chapter involves basic grammar and spelling, two very important aspects of good report writing. Written reports are essentially the official records of incidents. If the information contained in the report is vague, grammatically incorrect, or grossly misspelled, not only does it detract from the competence and professionalism of the Corrections Officer in question, but it also reflects poorly on the department as a whole. Well-written reports communicate better and serve to expedite, not hinder, the complaint-issuing process.

It is not the intention of this book to provide instruction in basic grammar. If you feel that this may be one of your weaker areas, there are volumes of material available at your local library dedicated to this subject. Rather, test questions comparable to those seen on past exams are given with answers and explanations.

This chapter also reviews a few basic spelling rules that can lend substantial assistance to those who struggle in this area. Additionally, an extensive list of words that have been seen on past exams, as well as those studied at various training academies, have been compiled and included in this section. This does not guarantee that words other than those compiled will not be seen on your exam; however, it will offer a fairly comprehensive study of the word base you will most likely encounter on the actual exam.

Read the following narrative and then refer to the blank booking form that immediately follows to answer questions 1–10. *(Note:* Answer sheets for this exercise are placed at the end of this section.)

On September 17, 1992, Michael J. Connors was arrested at his home at 2025 Parker Boulevard, Auburn, Washington, for the manufacture of and intent to deliver a controlled substance and for unlawful possession of a firearm by a felon, both of which are considered Class B felonies. Another person on the premises, Timothy Russell, who claimed to be a friend of the arrestee, was arrested for conspiracy to distribute a controlled substance. He was booked in the Auburn County Jail (see arrest report #15-503).

Officer John Halden, Badge Number 363, was the arresting officer. Officer Halden currently resides on Creston Drive in Auburn, Washington. One hundred and twenty grams of what is suspected to be cocaine and a .38-caliber pistol with the serial number 51105350 were placed in the evidence storage locker at Precinct 14 for future court exhibition. The arraignment of the suspect has been set for September 20, 1992, at 1:00 P.M. in Breston County District Court. Records indicate that the suspect has been convicted twice for assault and once for distribution of a controlled substance. He has served three years and two months in Humbolt Corrections and was paroled in October 1990, according to Officer Thurston Whitley, who was his probation officer at the time. Michael J. Connors has been known to have used the alias Mark E. Preston while engaging in drug-trade activity. Mr. Connors is a 37-year-old white male, 6', 195 pounds, with brown hair and hazel eyes. He is known to be a diabetic requiring insulin. One physical mark worth noting is a black eagle tattoo on his right forearm. Mr. Connors currently works for Hawthorne, Inc., located at 679 E. Marston Place, Auburn, Washington. His Social Security number is 508-27-4110, and another card found in his possession indicates that his stepmother, Andrea Stevens, who lives at 2042 Barrangton Avenue, Waverly, Iowa, should be contacted in case of an emergency. Her phone number is (319) 563-2751. Mr. Connors's two-tone white-on-blue 1990 Ford four-door station wagon was impounded by Hand K Towing at 4357 H Street, Auburn, Washington. Below are the names and addresses of people Mr. Connors asked to be notified pending his trial.

1. (Stepfather) George C. Nichols, 1459 E. Parkhurst, Federal Way, WA, home phone (206) 951-4321, business phone (206) 573-4444.

2. (Cousin) Arthur B. Gladstone, 160-D Magnuson Way Apartments, Colville, IA, home phone (515) 723-5678.

3. (Neighbor) Tina Weatherby, 2037 Parker Boulevard, Auburn, WA, home phone (206) 951-5541, business phone (206) 591-8741.

4. (Friend) Timothy Russell, 906 Forrest Drive, Auburn, WA, home phone (206) 933-5441.

① DATE OF REPORT	② BOOKING NO.	③ PRECINCT NO.	④ BADGE NO. OF ARRESTING OFFICER	⑤ TYPE F - FELONY M - MISDEMEANOR O - OTHER	⑥ EVIDENCE BOOKED ☐ YES ☐ NO	
					⑦ COMPLAINT FILED (CHARGES & COUNTS)	

⑧ INVESTIGATING OFFICER'S NAME & ADDRESS:	⑨ ARRAIGNMENT DATE	⑩ TIME	⑪ COURT

㉕ ARRESTEE'S NAME:	㉗ SSN	⑫ ARREST DISPOSITION:

㉖ ARRESTEE'S ADDRESS:	⑬ D.A. FELONY REFERRAL:
	⑭ 72-HOUR RELEASE:

㉘ SEX	㊲ SCARS, PECULIARITIES:	⑮ FELONY WARRANT SERVED:
㉙ AGE/DOB	㊳ EMPLOYER'S NAME & ADDRESS:	⑯ MISDEMEANOR WARRANT SERVED:
㉚ RACE		⑰ FELONY COMPLAINT FILED:
㉛ HAIR	㊴ IN CASE OF EMERGENCY CALL: NAME: ADDRESS: RELATION: PHONE NO.:	⑱ MISDEMEANOR COMPLAINT FILED:
㉜ EYES		⑲ OTHER:
㉝ HEIGHT	㊵ ARRESTEE'S VEHICLE: YR: MAKE: MODEL: COLOR:	⑳ PRIOR ARREST DISPOSITION:
㉞ WEIGHT	㊶ PRESENT LOCATION OR IMPOUNDMENT:	㉑ NAME OF PROBATION OFFICER:
㉟ MEDICAL PROBLEMS:		㉒ PRECINCT NO., IF AVAILABLE:
		㉓ TIME SERVED FOR OFFENSE:
㊱ ALIAS (AKAs):		㉔ PLACE WHERE TIME SERVED:

CODE	NAME	ADDRESS	HOME PHONE:	BUSINESS PHONE:

SEX:
0—MALE
Y—FEMALE

RACE:
1—CAUCASIAN
2—HISPANIC
3—AFRICAN AMERICAN
4—ASIAN AMERICAN
5—NATIVE AMERICAN

DATE OF BIRTH:
NUMERIC CODE SHOULD EXPRESS
MONTH-DAY-YEAR

EYES:
BROWN—BRO
BLUE—BE

GREEN—GE
HAZEL—HZ
GREY—GR
BLACK—B

HAIR:
BROWN—B
GREY—GE
BLACK—BA
BLONDE—BN
RED—R
BALD—NA

HEIGHT
WEIGHT
3 DIGIT NUMERIC CODE SHOULD
EXPRESS WEIGHT

SCARS/PECULIARITIES:
A—DEFORMITY
B—AMPUTATION
C—SCARS
D—TATTOO

LOCATION OF MARK:
1—FINGER
2—HAND
3—ARM
4—FOOT
5—LEG
6—CHEST
7—NECK
8—FACE

VEHICLE DESCRIPTION:
2 DOOR—2
4 DOOR—4
TRAILER—T
TRUCK—TK
VAN—N
STATION WAGON—W
CONVERTIBLE—K

CODES:
S—SPOUSE
A—BROTHER
D—SISTER
G—PARENT OR GUARDIAN
J—OTHER RELATIVE
M—FRIEND
O—ACCOMPLICE

ANY TIME ENTRIES IN THIS REPORT SHOULD BE EXPRESSED IN MILITARY FORM.

SAMPLE QUESTIONS FOR REPORT WRITING

1. According to the narrative, what information should be placed in Box 2 with regard to Mr. Connors's arrest?

    A. 15-503

    B. 511-05-5350

    C. 363

    D. None of the above

2. What information concerning Mr. Connors should be placed in Box 30 of this report?

    A. White

    B. Asian

    C. Black

    D. None of the above

3. What information concerning Mr. Connors should be placed in Box 33 of this report?

    A. 6'

    B. Brown

    C. 600

    D. 195 pounds

4. With regard to Mr. Connors's arrest, whose name should be inserted in Box 21?

    A. John Halden

    B. Thurston Whitley

    C. Arthur Gladstone

    D. Timothy Russell

5. The name Mark E. Preston would be appropriately inserted into what box on a booking report prepared for Mr. Connors?

    A. Box 36

    B. Box 39

    C. Box 42

    D. None of the above

6. What information would be placed in Box 10 with regard to Mr. Connors's arraignment?

    A. 9-17-92

    B. 9-20-92

    C. 1:00 P.M.

    D. None of the above

7. All of the following are true with respect to the booking report prepared on Mr. Connors except:

   A. 0, 1, 9-20-92, and B would be inserted in Boxes 28, 30, 29, and 31, respectively.

   B. Yes, Breston County District Court, 195 pounds, and HZ would respectively be inserted in Boxes 6, 11, 34, and 32.

   C. F, 363, conspiracy to distribute a controlled substance, and 508-27-4110 would be inserted in Boxes 5, 4, 7, and 27, respectively.

   D. Both A and C

8. All of the following are true with respect to the booking report prepared on Mr. Connors except:

   A. HZ, black-colored eagle tattooed on right forearm, 90-Ford-4-W-White/Blue and Humbolt Corrections would be inserted in Boxes 32, 37, 40, and 24, respectively.

   B. The name Andrea Stevens would be inserted in Box 39.

   C. Diabetic, N/A, Hand K Towing, 679 E. Marston Place, Auburn, WA, and the name George Nichols would be inserted in Boxes 35, 22, 41, and 42, respectively.

   D. All of the above are incorrect.

9. What would be the appropriate report code used by the authorities to indicate Mr. Timothy Russell's relation to Mr. Connors?

   A. G

   B. M

   C. A

   D. None of the above

10. What would be the appropriate report code used by authorities to indicate Mr. Arthur B. Gladstone's relation to Mr. Connors?

   A. O

   B. A

   C. J

   D. None of the above

Answer questions 11–20 on the basis of the following report.

GREENWALT CORRECTIONS
MAJOR OFFENSE REPORT

FILE # 6752-A

DATE SUBMITTED: OCTOBER 5, 1996
INMATE NAME: PHILLIP E. MORRIS
PRISONER ID#: 65715
CELL ASSIGNMENT: 615-MS
INCIDENT DETAILS: INMATE DUNLAP WAS
ASSAULTED BY INMATE MORRIS OVER AN
ALLEGED THEFT OF PERSONAL ITEMS. DUNLAP
RECEIVED TWO SERIOUS FACIAL CONTUSIONS
BUT OTHERWISE WAS UNHURT. TREATED AND
RELEASED SAME DAY.

OFFENSE/CHARGE: ASSAULT AND BATTERY
OFFENSE CODE: 62-05
DATE OCCURRED: OCTOBER 3, 1996
APPROXIMATE TIME OF INCIDENT: 11:45 AM
DATE REPORTED: OCTOBER 4, 1996
PLACE OF OFFENSE: EXERCISE YARD
  VICTIM(S) NAME AND ID:
    MR. CHARLES DUNLAP; INMATE # 65710
  WITNESS(ES) NAME AND ID:
    MR. CARL BERENSTEIN; INMATE # 63157
    MR. TREVOR BLACKSTON; INMATE # 68351

EVIDENCE SEIZED   ☑ YES   ☐ NO

EVIDENCE DESCRIPTION: 13 INCH LONG PIECE OF 1 INCH GALVANIZED PIPE

SIGNATURE OF REPORTING OFFICER: MATT CARLSON BADGE # 936

APPROVED BY: CAPTAIN DALE LEWISTON

REFERRED TO ADJUSTMENT COMMITTEE HEARING: ☑ YES   ☐ NO
  IF YES:

ASSIGNED A.C.H. REPORT NUMBER: 15-HY
DATE SUBMITTED: OCTOBER 7, 1996

COMMITTEE DECISION	
	☐ DISMISSAL
SUPERVISORY CHAIRPERSON'S NAME:	☐ NOT GUILTY
SHARON PRESTON	☑ GUILTY
DOUG BOSWELL	PENALTY CODE INVOKED:

CORRECTIONS REVIEW BOARD   ☐ SUSPENDED
      SIGNATURE: *Martha Jacobson*   ☐ DISAPPROVED
      TITLE: REGIONAL FACILITY DIRECTOR   ☑ APPROVED
      DATE: October 10, 1996

---

11. The information compiled in this report details an alleged offense committed by whom?

    A. Charles Dunlap

    B. Phillip Morris

    C. Doug Boswell

    D. Carl Berenstein

12. The alleged offense referred to in the previous question is which of the following selections?

    A. Assault and criminal mischief

    B. Assault and battery

    C. Reckless endangerment

    D. Abusive language directed at a staff member

13. What kind of physical evidence was documented as being confiscated?

    A. A shank or sharp metal object

    B. An unauthorized tool

    C. A small metal pipe

    D. Information to that effect was not provided.

14. Inmate #68351 is described within the report as being which of the following?

    A. Witness

    B. Victim

    C. Offender

    D. Committee chairperson

15. Who was noted in the offense report as being a regional facility director?

    A. Dale Lewiston

    B. Mark Chadwick

    C. Matt Carlson

    D. Martha Jacobson

16. According to the documentation provided, which of the following selections can be assumed as identifying Matt Carlson's immediate supervisor?

    A. Sharon Preston

    B. Dale Lewiston

    C. Doug Boswell

    D. Insufficient information provided to make such an assumption.

17. The alleged offense occurred at what time, according to the report?

    A. 11:05 A.M.

    B. 11:45 P.M.

    C. 12:15 P.M.

    D. None of the above

18. All of the following identification numbers belong to either witnesses or victims of the event detailed in the report except?

    A. 65715

    B. 63157

    C. 65710

    D. 68351

19. Which of the following dates represents the day the alleged offense was actually reported?

    A. 11-4-96

    B. 10-3-96

    C. 10-4-96

    D. 10-7-96

20. Inmate #65710 was reported as having been treated and released from the infirmary on which of the following dates?

    A. 10-4-96

    B. 10-10-96

    C. 10-3-96

    D. The information was not provided in the report.

ANSWER SHEET FOR SAMPLE REPORT-WRITING QUESTIONS

1. Ⓐ Ⓑ Ⓒ Ⓓ
2. Ⓐ Ⓑ Ⓒ Ⓓ
3. Ⓐ Ⓑ Ⓒ Ⓓ
4. Ⓐ Ⓑ Ⓒ Ⓓ
5. Ⓐ Ⓑ Ⓒ Ⓓ
6. Ⓐ Ⓑ Ⓒ Ⓓ
7. Ⓐ Ⓑ Ⓒ Ⓓ

8. Ⓐ Ⓑ Ⓒ Ⓓ
9. Ⓐ Ⓑ Ⓒ Ⓓ
10. Ⓐ Ⓑ Ⓒ Ⓓ
11. Ⓐ Ⓑ Ⓒ Ⓓ
12. Ⓐ Ⓑ Ⓒ Ⓓ
13. Ⓐ Ⓑ Ⓒ Ⓓ
14. Ⓐ Ⓑ Ⓒ Ⓓ

15. Ⓐ Ⓑ Ⓒ Ⓓ
16. Ⓐ Ⓑ Ⓒ Ⓓ
17. Ⓐ Ⓑ Ⓒ Ⓓ
18. Ⓐ Ⓑ Ⓒ Ⓓ
19. Ⓐ Ⓑ Ⓒ Ⓓ
20. Ⓐ Ⓑ Ⓒ Ⓓ

Answers can be found on pages 153–154.

SAMPLE QUESTIONS, GRAMMAR

Questions 21–40 are specifically designed to test your knowledge of proper English usage and grammar. This section is meant only as a basic review of what is traditionally taught in high school. If you feel unsure about some of the rules, it is strongly advised that you study supplemental material that addresses this subject. A quick refresher course in writing can always be beneficial, regardless of the potential exam implications.

Each question will provide four complete sentences. You will have to determine which sentence, if any, is grammatically correct. The answers to these questions, complete with explanations detailing why the incorrect sentence structures are wrong, are provided toward the back of this section.

21.   A.   The Policemen's Ball (an event established three years ago) has become a widely publicized festivity.

      B.   These kinds of preparatory study guides are instructive.

      C.   The grand jury has agreed on the verdict.

      D.   All of the above sentences are grammatically correct.

22.   A.   Detective Hanley is at his best in filing detailed field interview reports.

      B.   Officer Briggs was upset at me.

      C.   Rookie Corrections Officer Dan Clemms only made one error on his first assignment

      D.   None of the above sentences are grammatically correct.

23.   A.   Sergeant Hill has arrested a woman identified by the victim's mother as the person she saw leaving the scene of the crime.

      B.   The gang of juveniles fleed in several directions at the sight of Officer Jenkins.

      C.   After completing the accident report, the rest of the day was easy.

      D.   None of the above sentences are grammatically correct.

24.   A.   A gun was found lose in her purse.

      B.   The mayor effected many changes in police personnel.

      C.   The Thomas-Gains Community Service award was presented to both my partner and myself.

      D.   All of the above sentences are grammatically correct.

25.   A.   Its about time they implemented that policy.

      B.   The suspect was told to lay his gun down on the ground.

      C.   Everyone shaked my hand at the conference.

      D.   All of the above sentences are grammatically correct.

26.   A.   Officer Bartelli's response was quick and emphatic.

      B.   Steve Jones's nightstick was missing.

      C.   In general, it's relatively quiet out there.

      D.   All of the above sentences are grammatically correct.

27. A. To Lieutenant James, Patrolman Heath was borderline irresponsible.

    B. Each officer is bringing their own lunch.

    C. In summary: the prosecutor has proven a clear case of negligent homicide.

    D. None of the above sentences are grammatically correct.

28. A. The M.O. is very unique, but I cannot recall whom it is.

    B. This is the portable TV set that was knocked over during the argument.

    C. Detective Connelly remarked that "he felt fatigued."

    D. None of the above sentences are grammatically correct.

29. A. Richard and Sue said that their planning on a backpacking trip in October.

    B. "Your checkbook balance is wrong" she said, "add your deposit slips again."

    C. I have a partner who served three consecutive tours in Vietnam.

    D. All of the above sentences are grammatically correct.

30. A. To work effectively, a Corrections Officer should keep his firearm cleaned and oiled.

    B. Bill was real livid.

    C. There isn't an unbroken window in the abandoned warehouse.

    D. All of the above sentences are grammatically correct.

31. A. Judith Merriweather chairwoman of Crime Stoppers Blockwatch has announced the merger.

    B. We shall always remember him as a compassionate police officer, said the minister.

    C. Where has John Carrington been at?

    D. None of the above sentences are grammatically correct.

32. A. The nature of Corrections work both gave me excitement and satisfaction.

    B. The patrolman did not say whether he had completed the preliminary assessments.

    C. The applicant has had three years of undergraduate study at ohio state university.

    D. None of the above sentences are grammatically correct.

33. A. Steve and I attended the safety seminar sponsored by Kelso, Inc.

    B. Captain Felder has an leather recliner and an oak file cabinet he would like to sell.

    C. Carroll would like to join us to.

    D. All of the above sentences are grammatically correct.

34. A. The store manager payed little attention to the threat made by the suspect.

    B. How can you expect everyone to do his duty when you place them under intense scrutiny?

    C. Whom did you call?

    D. All of the above sentences are grammatically correct.

35. A. There is not no easy way of solving the problem of teenage drug abuse.

    B. Your official hiring date (once the background check proves satisfactory) will be the first Tuesday of next month.

    C. The new department policy was poorly planned, it lacked both insight and reality.

    D. None of the above sentences are grammatically correct.

36. A. Margarets new car has turned out to be a lemon.

    B. Talking, not arguing, is the best way to handle domestic disputes.

    C. That sort of trite remarks will ruin your career.

    D. All of the above sentences are grammatically correct.

37. A. Frank had a holier than thou attitude after tipping off authorities about an illegal gambling operation.

    B. A good Corrections Officer has courage, strength, and is patient.

    C. None of the administrators speaks well of Captain Martin.

    D. None of the above sentences are grammatically correct.

38. A. People seldom attend help sessions nevertheless they are proven to be extremely helpful for most.

    B. It almost seems impossible to meet the deadline established.

    C. Please fill out your job application form carefully, concisely, and truthfully.

    D. None of the above sentences are grammatically correct.

39. A. Before I worked for the department, I had never used a handgun.

    B. Officer Miller crouched besides the victim.

    C. Your going to the demonstration whether you like it or not.

    D. All of the above sentences are grammatically correct.

40. A. The Bill of Rights guarantees individual freedoms.

    B. The reason for Dave's absence was because he felt sick.

    C. Nobody else decisions are more respected than Sergeant Collin's.

    D. All of the above sentences are grammatically correct.

ANSWER SHEET FOR SAMPLE GRAMMAR QUESTIONS

21.	Ⓐ	Ⓑ	Ⓒ	Ⓓ	28.	Ⓐ	Ⓑ	Ⓒ	Ⓓ	35.	Ⓐ	Ⓑ	Ⓒ	Ⓓ
22.	Ⓐ	Ⓑ	Ⓒ	Ⓓ	29.	Ⓐ	Ⓑ	Ⓒ	Ⓓ	36.	Ⓐ	Ⓑ	Ⓒ	Ⓓ
23.	Ⓐ	Ⓑ	Ⓒ	Ⓓ	30.	Ⓐ	Ⓑ	Ⓒ	Ⓓ	37.	Ⓐ	Ⓑ	Ⓒ	Ⓓ
24.	Ⓐ	Ⓑ	Ⓒ	Ⓓ	31.	Ⓐ	Ⓑ	Ⓒ	Ⓓ	38.	Ⓐ	Ⓑ	Ⓒ	Ⓓ
25.	Ⓐ	Ⓑ	Ⓒ	Ⓓ	32.	Ⓐ	Ⓑ	Ⓒ	Ⓓ	39.	Ⓐ	Ⓑ	Ⓒ	Ⓓ
26.	Ⓐ	Ⓑ	Ⓒ	Ⓓ	33.	Ⓐ	Ⓑ	Ⓒ	Ⓓ	40.	Ⓐ	Ⓑ	Ⓒ	Ⓓ
27.	Ⓐ	Ⓑ	Ⓒ	Ⓓ	34.	Ⓐ	Ⓑ	Ⓒ	Ⓓ					

Answers can be found on pages 154–156.

SPELLING

Spelling questions can make up 5–10 percent of the Corrections Officer exam. Consequently, this area warrants a degree of review even by those who have fairly good spelling skills. A basic list of guidelines is provided that can be of assistance when the proper spelling of a word is in doubt. Pay particular attention to any exceptions pointed out in these guidelines—test questions often center around such exceptions. As mentioned earlier, a list of words that have been seen on past exams has been compiled for your study. There is a good chance that most of the spelling questions that may be seen on your actual exam will be included in this list.

Once you have studied these spelling rules and the list, move on to the sample spelling test questions that follow. Do not use a dictionary for reference, because you will not be allowed to use one during the actual exam. The answers to these sample questions are provided at the back of this chapter.

SPELLING GUIDELINES

1. If you add a suffix that begins with a vowel to a word that ends in the letter *e* (silent), you should drop the final *e*. For instance, the word *dine* and the suffix *-ing* are combined to form the word *dining*. Other examples would be *coming, loving, continuous, deplorable,* etc.

    However, if the word in question ends in soft *ge* or *ce,* the letter *e* may be kept before either *-able* or *-ous*. For instance, the word *manage* plus *able* is spelled *manageable*. Other examples would include *traceable, enforceable, advantageous, courageous,* etc.

    One other exception is to keep the letter *e* in the present participle of the words *singe, dye,* and *eye*: *singeing, dyeing,* and *eyeing*.

2. If you add a suffix that begins with a consonant (i.e., *-ment, -ly*), the spelling will not normally change. For instance, the words *movement, lonely, carelessness, extremely,* etc., illustrate this rule. Exceptions are *judgment, argument, acknowledgment,* and *truly*.

3. If a suffix is added to words that end in *y*, the *y* must be changed to *i* unless the suffix itself begins with *i*. For instance, *happy* and *-ness* are combined to spell *happiness*. Other examples include *business, merciless,* and *defiant*. However, words such as *study* or *carry* that end in *y* do not change with the addition of a suffix (*studying* and *carrying*).

4. The use of the suffix *-sede, -cede,* or *-ceed* is quite simple. *Supersede* is the only word spelled with *-sede. Succeed, proceed,* and *exceed* are the only words that incorporate *-ceed* as a suffix. All other comparable words are spelled with the *-cede* ending: *recede, intercede, precede,* etc.

5. In most cases, prefixes can be added to words without affecting the spelling of the word in question. For example, *mis-* added to *spell* produces *misspell*. Other examples would include *malcontent, unnecessary, inaccurate,* and *irreverent*.

6. Use *i* before *e* except after *c* or when it sounds like the name of the letter *a*. For instance, the words *believe, chief, yield, grief,* etc., demonstrate the proper spellings in the absence of *c. Receive, perceive,* and *deceit* are a few examples that reverse the order of *i* and *e*. Examples of words in which *ei* sounds like *a* are *neighbor, their, weight,* etc. They follow the same rules of spelling that apply to words having the letters *e* and *i* following *c*. Other words that seem to be an exception to these rules are *neither, seize, forfeit, either, leisure, weird, counterfeit,* and *foreign*.

7. If you intend to change the form of a single-syllable action word that ends in a consonant preceded by a vowel, you must double the final consonant. For instance, *plan, sad,* and *sit* change to *planning, sadden,* and *sitting.*

    The final consonant must be doubled to change the form of a two-syllable word that ends in a consonant preceded by a vowel and that is accented on the second syllable. For instance, the words *refer, remit,* and *occur* can have their respective spellings changed to *referring, remittance,* and *occurring.* However, if you are using a two- or three-syllable word and the addition of a suffix results in the change of accent from the final syllable to a preceding one, you should not double the final consonant. For instance, the words *travel, refer,* and *cancel* would be spelled *traveling, reference,* and *canceling* according to this rule.

8. Adjectives that end with the letter *l* may be changed to a corresponding adverb by simply adding *-ly* to the word. For instance, *legal, accidental,* and *unusual* may be changed to *legally, accidentally,* and *unusually.*

    If you desire to combine suffixes and prefixes that end in *ll,* usually one *l* is dropped from the word. For instance, the words *all together, all ready,* and *mind full* would appropriately be combined to spell *altogether, already,* and *mindful.*

9. If the intent is to make a singular word plural, this can usually be accomplished by simply adding *s* to the word; for instance, *chips, rules, times,* etc. If the word in question ends in *s* or an *s*-like sound (i.e., *sh, ch, ss, x,* and *z*), then a plural may be formed by adding *es;* for instance, *crushes, annexes, dishes,* etc. Be aware, however, that some words require irregular changes to become plural. For instance, *alumnus* to *alumni, thief* to *thieves, woman* to *women,* and *crisis* to *crises,* just to name a few.

10. If you are unsure of whether a word's ending is properly spelled *-ise* or *-ize,* you can be relatively assured that the latter choice is correct more often than it is wrong. American usage seems to prefer *-ize* in most instances. *Advise, despise, surprise,* and *supervise* are just a few of the *-ise* exceptions. *Organize, utilize, centralize,* and *authorize* are typical words that incorporate *-ize.*

    There are, of course, other minor spelling rules that have not been discussed here. However, this list of guidelines encompasses most of what will concern you on the actual exam. Keep this list in mind as you work through the sample questions provided.

SAMPLE QUESTIONS, SPELLING

41. Prior to the Miranda case, police officers felt that it was <u>unnecessery</u> to explain to a defendant his or her rights at the time of the arrest. How should the word underlined in this sentence be spelled?

    A. Unecessary

    B. Unneccessary

    C. Unnecessary

    D. No change is required because the word in question is spelled correctly.

42. Most people probably <u>exsede</u> the speed limit by five-to-ten miles per hour. How should the word underlined in this sentence be spelled?

    A. Exceed

    B. Excede

    C. Exseed

    D. No change is required because the word in question is spelled correctly.

43. Kids learning to drive seem to have difficulty with the aspects of <u>parallel</u> parking. How should the underlined word be spelled?

    A. Parralel

    B. Paralell

    C. Pearallel

    D. No change is required because the word in question is spelled correctly.

44. Sex offenders need to be <u>superviced</u> closely. How should the underlined word be spelled?

    A. Supervized

    B. Supervised

    C. Supervizzed

    D. No change is required because the word in question is spelled correctly.

45. The witness claims to <u>reckinize</u> two of the three people we have in custody. How should the underlined word be spelled?

    A. Recognise

    B. Recognize

    C. Rekognize

    D. No change is required because the word in question is spelled correctly.

46. Howard wants the reports on his desk no later than <u>Wensday</u>. How should the underlined word be spelled?

    A. Wendsday

    B. Wedsday

    C. Wednesday

    D. No change is required because the word in question is spelled correctly.

47. It was very difficult to tell the difference between the <u>counterfiet</u> and the real thing. How should the underlined word in the sentence be spelled?

    A. Countorfeit

    B. Counterfit

    C. Counterfeit

    D. No change is required because the word in question is spelled correctly.

48. The defense attorney hoped that his client would receive a lenient <u>judgement</u> since it was a first-time offense. How should the underlined word in this sentence be spelled?

    A. Judgment

    B. Jugment

    C. Judgmente

    D. No change is required because the word in question is spelled correctly.

49. The whole incident proved to be <u>embarrassing</u>.

    A. Embarassing

    B. Embarrasing

    C. Emberrassing

    D. No change is required because the word in question is spelled correctly.

50. Only recently have repeat offenders <u>receeved</u> harsher sentences. How should the underlined word be spelled?

    A. Received

    B. Recieved

    C. Reccived

    D. No change is required because the word in question is spelled correctly.

51. Considering the circumstances, her actions seemed <u>justafiable</u>. How should the underlined word be spelled?

    A. Justifyable

    B. Justefiable

    C. Justifiable

    D. No change is required because the word in question is spelled correctly.

52. <u>Ocasionally</u>, you will be required to put in overtime. How should the underlined word be spelled?

    A. Ocassionally

    B. Occasionally

    C. Occasionaly

    D. No change is required because the word in question is spelled correctly.

53. After chasing the suspect for several blocks, Officer Miller had to stop to catch his <u>breathe</u>. How should the underlined word in this sentence be spelled?

    A. Breath

    B. Breeth

    C. Breathe

    D. No change is required because the word in question is spelled correctly.

54. Most defendants in a court of law have the assistance of <u>counsul</u>. How should the underlined word in the sentence be spelled?

    A. Council

    B. Counsell

    C. Counsel

    D. No change is required because the word in question is spelled correctly.

55. She had a lot of <u>miscellaneous</u> items in her purse. How should the underlined word in this sentence be spelled?

    A. Misscellaneous

    B. Miscelaneous

    C. Miscellanious

    D. No change is required because the word in question is spelled correctly.

56. Mayor Blackmore has received a lot of <u>correspondence</u> on this issue. How should the underlined word be spelled?

    A. Corraspondence

    B. Correspondents

    C. Corespondance

    D. No change is required because the word in question is spelled correctly.

57. Madison is a large <u>municpality</u>. How should the underlined word in this sentence be spelled?

    A. Municsipality

    B. Municipality

    C. Munecapality

    D. No change is required because the word in question is spelled correctly.

58. Her testimony seemed <u>contredictory</u> to statements she made earlier. How should the underlined word in the sentence be spelled?

    A. Contradictory

    B. Contradictery

    C. Contradictary

    D. No change is required because the word in question is spelled correctly.

59. Officer Blaine <u>personaly</u> took responsibility for the incident. How should the underlined word in this sentence be spelled?

    A. Personelly

    B. Personoly

    C. Personally

    D. No change is required because the word in question is spelled correctly.

60. The severity of the accident made it difficult to determine the <u>identafication</u> of the victims involved. How should the underlined word in the sentence be spelled?

    A. Identification

    B. Identifacation

    C. Idintification

    D. No change is required because the word in question is spelled correctly.

ANSWER SHEET FOR SAMPLE SPELLING QUESTIONS

41. Ⓐ Ⓑ Ⓒ Ⓓ 48. Ⓐ Ⓑ Ⓒ Ⓓ 55. Ⓐ Ⓑ Ⓒ Ⓓ
42. Ⓐ Ⓑ Ⓒ Ⓓ 49. Ⓐ Ⓑ Ⓒ Ⓓ 56. Ⓐ Ⓑ Ⓒ Ⓓ
43. Ⓐ Ⓑ Ⓒ Ⓓ 50. Ⓐ Ⓑ Ⓒ Ⓓ 57. Ⓐ Ⓑ Ⓒ Ⓓ
44. Ⓐ Ⓑ Ⓒ Ⓓ 51. Ⓐ Ⓑ Ⓒ Ⓓ 58. Ⓐ Ⓑ Ⓒ Ⓓ
45. Ⓐ Ⓑ Ⓒ Ⓓ 52. Ⓐ Ⓑ Ⓒ Ⓓ 59. Ⓐ Ⓑ Ⓒ Ⓓ
46. Ⓐ Ⓑ Ⓒ Ⓓ 53. Ⓐ Ⓑ Ⓒ Ⓓ 60. Ⓐ Ⓑ Ⓒ Ⓓ
47. Ⓐ Ⓑ Ⓒ Ⓓ 54. Ⓐ Ⓑ Ⓒ Ⓓ

Answers can be found on pages 156–157.

For your convenience, a reference list of words seen on various Corrections Officer exams follows. It should be noted that this list of words does not preclude the possibility of seeing other words or variations of the same word on the actual exam. However, this reference list should account for a majority of spelling questions most likely encountered on the test.

abandoned	artificial	cartridge	corporation
abduction	asked	cashier	corps
academy	asphyxiated	casualty	corpse
accelerator	assault	ceiling	correctional
accessories	assistance	cemetery	corrective
accident	assistants	chauffeur	corroborate
accomplice	associate	chief	cough
accountability	assortment	cigarette	council
accurate	athletics	circle	counsel
acquaintance	attorney	circumstance	counterfeit
acquitted	attraction	citizen	coupon
across	attribute	coarse	court
adjacent	authorization	cocaine	courteous
administrative	automatic	coerce	credibility
admissible	available	coherent	criminal
admission	backward	collaborate	criteria
admonition	bail	collar	cruising
adultery	bale	collision	curfew
affidavit	bandage	colonel	current
affirmation	barricade	combative	custody
aggravated	beaten	coming	cylinder
aggressive	beginning	commercial	damage
alcohol	behavior	commissary	dangerous
allege	beige	commission	deceased
always	believe	committed	decent
ammunition	belligerent	committee	decision
analysis	bicycle	communication	defendant
anonymous	borderline	community	delinquent
answer	boulevard	complainant	delusion
apparent	brake	comply	demeanor
appeal	break	concealed	depression
application	breathalyzer	confusion	descent
appoint	bruise	conscience	describe
appraise	building	conscious	description
apprehend	bulletin	consent	detached
approximately	bureau	consistent	detention
argument	burglary	conspiracy	deterrent
arraignment	business	construction	diabetic
arrangement	cache	continue	diesel
arrest	calendar	contraband	different
arson	campaign	conviction	disabled
arterial	captain	cooperate	disagree
artery	carnal	coordinate	disappear
article	carrying	coroner	disappointed

discipline	foreign	incident	latent
disoriented	forfeit	incorrigible	lawyer
dispatched	forgery	incriminate	legal
dispense	forth	indecent	leisure
disperse	forty	indicate	length
disposition	fourteen	indict	lethal
disseminate	fourth	indigent	liability
dissent	fracture	individual	likable
district	fraudulent	informant	liaison
disturbance	frequent	infraction	libel
duress	frequently	ingest	liberty
during	friend	inhaled	license
educational	frisk	inherent	lieutenant
eight	fugitive	inherit	liquor
elementary	furniture	initial	loiter
eliminate	gambling	injured	loose
embarrass	garbage	inquiry	lose
embezzlement	gauge	inscribed	loss
emergency	genuine	instead	malicious
emphasize	government	instinct	manipulate
employee	grabbed	institutional	manual
enforcement	grazed	insufficient	marijuana
epileptic	grease	insulted	marital
equipment	grievance	insurance	maximum
erratic	guardian	intelligent	medal
escape	gymnasium	intercourse	medical
escorted	handkerchief	interest	menace
evidence	hazard	interrogate	metal
examination	headache	intersection	metropolitan
exceed	hemorrhage	intervention	microfiche
excellent	heroin	interview	microphone
except	history	intimidation	mileage
excite	holster	intoxicating	minor
exclude	homicide	investigation	minute
exercise	horizontal	its	Miranda
exhaust	hostage	it's	miscellaneous
experience	hurrying	jealous	mischief
explanation	hydrant	jewelry	misdemeanor
explosion	identified	judge	misspelled
expression	illegal	judgment	mistaken
extension	illiterate	judicial	mitigate
extortion	imitation	jury	molest
extradite	immediately	juvenile	motorcycle
familiar	impact	khaki	municipal
felony	impaired	knife	muscle
feminine	implementation	knowledge	mustache
fighting	impossible	label	naive
financial	impression	laboratory	narcotics
forcibly	incest	larceny	nausea

necessary	perjury	psychiatrist	retaliate
negative	permanent	psychology	retribution
neglect	permit	public	revoked
negligent	persecute	pulse	revolver
negotiable	persistent	pungent	rhythmic
neighbor	personal	punitive	riot
nervous	personnel	purpose	robbery
neurotic	perspiration	pursue	routine
niece	physical	pursuit	sacrifice
ninety	physician	putrefy	sanitary
noisy	piece	pyrotechnic	satisfactory
noticeable	plaintiff	quality	Saturday
notify	planning	quantity	scene
obligation	pneumatic	questionnaire	schedule
obnoxious	policies	quiet	scheme
obscene	polygamy	quite	schizophrenic
observed	polygraph	racial	search
obsolete	positive	radical	secretary
obstacle	possession	raid	security
occasion	potential	rally	seen
occupant	pregnancy	ramification	segregate
occur	prejudice	rationalization	seize
occurred	prejudiced	raucous	semiautomatic
odor	preliminary	react	sense
offender	premises	realize	sentence
official	prescription	receipt	sequester
operator	preservation	receive	sergeant
opinion	previous	reckless	serial
opportunity	principal	recognize	several
opposite	principle	recommendation	severely
ordinance	prisoner	recurrence	sexual
organize	private	reference	sheriff
original	privileges	refuse	shining
oxygen	probably	registration	shone
painful	probationary	regrettable	shown
parallel	procedure	rehabilitation	sieve
parole	proceeded	reimburse	signature
participate	process	relevant	silhouette
passed	profane	reliable	similar
passenger	professional	religious	simultaneous
past	prohibitive	remember	since
patience	promiscuous	renewal	sincerity
patients	promotional	representation	siphon
peace	proposition	reputation	skeleton
pedestrian	prosecute	request	skeptical
penalty	prosecutor	resistance	skidded
penitentiary	prostitution	respiration	sleight
perform	provoke	responsible	slight
perimeter	proximity	restitution	sobriety

socialize	supervisor	tissue	vicinity
sodomy	surveillance	to/too/two	vicious
sophisticated	susceptible	together	victim
specimen	suspect	tongue	violate
spontaneous	suspicion	tourniquet	visible
sprain	symptom	toxicology	volume
statement	tactical	traffic	voluntary
stationary	tamper	transferred	waist
stationery	tattoo	translucent	warehouse
statute	technician	trespassing	warrant
sterilize	telephone	truancy	waste
stomach	temperature	Tuesday	weapon
strangulate	temporary	typewriter	weather/whether
strictly	terrorism	ultimatum	Wednesday
striped	testimony	unconscious	weight
stripped	theater	uniform	welfare
subject	theft	unnecessary	whiskey
submitting	their	urgent	whole
subpoena	there	using	whore
substantiate	they're	utility	witness
subtle	thieves	vacuum	women
succeed	thorough	vagrancy	wounded
successful	thought	valuable	wrapper
suffocate	threaten	vehicle	wreck
suicidal	threw	velocity	yield
summons	throat	verify	you're
superintendent	through	version	young
superior	tier	vertical	your/you're

ANSWERS TO SAMPLE REPORT-WRITING QUESTIONS

1. *D*   A booking report number had not been specifically given in the reading. Selection A represents an arrest report number for Mr. Russell.

2. *D*   Reference Code Number 1 should be used, according to the report. Selection A is a correct description; however, it is procedurally wrong to state the fact this way since applicable booking codes have been provided.

3. *C*   The report specifically mentions that height must be expressed as a three-digit number expressing both feet and inches. Therefore, selection C is the correct choice.

4. *B*   Thurston Whitley was Mr. Connors's probation officer. Selection A names the arresting officer involved.

5. *A*   This name is an alias used by Mr. Connors. Box 36 would be the correct place for this information.

6. *D*   Selection C is correct with respect to the appointed time; however, the booking report makes specific reference to the fact that all time entries must be expressed in military form. Therefore, 1300 hours would be the correct information to insert in Box 10.

    (*Note:* It should be mentioned here that many exams seen recently vacillate between the use of military time and regular [civilian] time. Many Police and Corrections departments utilize military time in filling out various reports. Therefore, you should be aware of both uses. Military time is figured on a 24-hour clock: 0100 hours represents 1:00 A.M., 0200 hours represents 2:00 A.M., 1200 hours represents noon, 1600 hours represents 4:00 P.M., 2200 hours represents 10:00 P.M., and so on. Minutes are figured the same as for civilian time. For instance, 0830 hours represents 8:30 A.M., 0945 hours represents 9:45 A.M., 1515 hours represents 3:15 P.M., etc. Be aware of both forms of time because invariably you will be expected to understand the differences.)

7. *D*   Selection A is incorrect in placing 9-20-92 in Box 29. This would reflect Mr. Connors's arraignment date, not his date of birth. Mr. Connors's age was given to be thirty-seven. Selection C is incorrect in the charges filed against Mr. Connors. Instead, this lists what was filed against Mr. Russell. Both manufacture of and intent to deliver a controlled substance, plus unlawful possession of a firearm by a felon, should be placed in Box 7.

8. *D*   Even though the description is correct, selection A is incorrect because it does not use the code D-3 to establish the location of the scar or peculiarity. Selection B is incomplete. Andrea Stevens's relation to Mr. Connors, home address, and home phone number should be completed since the information is available. Selection C incorrectly states Hand K Towing's impoundment yard as being located at 679 E. Marston Place; this is the address where Mr. Connors is employed. The correct insertion made into Box 41 is Hand K Towing, 4357 H Street, Auburn, WA.

9. *D*   Mr. Connors made reference to Mr. Russell as a friend. Mr. Russell was, in fact, arrested for conspiracy to distribute a controlled substance at the same time Mr. Connors was arrested. Therefore, from the authorities' perspective, Mr. Timothy Russell would be considered an accomplice. The code O is not offered as an option for the question.

10. *C*   Mr. Connors made reference to Mr. Gladstone as his cousin. Selection C best describes the relationship.

11. *B*   Phillip Morris was the alleged perpetrator as documented in the offense report.

12. *B*   Assault and battery

13. *C*   A small metal pipe

14. *A* Inmate #68351, Trevor Blackston, was a witness to the incident.

15. *D* Martha Jacobson's title is Regional Facility Director.

16. *B* Since Captain Dale Lewiston is stated within the report as having approved Matt Carlson's work, it can be assumed that he is an immediate superior involved in the matter.

17. *D* The assault was documented as having taken place at 11:45 A.M., which is not a choice among the selections offered.

18. *A* 65715 is the ID number of the alleged offender.

19. *C* The date that the offense was actually reported was October 4, 1996.

20. *C* It was stated in the report that inmate Dunlap was treated and released the same day of the incident, which was reported as having occurred on 10-3-96.

ANSWERS TO SAMPLE GRAMMAR QUESTIONS

21. *D* A. Parentheses can be used to enclose explanations within a sentence.
   B. The word *these* is plural and correctly modifies the plural noun *study guides.*
   C. *Grand jury* is considered a collective noun and therefore requires the singular word *has.*

22. *A* The sentence correctly uses the present tense to illustrate a point.
   B. The word *at* exemplifies the incorrect use of a preposition. The work *with* would be considered appropriate.
   C. *Only made* exemplifies the incorrect placement of an adverb. It should be turned around to read *made only.*

23. *A* This sentence correctly uses a subordinate clause in stating what happened.
   B. The word *fleed* does not exist; the appropriate word should be *fled.*
   C. The sentence contains an inappropriate dangling modifier that fails to identify who filled out the accident report. One way to write this sentence better would be: *After he completed the accident report, he found the rest of the day easy.*

24. *B* *Affect* means "influence"; here *effect* ("cause," "bring about") is needed.
   A The word *lose* is considered a verb that means the opposite of win. The proper adjective to use in this case is *loose*, which means unrestrained.
   C. *Myself* is a reflexive pronoun that should not be substituted for *I* or *me.*

25. *B* *Lay* is the correct transitive verb to be used in this statement.
   A. *It's* is a contraction of "it is." An apostrophe is needed between the letters *t* and *s*. *Its* is a possessive pronoun.
   C. *Shaked* is not recognized as a word. *Shook* is the appropriate word needed in this sentence.

26. *D* A. The apostrophe is correctly used to indicate possession.
   B. With a singular noun that ends in *s,* in this case *Jones,* it would be correct to indicate possession either by adding an apostrophe after *s* in *Jones (Jones')* or by adding an apostrophe and *s (Jones's).* However, it would have been incorrect to write *Joneses.*
   C. The comma is appropriately used to set apart the introductory phrase, and the apostrophe is used correctly to indicate the contraction.

27. *D* The comma is appropriately used in the sentence after the introductory phrase. Without it, the sentence seems confused and may be misunderstood.
   B. There must be agreement between the pronoun and what it stands for. *His* or *hers* would be considered correct instead of *their.*
   C. The colon is used correctly; however, the first word of a complete sentence/statement that follows a colon should be capitalized.

28. *B*   *That* is the appropriate pronoun since it refers to an object, in this case a TV set.

       A. *Who* and *whom* can refer only to people. Since a method of operation instead of people is being described, the word *whose,* which is a possessive of *who,* would be considered the correct choice, referring to the person with that M.O.

       C. Quotation marks should not be used to set off indirect quotations. The absence of quotation marks would be acceptable.

29. *C*   The adjective clause is appropriately introduced by the pronoun *who.*

       A. *Their* is a possessive of *they.* Instead, the contraction *they're* is needed.

       B. A comma splice should not be used in divided quotations. A period after *said* and capitalizing *add* would be one correct revision.

30. *C*   The singular verb agrees with the singular noun.

       A. This statement sounds ridiculous, not to mention that a modifier must modify something. A more appropriate statement would read, "The Corrections Officer should keep his firearm cleaned and oiled to make it work effectively."

       B. Adverbs modify adjectives, verbs, and other adverbs. Therefore, it should read, "Bill is very livid."

31. *D*   A. Commas were not used to set off words in parenthetical apposition. Commas should be placed at "Merriweather, chairwoman" and "Blockwatch, has."

       B. Quotation marks should always be used to enclose a quotation. They should be placed prior to the word *We* and after the word *officer.*

       C. "Where has John Carrington been?" This would be a more appropriate way of asking the question. *At* is unnecessary and ungrammatical.

32. *B*   *Whether* is properly used as a conjunction in this statement.

       A. A correlative conjunction was not appropriately placed next to the words it connects. A better way to restructure this sentence would be this: "The nature of Corrections work gave me both excitement and satisfaction."

       C. Ohio State University is considered to be a proper name and should therefore be capitalized.

33. *A*   I (instead of *me*) is the correct choice of first-person pronoun as the subject of *attended.*

       B. *A* instead of *an* should be used before *leather recliner.*

       C. *To* is a preposition that expresses motion or direction toward something. Instead, the adverb *too* should be used to indicate "in addition."

34. *C*   *Whom* is the proper pronoun to use instead of *who.*

       A. *Paid* is the correct substitute.

       B. *His* is considered singular, and, therefore, *them* should be replaced by *him.*

35. *B*   Commas would have worked as well; however, parentheses are suitable to set off parenthetical expressions.

       A. *Not* should be left out of the sentence. *Not* and *no* combined in a statement can render an expression ineffective.

       C. A colon should be used instead of a comma when there is a restatement of the idea.

36. *B*   Commas are effectively used to set off contrasted phrases.

       A. There is need for an apostrophe to demonstrate possession (*Margaret's*).

       C. Plural adjectives must be used to modify plural nouns. Therefore, *that* should be replaced with *those.*

37. *D* A. *Holier than thou* is intended to be a single compound unit and therefore requires hyphenation (*holier-than-thou*).
    B. Ideas within a sentence must be parallel or presented in the same form. The correct way of expressing the same idea is this: A good Corrections Officer has courage, strength, and patience.
    C. *Speaks* fails to agree with the plural subject, *administrators*. *Speak* would be correct.

38. *C* The descriptive words in the statement are in complete agreement with one another.
    A. Anytime there are two complete thoughts within a sentence that uses the connecting word *nevertheless,* it should be preceded with a semicolon and followed by a comma.
    B. An adverb should be placed close to the word it modifies. *Seems* and *almost* should be reversed.

39. *A* Punctuation and tense are correctly used in this statement.
    B. *Besides* is an adverb that means "in addition to." On the other hand, *beside* is a preposition that means "by the side of."
    C. *Your* is a possessive of *you. You're,* which is a contraction of *you are,* is what is needed in this statement.

40. *A* *Bill of Rights* is appropriately capitalized.
    B. *Because* makes poor use of a conjunction. *That* would be more appropriate.
    C. *Else* must illustrate possession by adding an apostrophe and *s* (*else's*).

ANSWERS TO SAMPLE SPELLING QUESTIONS

41. *C* Unnecessary

42. *A* Exceed

43. *D* Parallel

44. *B* Supervised

45. *B* Recognize

46. *C* Wednesday

47. *C* Counterfeit

48. *A* Judgment

49. *D* Embarrassing

50. *A* Received
    (*Note:* Sometimes the very word that you are trying to determine the correct spelling for may exist elsewhere in the text. In this case, *received* was used in the previous question. While this may be atypical of the actual exam, be mindful of the fact that this method may serve as a cross-check of your word.)

51. *C* Justifiable

52. *B* Occasionally

53. *A* *Breath* is the proper spelling of the noun that refers to respiration. *Breathe* is the proper spelling of the verb that refers to inhaling and exhaling. (*Note:* You may be given spelling questions that may require not only correct spelling, but vocabulary discernment as well. This question is a prime example of what could be involved. First, determine which word is applicable to the context of the sentence, and then select the correct spelling.)

54. *C* Counsel
     Selection A is the correct spelling for a conference group or assembly.

55. *D* Miscellaneous

56. *D* Correspondence
     Selection B is the proper spelling of the noun that refers to writers.

57. *B* Municipality

58. *A* Contradictory

59. *C* Personally

60. *A* Identification

Your score for this exercise would rate as follows:

    54–60 correct — Excellent
    47–53 correct — Good
    40–46 correct — Fair
    Less than 40 correct — Poor

Chapter 7

Mathematics

As a Corrections Officer, you will need to have good mathematical ability to determine everything from inmate counts to blood alcohol levels. Mathematics is important beyond your career, as well. The implications in your personal life can be as far-reaching as calculating depreciation values on real estate for tax purposes to simply balancing your checkbook.

Mathematics treats exact relations existing between quantities in such a way that other quantities can be deduced from them. In other words, you may know a basic quantity, but to derive further use from that quantity, it is necessary to apply known relationships (that is, formulas).

For example, let's say you wanted to know how many revolutions a tire would have to make to roll a distance of exactly 20 feet. Outside of physically rolling the tire itself and using a tape measure, it would be impossible to solve such a problem without mathematics. However, by applying math, we can exploit known relationships to derive the answer.

If we know that the diameter of the tire is 40 inches, we can easily determine the tire's perimeter or circumference. In geometric terms, the tire is a circle and the known formula for determining the circumference of a circle is to multiply the diameter by π (which is 3.1416). The symbol π is referred to in mathematics as *pi*. Therefore, our tire's circumference is $40 \times 3.1416 = 125.66$ inches.

Since we now know that the circumference of the tire is 125.66 inches, we can learn how many revolutions a tire with this circumference would need to go exactly 20 feet. However, we cannot simply divide 125.66 inches into 20 feet because we are dealing with two entirely different units of measure, inches and feet.

Therefore, we need to convert feet into inches. We know that there are 12 inches in 1 foot, so 20 feet $\times$ 12 inches = 240 inches. Now we can divide 125.66 inches into 240 inches to find the answer we need. In this case, the tire would have to make 1.91 revolutions to roll exactly 20 feet. You can see by this example how known relationships can help find an unknown.

This chapter is designed with the purpose of reviewing only those aspects of math that have been predominantly seen on past exams. If you find any areas of weakness after completing the exercises, it would be in your best interest to get additional reference material from your library.

The subjects reviewed in this section include fractions, decimals, ratios, proportions, and geometry. Each of these areas is discussed briefly, and some examples demonstrate its application. At the end of this section, there are practice exercises for you to complete. Answers and explanations are provided separately so you can check your performance.

MATHEMATICAL PRINCIPLES

A. FRACTIONS

Fractions are essentially parts of a whole. If you have $1/2$ of something, this means you have 1 of 2 equal parts. If you have $7/8$ of something, this means you have 7 of the 8 equal parts available.

The 1 of $^1/_2$ is the *numerator*, which tells the number of parts used. The 2 is the *denominator*, which tells how many parts the whole has been divided into. As a general rule, if the numerator is less than the denominator, the fraction is called *proper*. On the other hand, if the numerator is greater than or equal to the denominator, the fraction is called *improper*. See the examples below:

$^1/_3$ is a proper fraction.

$^2/_3$ is a proper fraction.

$^3/_3$ is an improper fraction (Note: this fraction has a value of 1).

$^7/_3$ is an improper fraction.

A mixed number is simply a whole number plus a fractional part. For example, $2^1/_3$ is a mixed number. If there is a need to change a mixed number into an improper fraction, simply multiply the whole number by the denominator of the fraction and add the resulting product to the numerator. For example:

$2^1/_3 = (2 \times 3) + 1$ divided by $3 = {}^7/_3$, an improper fraction

If it is necessary to change an improper fraction into a mixed number, simply divide the numerator by the denominator. The quotient is the whole number; the remainder is left over the denominator, and this remaining fraction is reduced to its lowest terms. For example:

$^{15}/_{10} = 1^5/_{10} = 1^1/_2$

The fraction $^{15}/_{10}$ is improper, and 15 divided by 10 is 1 with 5 left over, so $1^1/_2$ is the resulting mixed number reduced.

When we need to add, subtract, divide, or multiply fractions, certain rules need to be understood and followed. One basic rule is that multiplication or division should be done prior to addition or subtraction.

To start, when you add or subtract fractional numbers, you must always use a common denominator. For example:

$^1/_4 + {}^2/_4 = {}^3/_4$

$^3/_6 - {}^1/_6 = {}^2/_6$

Notice that the solution's denominator remains the same, while the variable is the numerator (that is, $^1/_4 + {}^2/_4$ does not equal $^3/_8$, nor does $^3/_6 - {}^1/_6 = {}^2/_0$ or 0).

The same thing applies to mixed numbers as well.

$2^1/_4 + 1^3/_4 = 3^4/_4$

$^4/_4$ is an improper fraction that can be reduced to 1. Therefore:

$2^1/_4 + 1^3/_4 = 4$

But what happens when you have to add or subtract two fractions that have different denominators? Look at two such examples below:

$^3/_7 + {}^1/_2 = X$

$^5/_8 - {}^1/_3 = X$

Before anything can be figured out, it is essential that we find the least common denominator (LCD) for each problem. Looking at the former example ($^3/_7 + {}^1/_2 = X$), we need to find the LCD for 7 and 2. In this case, it happens to be 14 (that is, 7 and 2 each divide evenly into 14, and 14 is the smallest number for which that is true). Now that we are working the problem in units of fourteenths, it is easy to figure the values of the numerators involved. For example:

$^3/_7 = {}^x/_{14}$

To find X, you need to divide 7 into 14 and multiply the resulting quotient by the numerator:

$$14 \div 7 = 2, 2 \times 3 = 6; \text{ therefore, } 3/7 = 6/14$$

Work in a similar manner for all fractions.

$$1/2 = x/14, 14 \div 2 = 7, 7 \times 1 = 7, \text{ therefore } 1/2 = 7/14$$

Now that we have a common denominator, we can add or subtract numbers as we please. In this case,

$$6/14 + 7/14 = 13/14$$

This is a proper fraction that cannot be reduced any further.

Try your hand at the second example, $5/8 - 1/3 = X$. If you followed the format below to arrive at the answer of $7/24$, you were correct.

$$5/8 = x/24, 24 \div 8 = 3, 3 \times 5 = 15; \text{ therefore } 5/8 = 15/24$$
$$1/3 = x/24, 24 \div 3 = 8, 8 \times 1 = 8, \text{ therefore, } 1/3 = 8/24$$
$$15/24 - 8/24 = 7/24$$

This is a proper fraction that cannot be reduced further.

To add or subtract mixed numbers with different fractions, the same rule applies. The only difference is that whole numbers can be treated as fractions themselves if they need to be borrowed from. For example,

$$5\,2/8 - 3\,3/4 = X$$

First, we need to convert the fractions separately. The LCD for both fractions is 8. Therefore, we calculate that $3/4 = 6/8$.

Since $2/8 - 6/8$ would leave us with a negative number, we need to borrow from the whole number (which is 5). Therefore, we can look at $5\,2/8$ as $4\,10/8$. Thus, the problem now reads $4\,10/8 - 3\,6/8 = X$.

As the problem now reads, we can subtract the whole numbers (4 and 3) separately, thus $4 - 3 = 1$. The fractions $10/8$ and $6/8$ can be subtracted separately as well; thus $10/8 - 6/8 = 4/8$ or $1/2$.

Now, put the whole number answer and the fractional answer together and we arrive at the total solution, $X = 1\,1/2$.

To multiply fractions or mixed numbers it is not necessary to determine an LCD. Rather, the product of the numerators is divided by the product of the denominators. Several examples are shown below:

$$6/7 \times 5/8 = \frac{6 \times 5 = 30}{7 \times 8 = 56} = 30/56$$

which is equivalent to (or *reduces to*) $15/28$

$$4 \times 7\,1/3 = 4/1 \times 22/3 = \frac{4 \times 22 = 88}{1 \times 3 = 3} = 29\,1/3$$

When you need to divide fractions or mixed numbers, convert the divisor to its reciprocal (reverse numerator and denominator) and then multiply. For example:

$$7/8 \div 1/2 = X$$

($2/1$ is the reciprocal of $1/2$). Thus,

$$7/8 \times 2/1 = 14/8, \text{ or } 1\,3/4, \text{ reduced}$$

Another example involving mixed numbers is

$$6\,5/8 - 3\,1/3 = X$$

This equals $53/8 \times 3/10$ (reciprocal of $3\,1/3$) $= 159/80$, or $1\,79/80$, reduced.

B. DECIMALS

Decimals are basically another means to represent fractional numbers. The difference is that in decimals all fractions are expressed in factors of 10. The placement of the decimal point determines if it is a measure concerning tenths, hundredths, thousandths, ten thousandths, etc., and directly influences the size of the whole numbers involved. Look at the illustration below, which depicts the same number with different decimal placements, and examine the consequent change in value:

$4{,}459.1340 =$ Four thousand four hundred fifty-nine and one hundred thirty-four thousandths

$44{,}591.340 =$ Forty-four thousand five hundred ninety-one and thirty-four hundredths

$445{,}913.40 =$ Four hundred forty-five thousand nine hundred thirteen and four tenths

$4{,}459{,}134.0 =$ Four million four hundred fifty-nine thousand, one hundred thirty-four

When conducting addition or subtraction of decimals, the place values (that is, decimal points) of decimals must be in vertical alignment. Just as mixed numbers require a common denominator, so decimals require this alignment. In this respect, the common denominator is that tenths are under tenths, hundredths are under hundredths, etc., so that you are adding or subtracting comparable units. For example:

$$\begin{array}{r} 6.5432 \\ + 73.43 \\ \hline 79.9732 \end{array} \quad \text{or} \quad \begin{array}{r} 50.432 \\ - 12.07 \\ \hline 38.362 \end{array}$$

When multiplying decimals, it is necessary to treat them as whole numbers. Once you have determined the product, the decimal point is moved to the left the same number of places as there are numbers after the decimal point in both the decimals being multiplied. For example:

$$\begin{array}{r} 5.678 \\ \times .02 \\ \hline 11356 \\ 0000 \\ \hline 0.11356 \end{array}$$

In this case, there are 5 numbers to the right of the decimal (678 and 02); therefore, 11356 should have the decimal placed in front of the first 1. The final number is 0.11356.

Dividing decimals is as simple as multiplication. When utilizing long division, simply move both place values to the right so that the divisor becomes a whole number. The decimal point then needs to be placed in the quotient above the place it has been moved to in the number being divided. At that point, each of the numbers can be treated as whole numbers and ordinary long division can be used. For example:

$$7.62 \div 3.11 = X$$

$$3.11\overline{)7.62} = X$$

We need to move the decimal point over two places to render the divisor a whole number. Note the placement of the decimal in the quotient.

$$311\overline{)762.} = X$$

Then,

$$
\begin{array}{r}
2.450 \\
311\overline{)762.} \\
\underline{622} \\
1400 \\
\underline{1244} \\
1560 \\
\underline{1555} \\
5
\end{array}
$$

and $X = 2.450$

With this rule in mind, it is very easy to convert fractions to decimals. Use the example below, and observe the placement value.

The fraction $16/23$ is proper. But, when using long division to determine a decimal, we would divide 23 into 16.

$$
\begin{array}{r}
.6956 \\
23\overline{)16.0} \\
\underline{138} \\
220 \\
\underline{207} \\
130 \\
\underline{115} \\
150 \\
\underline{138} \\
12
\end{array}
$$

or 0.696, rounded off

C. PERCENTAGES

The term *percentage* by itself means "divided by one hundred." For example, 15% means 15 ÷ 100. A percentage shows what portion of 100 a given number constitutes. For example, if someone had 100 plants and gave away 20 to a friend, that would mean he or she gave away $20/100$ or 0.20 of the stock. To determine the percentage of plants given away, we would simply multiply 0.20 by 100, giving us 20%.

Let's look at another problem and determine the percentages involved:

> If a fire truck had 300 feet of $1\,1/2$ inch hose and 3 firefighters took 100 feet, 75 feet, and 125 feet respectively to attend to a fire, what percentage of hose did each firefighter carry?

Since we already know the total length of hose involved, it is a simple matter to determine the percentages.

Firefighter A	Firefighter B	Firefighter C
$\dfrac{100 \text{ feet}}{300 \text{ feet}} \times 100$	$\dfrac{75 \text{ feet}}{300 \text{ feet}} \times 100$	$\dfrac{125 \text{ feet}}{300 \text{ feet}} \times 100$
= 33%	= 25%	= 42%

When you add these percentages together, you get 100% of hose used.

D. RATIOS AND PROPORTIONS

A ratio is simply two items compared by division. For instance, it is known that there are 3500 residents for every 1 patrolman in the city of Birmingham. If this were to be properly expressed as a ratio, it would be 3500:1 or 3500/1. As a rule, if a ratio is expressed as a fraction, it should be reduced. One other rule to remember is that a ratio should not be expressed as a mixed number.

A proportion, on the other hand, is an equation that shows that two ratios are equal. One of the more common types of questions seen on past exams concerns speed and distance proportions. For example, if a car can travel 5 miles in 6 minutes, how far can it travel in 30 minutes, assuming that the same speed is maintained? This kind of problem would first be set up as two separate ratios and then placed in a proportion to determine the unknown.

$$\text{RATIO 1 } \frac{5 \text{ miles}}{6 \text{ minutes}} \qquad \text{RATIO 2 } \frac{X \text{ miles}}{30 \text{ minutes}}$$

$$\text{In proportional form we then have: } \frac{5 \text{ miles}}{6 \text{ minutes}} = \frac{X \text{ miles}}{30 \text{ minutes}}$$

Once the proportion is established, you can cross multiply the proportion figures and obtain this:

$$6X = 5 \times 30$$

To solve for X, one of two basic algebraic laws needs to be applied. The addition law for equations states that the same value can be added or subtracted from both sides of an equation without altering the solution. The second basic law is the multiplication law for equations. This states that both sides of an equation can be multiplied or divided by the same number without changing the final solution.

These two laws are used to solve equations that have only one variable. In the case of $6X = 5 \times 30$, we will implement the multiplication/division law to determine X. If we divide both sides of the equation by 6, we can then figure how many miles the car would travel in 30 minutes.

$$\frac{6X}{6} = \frac{5 \times 30}{6}$$

$$X = \frac{150}{6}$$

$$X = 25 \text{ miles}$$

When working with direct proportions like this, you have to be careful not to confuse them with inverse proportions. An example would be two gears with differing numbers of teeth that run at a given number of revolutions per minute (rpm).

Let's say one gear has 30 teeth and runs at 60 rpm, while the other gear has 20 teeth and runs at X rpm. Find X.

We could set it up as a direct proportion:

$$\frac{30 \text{ teeth}}{20 \text{ teeth}} = \frac{60 \text{ rpm}}{X \text{ rpm}}$$

$$30X = 60 \times 20$$

$$X = \frac{1200}{30}$$

$$X = 40 \text{ rpm}$$

Since we recall from mechanical principles that a gear with fewer teeth turns faster than a gear with more teeth, we know that the ratios demonstrated by this proportion are incorrect. Rather, it should be inversely proportional. Therefore, it is important when coming across a question of this nature to utilize the reciprocal of one of the ratios in the equation to set up the proportion. For example:

$$\frac{20 \text{ teeth}}{30 \text{ teeth}} = \frac{60 \text{ rpm}}{X \text{ rpm}}$$

or

$$\frac{30 \text{ teeth}}{20 \text{ teeth}} = \frac{X \text{ rpm}}{60 \text{ rpm}}$$

Both of these are correct proportions.

$$20X = 30 \times 60$$

$$X = \frac{1800}{20}$$

$$X = 90 \text{ rpm}$$

$X = 90$ rpm is the correct answer, given the fact that this gear has the smaller number of teeth.

E. GEOMETRY

(*Note:* Even though geometry problems are rarely seen on Corrections Officer exams, the review of very basic rules is warranted. If, by chance, you run across such questions on your exam, you will then be that much better prepared.)

Any object that requires space has dimensions that can be measured in length, width, and height. If all three of these measurements are used to quantify the size of a given object, it can be said that it is three-dimensional, or solid. If only two measurements, such as length and width, can be determined, it is considered to be two-dimensional, or a plane. A line is essentially a one-dimensional figure because it has no height or width, only length.

Two-dimensional objects frequently seen in geometry are:

1. *Rectangle:* a plane formed from two pairs of parallel lines that are perpendicular to one another. Its area can be determined by multiplying length by width. For example, a rectangle measuring 9 feet by 6 feet has an area of 54 square feet.

2. *Square:* a rectangle with sides of equal length. The area of a square is found in the same way as for a rectangle.

3. *Triangle:* a closed plane shape that has three sides. Its area can be determined by multiplying $\frac{1}{2}$ times the base times the height. For example, a triangle with a 10-foot base and 5-foot height has an area of 25 square feet ($\frac{1}{2} \times 10 \times 5$). (A right triangle has one angle that is 90 degrees; that is, two sides are perpendicular.)

4. *Circle:* a closed plane curve whose circumference is equidistant from the center. A line from the center of the circle to its circumference is a radius. The diameter of a circle is the radius times two. The area of a circle is equal to πR^2 ($\pi = 3.1416$). For example, a circle with a radius of 10 feet has an area of $\pi \times 10^2 = 314.16$ square feet. If, on the other hand, we wanted to determine the circumference, we would multiply π by the diameter, or $\pi 2R$. In this case, the circumference $= 3.1416 \times 10 \times 2$, or 62.83 feet.

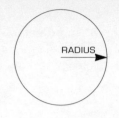

The space occupied by a three-dimensional object is called its volume. If we want to know the volume of a rectangular solid, we take the area of a rectangle times its height. For example, this rectangular solid has an area of 50 square feet (that is, 10 feet $\times$ 5 feet). When we multiply 50 square feet $\times$ 3 feet, we can determine its volume, which in this case is 150 cubic feet.

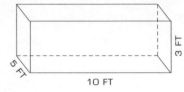

A square solid is a cube. Since all sides are equal in length, we can simply cube the length (L^3) to determine its volume.

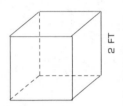

For example, let's say one side measures 2 feet in length. The volume of this cube would equal 2 feet $\times$ 2 feet $\times$ 2 feet, or 8 cubic feet.

The volume for a sphere is found by using the equation

$$V = {}^4\!/_3\, \pi\, R^3$$

For example, if the radius of a ball is 3 inches, what would its volume be?

$$(^4\!/_3) \times (3.1416) \times (3)^3 = {}^4\!/_3 \times 3.1416 \times 27 = 113.1 \text{ cubic inches}$$

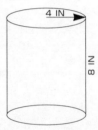

The volume of a cylinder is found by using the equation

$$V = \pi\, R^2 \text{ Height}$$

For example, if a tin can has a radius of 4 inches and a depth of 8 inches, what is its volume?

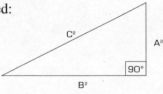

$$(3.1416) \times (4)^2 \times (8) = 3.1416 \times 16 \times 8 = 402.12 \text{ cubic inches}$$

One other aspect of geometry that may be seen on Corrections Officer exams concerns right triangles. The Pythagorean theorem states that the square of the side opposite the right angle equals the sum of the squares of the other sides, or $C^2 = A^2 + B^2$. For example,
If side $A = 5$ feet and side $B = 10$ feet, then side C can be determined:

$$C^2 = 5^2 + 10^2$$
$$C^2 = 25 + 100$$
$$C^2 = 125$$

Therefore, C is equal to the square root of 125, or 11.2.

Next, you will find some sample questions on mathematical principles so you can test your skills in this area. Solutions to the problems are given at the end of the exercise to verify your work.

SAMPLE QUESTIONS FOR MATHEMATICS

1. $17^3/4 - 8^1/4 = X$. Which of the following equals X?

   A. $9^2/4$ B. $9^1/8$ C. $9^1/2$ D. 9

2. $9 - {}^3/8 = X$. Which of the following equals X?

   A. $8^3/8$ B. $8^5/8$ C. 9   D. $7^3/8$

3. $9^1/4 + 18^2/4 + 20^1/4 = X$. Which of the following equals X?

   A. $48^1/4$ B. $48^1/2$ C. $43^1/4$ D. 48

4. $6^1/3 - 4^5/6 = X$. Which of the following equals X?

   A. $1^1/4$ B. $1^1/2$ C. $1^3/4$ D. $1^3/6$

5. $4^2/3 + 1^1/6 - 2^1/8 = X$. Which of the following equals X?

   A. $3^{17}/24$ B. $3^1/4$ C. $3^3/16$ D. $3^5/18$

6. $12^3/8 \times 2^5/7 = X$. Which of the following equals X?

   A. $32^{33}/25$ B. $32^{17}/18$ C. $33^{33}/56$ D. $34^1/3$

7. $7 \times {}^1/2 \times {}^3/7 = X$. Which of the following equals X?

   A. $1^3/7$ B. $1^1/4$ C. $1^3/4$ D. $1^1/2$

8. $8^3/4 \div 2^1/2 = X$. Which of the following equals X?

   A. $1^7/8$ B. $3^1/8$ C. $3^1/2$ D. $4^1/{10}$

9. If the number $5^2/3$ is changed from a mixed number to a decimal, which of the following is correct, assuming it is rounded off to hundredths?

   A. 5.67   B. 5.66   C. 5.6   D. 5.7

10. $6.71 \times 0.88 = X$. Which of the following equals X?

    A. 5.0948   B. 5.887   C. 5.91   D. 5.9048

11. $132.069 - 130.69 = X$. Which of the following equals X?

    A. 0.379   B. 1.379   C. 1.739   D. 1.793

12. $8.53 + 17.671 = X$. Which of the following equals X?

    A. 16.524   B. 23.102   C. 26.201   D. 25.012

13. $15.75 \div 4.12 = X$. Which of the following equals X?

    A. 3.823   B. 3.283   C. 3.023   D. 3.803

14. $6.75 + 8.372 \times 3.14 = X$. Which of the following equals X?

    A. 47.48   B. 33.04   C. 37.48   D. 34.03

15. $9 \times 5.2 \div 18.76 = X$. Which of the following equals X?

    A. 0.40   B. 15.75   C. 28.06   D. 2.49

16. $17 - 14.87 \div 2.5 + 3.61 = X$. Which of the following equals X?

    A. 4.46   B. 0.35   C. 14.66   D. 4.64

17. If 23.6 were changed into a percentage of its relationship to the number 1, which of the following would be correct?

    A. 23.6%   B. 0.236%   C. 236%   D. 2360%

18. The fraction $^3/_7$ represents what percentage?

    A. 41.85%   B. 42.85%   C. 48.25%   D. 43.35%

19. If someone were to withdraw $237.00 from a savings account that totaled $3,000.00, what percent of the money would be left in the account?

    A. 92.1%   B. 83.7%   C. 94.1%   D. 89.7%

20. The number 13 is 75% of what number?

    A. 15.49   B. 16.35   C. 16.99   D. 17.33

21. If a screw has a pitch that requires it to be turned 30 times to advance it 2 inches, what ratio correctly reflects the relationship?

    A. 2:30   B. 30:2   C. 2:15   D. 15:1

22. According to the directions on a bottle of liquid fertilizer, it is supposed to be mixed in water at the rate of 3 tablespoons per gallon before applying to a garden. How many tablespoons of fertilizer would be required for 20 gallons of water?

    A. 20   B. 40   C. 60   D. 80

23. $\dfrac{5}{8} = \dfrac{X}{32}$ Which of the following equals X?

    A. 10   B. 20   C. 25   D. 30

24. $\dfrac{3/5}{1/2} = \dfrac{X}{15}$ Which of the following equals X?

    A. 18   B. 16.5   C. 19.2   D. 16

25. What is the area of a rectangle if it is 6 feet long by 4 feet wide?

    A. 10 square feet

    B. 64 square feet

    C. 24 cubic feet

    D. 24 square feet

26. If a township is a square section of territory and one side is known to be 6 miles in length, how many square miles does the township occupy?

    A. 16 square miles

    B. 18 square miles

    C. 36 square miles

    D. 42 square miles

27. What is the circumference of a gear that has a 5 $^7/_8$ inch diameter?

    A. 18.05 inches

    B. 16.57 inches

    C. 19.45 inches

    D. 18.46 inches

28. If a triangle had a base of 8 feet and a height of 3.5 feet, what would its area be?

    A. 12 square feet

    B. 14 square feet

    C. 16 square feet

    D. 20 square feet

29. If a rectangular object is 20 feet long by 15 feet wide and has a height of 4 inches, what is its approximate volume?

    A. 1200 cubic feet

    B. 1200 square feet

    C. 100 cubic feet

    D. 100 square feet

30. If one side of a cube measures 36 inches, what is its volume?

    A. 46,000 cubic inches

    B. 46,656 square inches

    C. 46,656 cubic yards

    D. 1 cubic yard

31. If a fully inflated basketball has a diameter of 12 inches, how much volume does it occupy?

    A. 904.78 cubic inches

    B. 673.54 cubic inches

    C. 509.78 cubic inches

    D. 475 cubic inches

32. If a can has a height of 16 inches and a volume of 1256.64 cubic inches, what is its diameter?

    A. 10 inches

    B. 11 inches

    C. 12 inches

    D. 12.5 inches

33. The Pythagorean theorem concerns what kind of geometric shape?

    A. Equilateral triangle

    B. Scalene triangle

    C. Right triangle

    D. Acute triangle

34. If the length of side *A* of a right triangle is 8 feet and the length of side *C* (the hypotenuse) is 12.8 feet, what is the length of side *B*?

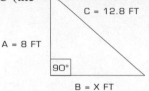

C = 12.8 FT

A = 8 FT

90°

B = X FT

   A. 8 feet

   B. 10 feet

   C. 12 feet

   D. 12.3 feet

35. What is the area of the figure below?

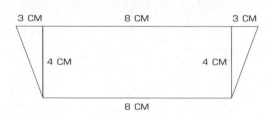

3 CM   8 CM   3 CM

4 CM   4 CM

8 CM

   A. 44 square centimeters

   B. 46 square centimeters

   C. 48 square centimeters

   D. 50 square centimeters

36. If a basement's floor plan has the dimensions shown below, how many square feet would it cover?

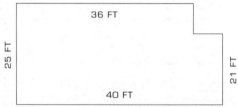

36 FT

25 FT

21 FT

40 FT

   A. 1000

   B. 995

   C. 988

   D. 984

37. What is the length of a diagonal line inside a square that measures 81 square feet?

   A. 9.82 feet

   B. 10.38 feet

   C. 12.73 feet

   D. 14.71 feet

38. If 34 inches represents 34% of the diameter of a particular circle, what is the area of the circle?

   A. 4,891 square inches

   B. 5,432 square inches

   C. 6,971 square inches

   D. 7,854 square inches

39. If you were told that a specific tire could roll 200 yards in 27.28 revolutions, what is the radius of the tire?

   A. 42 inches

   B. 84 inches

   C. 37.5 inches

   D. 75 inches

40. What is the volume of the figure shown below? (Hint: Look at this diagram as half of a cylinder on top of a rectangular solid.)

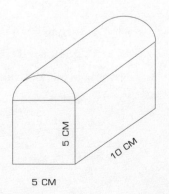

5 CM

10 CM

5 CM

   A. 376.7 cubic centimeters

   B. 348.2 cubic centimeters

   C. 336.7 cubic centimeters

   D. 329.8 cubic centimeters

ANSWER SHEET FOR SAMPLE MATHEMATICS

1. (A) (B) (C) (D)   15. (A) (B) (C) (D)   29. (A) (B) (C) (D)

2. (A) (B) (C) (D)   16. (A) (B) (C) (D)   30. (A) (B) (C) (D)

3. (A) (B) (C) (D)   17. (A) (B) (C) (D)   31. (A) (B) (C) (D)

4. (A) (B) (C) (D)   18. (A) (B) (C) (D)   32. (A) (B) (C) (D)

5. (A) (B) (C) (D)   19. (A) (B) (C) (D)   33. (A) (B) (C) (D)

6. (A) (B) (C) (D)   20. (A) (B) (C) (D)   34. (A) (B) (C) (D)

7. (A) (B) (C) (D)   21. (A) (B) (C) (D)   35. (A) (B) (C) (D)

8. (A) (B) (C) (D)   22. (A) (B) (C) (D)   36. (A) (B) (C) (D)

9. (A) (B) (C) (D)   23. (A) (B) (C) (D)   37. (A) (B) (C) (D)

10. (A) (B) (C) (D)   24. (A) (B) (C) (D)   38. (A) (B) (C) (D)

11. (A) (B) (C) (D)   25. (A) (B) (C) (D)   39. (A) (B) (C) (D)

12. (A) (B) (C) (D)   26. (A) (B) (C) (D)   40. (A) (B) (C) (D)

13. (A) (B) (C) (D)   27. (A) (B) (C) (D)

14. (A) (B) (C) (D)   28. (A) (B) (C) (D)

Answers can be found on pages 173–178.

ANSWERS TO MATHEMATICS SAMPLE QUESTIONS

1. C $3/4 - 1/4 = 2/4$ and should be reduced to $1/2$.
   $17 - 8 = 9$; therefore, $X = 9\,1/2$.

2. B $9 - 3/8 = X$; $9 = 8\,8/8$; then, $8/8 - 3/8 = 5/8$;
   therefore, $X = 8\,5/8$.

3. D $9\,1/4 + 18\,2/4 + 20\,1/4 = X$;
   $1/4 + 2/4 + 1/4 = 1$; $9 + 18 + 20 = 47$; therefore,
   $X = 47 + 1 = 48$.

4. B $6\,1/3 - 4\,5/6 = X$; $1/3 = 2/6$, therefore,
   $5\,8/6 - 4\,5/6 = X$; $5 - 4 = 1$ and $8/6 - 5/6 = 3/6$;
   $3/6$ is reduced to $1/2$; therefore, $X = 1\,1/2$. Choice D is the correct answer also, but it is not in reduced form.

5. A $2/3, 1/6, 1/8$ have the LCD of 24; therefore,
   $2/3 = 16/24$, $1/6 = 4/24$, $1/8 = 3/24$

   $$\frac{16}{24} + \frac{4}{24} = \frac{20}{24} \quad \frac{20}{24} - \frac{3}{24} = \frac{17}{24}$$

   $(4 + 1) = 5$; $(5 - 2) = 3$; therefore $X = 3\,17/24$.

6. C $12\,3/8 = 99/8$; $2\,5/7 = 19/7$;
   $99/8 \times 19/7 = 1881/56 = 33\,33/56$

7. D $$\frac{7}{1} \times \frac{1}{2} = \frac{7}{2} \quad \frac{7}{2} \times \frac{3}{7} = \frac{21}{14}$$

   $21/14 = 1\,7/14$; when this is reduced, $X = 1\,1/2$.

8. C $8\,3/4 = 35/4$; $2\,1/2 = 5/2$;
   $35/4 \div 5/2 = 35/4 \times 2/5 = 70/20$;
   $70/20 = 3\,10/20$, or $3\,1/2$ when reduced; therefore, $X = 3\,1/2$.

9. A The whole number 5 remains unchanged; however, $2/3$ is the same as saying 2 divided by 3. Therefore, when rounded off to hundredths, the fraction is 0.67. Thus, the decimal should be 5.67. Choice B is correct, except that it has not been rounded off as requested. Choices C and D are not correct because both are rounded off to tenths, not hundredths.

10. D $6.71 \times .88 = X$; therefore, $X = 5.9048$

11. B 132.069
    $-$ 130.690
    _____
          1.379

    Therefore, $X = 1.379$.

12. C 17.671
    $+$ 8.53
    _____
        26.201

    Therefore, $X = 26.201$.

13. *A* 15.75 divided by 4.12 should be looked at as 1575 divided by 412; then, the decimals are reinserted. The answer is 3.8223, or 3.822 rounded off to thousandths.

14. *B* You should remember that multiplications and divisions are always carried out before additions or subtractions. Another similar rule states that when several multiplications and divisions occur together, you should do them in the order they are given. In this case, we first multiply 8.372 by 3.14, giving us 26.29. Now, add 26.29 to 6.75. Therefore, $X = 33.04$.

15. *D* Multiply $9 \times 5.2 = 46.8$; $46.8 \div 18.76 = 2.4946695$; therefore, $X = 2.49$ rounded off to hundredths.

16. *C* Remembering the rules discussed in answer 14, division must be done first; 14.87 divided by 2.5 should be looked at as 148.7 divided by 25, or 5.95. Thus,

$$17 - 5.95 + 3.61 = X$$

$$
\begin{array}{ll}
17.00 & 11.05 \\
-5.95 & +3.61 \\
\hline
11.05 & 14.66
\end{array}
$$

$$X = 14.66$$

17. *D* 23.6 multiplied by $100 = 2360\%$.

18. *B* 3.0 divided by $7 = 0.4285$; then, 0.4285 multiplied by $100 = 42.85\%$.

19. *A*
$$
\begin{array}{l}
3000.00 \\
-237.00 \\
\hline
2763.00
\end{array}
$$

then, 2763.0 divided by $3000 = 0.921$. Finally, 0.921 multiplied by $100 = 92.1\%$.

20. *D* This kind of percentage problem needs to be worked as a proportion. We would get the following:

$$\frac{75}{100} = \frac{13}{X}; \quad 75X = 1300$$

$$X = \frac{1300}{75} = 17.33$$

21. *D* Since the ratio is 30/2, as with fractions, it should be reduced as low as possible, preferably to 1. In this case, 30:2 can be reduced to 15:1.

22. *C* The ratio is 3:1 in this problem. Therefore,

$$\frac{3\ \text{Tbsp}}{1\ \text{gal}} = \frac{X\ \text{Tbsp}}{20\ \text{gal}}$$

$$X = 3 \times 20, \ \text{which is } 60.$$

23. *B* $\dfrac{5}{8} = \dfrac{X}{32}$

$8X = 160$

$X = \dfrac{160}{8} = 20$

24. *A* $\dfrac{\frac{3}{5}}{\frac{1}{2}} = \dfrac{X}{15}$; $\frac{1}{2}X = 9$; thus, $\frac{1}{2}X \times 2 = 9 \times 2$;

therefore, $X = 18$.

25. *D* A rectangular area is determined by the following equation:

A = length × width

Therefore, 6 feet × 4 feet = 24 square feet.

26. *C* Since the area of a square is equal to the length of one side squared, we simply square 6 miles (that is, 6^2), giving us 36. Therefore, the township occupies 36 square miles.

27. *D* The first step in this problem is to change the fraction $7/8$ into a decimal since π is in decimal form. Thus, we divide 7 by 8, giving us .875. The gear's diameter is 5.875 in decimal form. Circumference = diameter × π (3.1416). Therefore,

5.875 diameter × 3.1416 = 18.4569 inches, or 18.46 inches (rounded to hundredths).

28. *B* Since the area of a triangle is equal to $1/2$ × base × height, we can plug in the numbers accordingly, giving us the following:

$(1/2)(8)(3.5)$ = 14 square feet

The area is 14 square feet.

29. *C* The volume of a rectangle is found by using the formula A = length × width × height. Before we use this equation, all units must be the same (that is, inches or feet). In this case, it is easier to convert the height to feet.

$\dfrac{4 \text{ inches}}{12 \text{ inches/feet}} = .3333$ feet

Area = 20 feet × 15 feet × .33 feet = 99.90 cubic feet, or approximately 100 cubic feet.

30. *D* The easiest way to solve this problem is to recognize that 36 inches = 1 yard. Since 36^3 is a sizable number to multiply, we will use the simpler alternative of 1^3. Therefore, $1^3 = 1$ cubic yard. This is a common unit of measure in the construction field when ordering specific volumes of dirt, rock, concrete, etc. Choice B would be correct if the number were in cubic inches. Square inches determine only the area of a two-dimensional shape.

31. *A*   A basketball fully inflated can be thought of as a sphere. To determine its volume, we need to use the equation

$$4/3 \times \pi \, (3.1416) \times R^3$$

The diameter is given as being 12 inches; therefore, its radius is equal to 1/2 the diameter (that is, 6 inches).

$$\frac{4}{3} \times \frac{3.1416}{1} = \frac{12.5664}{3} = 4.1888$$

$6^3 = 6 \times 6 \times 6 = 216$ cubic inches;
$4.1888 \times 216 = 904.78$ cubic inches, rounded to hundredths.

32. *A*   Since the geometric shape in the question is a cylinder, we need to examine the equation volume $= \pi \, R^2 \, H$. If we plug our known values into this equation, it would read

$$1256.64 = \pi \, (3.1416)(X)^2 \, (16 \text{ inches})$$

$$\frac{1256.642}{3.1416 \times 16} = X^2$$

$25 = X^2$; therefore, $X = 5$.

Remember, 5 inches represents only the radius; the diameter would equal $5 \times 2 = 10$ inches.

33. *C*   Right triangle

34. *B*   Implementing the Pythagorean theorem, $A^2 + B^2 = C^2$, we can determine X with simple algebra to solve for one variable.

$$A^2 = 8^2 = 64$$
$$C^2 = 12.8^2 = 163.84$$
$$64 + X^2 = 163.84$$
$$X^2 = 163.84 - 64$$
$$X = \sqrt{99.84}$$

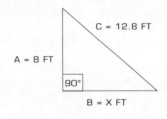

Therefore, $X = 10$ feet.

35. *A*   In geometric terms this is considered to be a trapezoid, which is a quadrilateral with two sides parallel and the other two sides not parallel. To figure the area, we can see it as one rectangle (*A*) and two triangles (*B*) and (*C*).

The rectangular area is equal to length × width; therefore,

$8 \times 4 = 32$ square centimeters (cm)

The triangle areas are equal to $1/2 \times$ base × height

$1/2 \times 3 \times 4 = 6$ square cm

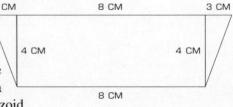

Since triangles B and C have the same dimension, we just multiply $6 \times 2 = 12$ to determine their total area combined. Therefore, A + B + C = total area of trapezoid.

32 square cm + 12 square cm = 44 square cm

36. *D* With the dimensions given, we can assume it has a rectangular shape. The easiest way to approach this question is to figure the total area of the basement as a rectangle and subtract the area missing in the corner.

40 feet × 25 feet = 1,000 square feet

Side *A* = 25 feet − 21 feet, or 4 feet

Side *B* = 40 feet − 36 feet, or 4 feet

The area of the missing corner is 4 feet × 4 feet, or 16 square feet. Therefore, this basement's total area is

1000 square feet − 16 square feet = 984 square feet

37. *C* The area of a square is the length of one side squared. If the square given is 81 square feet in area, then the square root of 81 will give us the length of the square's side, which, in this case, is equal to 9. Since we are dealing with right angles in the square, we can apply the Pythagorean theorem to determine the length of the diagonal. Therefore,

$9^2 + 9^2 = X^2$

$81 + 81 = X^2$

$162 = X^2$; therefore, $X = 12.73$ feet.

38. *D* First, we need to figure the diameter. If we know that 34 inches is 34% (that is, .34) of the diameter, we can set up a proportion to solve it. Our proportion would be

$$\frac{34 \text{ inches}}{.34} = \frac{X}{1.00}$$

$$\frac{.34X}{.34} = \frac{34}{.34}$$

Therefore, $X = 3,400$ divided by 34.

Since the diameter is 100 inches, the following formula can be applied to determine the area of the circle in question.

$A = \pi R^2$

The radius is equal to $1/2$ the diameter, or, in this case, $100 \times .50 = 50$ inches.

Therefore,

A = 3.1416 × 50² inches
A = 3.1416 × 2,500 square inches
A = 7,854 square inches.

39. *A*   First, if we divide 27.28 revolutions into 200 yards, we can determine how many yards (or inches) this tire would travel after 1 revolution. We arrive at 7.33 yards. Then, since the diameter of this tire is referred to in inches, not yards, we simply multiply 7.33 yards × 36 inches/yard to give us 263.88 inches. In other words, for every 1 revolution this tire makes, it can travel 263.88 inches. This number is the tire's circumference. If we know the tire's circumference, using the equation

diameter × 3.1416 = circumference

we can easily figure the tire's diameter.

$$X \times 3.1416 = 263.88 \text{ inches}$$

$$\frac{X \times 3.1416}{3.1416} = \frac{263.88 \text{ inches}}{3.1416}$$

$$X = 83.99, \text{ or } 84 \text{ inches, in diameter}$$

Since the question asked for the radius of the tire, we can simply divide the diameter by 2, giving us an answer of 42 inches.

40. *B*   The volume of the rectangular solid is equal to its length × width × height.

10 cm × 5 cm × 5 cm = 250 cubic centimeters

The volume of a cylinder is equal to π × radius squared × height. Since the width of the rectangular solid can be considered the diameter of the cylinder, the radius is $1/2$ the diameter, or, in this case, 5 cm divided by 2 = 2.5 cm. The length of the rectangular solid can be considered the height of the cylinder. Therefore,

3.1416×2.5^2 cm × 10 cm = volume of cylinder
3.1416×6.25 cm × 10 cm = 196.35 cubic cm

However, there is only half of a cylinder on top of the rectangular solid, so the cylinder represents only 98.2 cubic cm volume in the illustration shown. Now, add both volumes to give the total volume of this geometric shape.

250 cubic cm + 98.2 cubic cm = 348.2 cubic cm

Chapter 8

Practice Exam 1

The time allowed for the entire examination is two and a half hours. Each question has four answers, lettered A, B, C, and D. Choose the best answer and then, on the answer sheet provided on pages 213–214 (which you can remove from the study guide), find the corresponding question number and darken the circle corresponding to the answer you have selected.

Study the following narrative for fifteen minutes. Do not exceed the time allowed; if you do, you will forfeit the true sense of how an exam is actually conducted. When your time is up, turn to questions 1–15 without making further reference to this reading.

A JUDICIAL SUMMARY OF A CRIMINAL CASE IN SUPERIOR COURT

Basically, each municipality has its own police department, which responds to calls within its jurisdiction. Unincorporated areas are usually served by some other agency or multijurisdictional law-enforcement task force. Criminal cases begin when the police are called to respond to an incident. Typically, an officer travels to the crime scene and fills out an incident report that describes the circumstances involved and lists the names and addresses of prospective witnesses. This incident report is then filed with the department and subsequently forwarded to the appropriate detective division responsible for investigating that type of crime. Detectives formalize the process by taking written statements from any witness, obtaining evidence, and writing a report detailing the known facts of the case. This information is then given to the prosecuting attorney. A filing-unit clerk logs the case in and assigns a case number to it. At this point, a senior deputy prosecuting attorney will either approve the filing of formal charges or move to dismiss. If the senior deputy feels that sufficient evidence exists to prosecute the crime successfully, he or she pursues the case. Court clerks type the formal documentation required for the senior deputy's final approval. After approval, the documentation is given to a legal desk clerk who assigns a superior court case number as a permanent record. After it has been signed by an appropriate magistrate, the compiled paperwork is then processed by the information and records department.

A defendant must be identified before charges are formally filed. Custody is not at issue here. The defendant may have already been arrested and placed in custody for the crime, or he or she may remain at large; identification is the important issue.

Once the person in question is arrested and subsequently taken to jail, he or she has the right to appear before a judge within twenty-four hours to seek a release. If a judge is reasonably assured that the defendant will honor a promise to return for the hearing, he or she is released without bail, or, in other words, on personal recognizance. If, on the other hand, a defendant has a dangerous criminal history, he or she may be asked to post significant bail.

In either case, the presiding magistrate must render a decision concerning the defendant's disposition by 2:00 P.M.

The Administrative Recognizance Release Program (ARRP) is a fairly recent innovation that attempts to streamline this process. If a suspect is determined to be nonviolent and has demonstrated past reliability, he or she may be released on personal recognizance prior to the hearing. If the bond set by the magistrate cannot be met by the defendant, he or she has the right to petition the court for a reduction of bail.

Once charges have been formally filed, the defendant is summoned to appear for arraignment. The arraignment is basically a formal hearing of the charges levied against the defendant. At the arraignment, it is explained that an attorney is needed (if one has not already been retained) and that if the defendant cannot afford one, a court-appointed defense attorney is made available at state expense.

Within two weeks of this hearing, the defendant has to appear for another hearing called an *omnibus*. It is at this point that a plea is entered and a trial date is formally set. During the course of this hearing, both the defense attorney and the prosecuting attorney must exchange information pertinent to the case. In legal parlance, this is referred to as *discovery*; it allows all parties concerned equal access to information for formal case preparation.

A defendant who wishes to plead guilty in exchange for a lesser charge or dismissal of certain counts (plea bargaining) must do so prior to or during the omnibus hearing. If the judge accepts the plea, the defendant waives the right to trial and is convicted of the lesser charges set by the prosecution. If plea bargaining is not utilized and the defendant pleads not guilty and is in custody, a trial date must be set within sixty days of arraignment. If the defendant has been released pending trial, the trial date must be established within ninety days. These time limits preserve the defendant's right to a speedy trial. While waiting for the trial, the deputy prosecutor assigned to the case issues subpoenas for any witnesses. These subpoenas state specifically when and where witnesses must appear.

Pretrial hearings may also be required to determine whether certain incriminating evidence, offered voluntarily by the defendant after being duly informed of his or her constitutional rights, can be used by the prosecution. Court rule 3.5 establishes that a hearing (*3.5 hearing*) must be held to determine the admissibility of such evidence.

Another form of pretrial hearing occurs when a defendant attempts to prove that the evidence against him or her was seized illegally and is thus inadmissible in court. If the constitutional rights of the defendant were violated, the suppression hearing rules in favor of the defendant.

Prior to the actual trial date, either the defense or the prosecution may ask to have the trial delayed (or *continued*) for various reasons. If either party wishes to avoid a deferment, a presiding judge determines if it is warranted. If there are sufficient grounds to justify it, everyone who has been subpoenaed is informed of the new place and time of the trial. Otherwise, the case is heard as scheduled.

The court may have to hear several cases in a day; however, criminal cases usually take precedence over civil cases and are assigned accordingly. Once the trial actually begins, the defendant must choose whether to have a jury hear the case or to waive that right. If the defendant prefers the jury trial, the attorneys conduct jury selection, referred to as *voir dire*. Prospective jurors are interviewed by both counsels and accepted or eliminated depending on the attitudes they exhibit toward the defendant. At the close of jury selection, the trial begins. Attorneys make opening statements and call witnesses to testify under oath about what they know of the defendant and their connection to the crime involved. Witnesses are allowed to be cross-examined by opposing counsel.

When this phase of the trial has ended, the defendant may elect to take the stand to further defend him- or herself. The state has the right to call rebuttal witnesses at the completion of such testimony. The jury is then instructed by the judge and both attorneys about what the law requires and what their duty involves. Final statements are rendered first by the prosecutor and then by the defense before deliberations begin.

A unanimous decision by jurors is required to convict the defendant. A jury that fails to agree is referred to as a *hung jury*. Depending on state discretion, the case will either be dismissed or retried at a later date. Hung juries are usually the consequence of insufficient evidence. The state must prove its charge beyond a reasonable doubt to effect a conviction. If a conviction is handed down in superior court, a judge issues a sentence approximately four to six weeks later. State sentencing guidelines normally dictate that the punishment be appropriate for the crime. This can come either in the form of serving time in a state prison or as probation.

Answer questions 1–15 on the basis of the narrative just studied. *Do not refer to the reading.*

1. Which of the following correctly identifies the title of the passage?
   A. A Summary of Criminal Case Proceedings in Superior Court
   B. A Judicial Review of Criminal Cases in Superior Court
   C. A Judicial Summary of a Criminal Case in Superior Court
   D. A Judicial Review of Civil Cases in District Court

2. What kind of crimes were specifically addressed within the context of the reading?
   A. Felonies
   B. Misdemeanors
   C. Traffic citations
   D. None of the above

3. According to the reading, what is another term for jury selection?
   A. *Voir dire*
   B. Preliminary hearing
   C. Omnibus
   D. Probationary discretion

4. The acronym ARRP was explained in the narrative as meaning?
   A. Assessment for Responsible Release Program
   B. Administrative Recognizance Release Program
   C. Accountability Recognizance Release Program
   D. None of the above

5. According to the reading, plea bargaining arrangements must be made prior to or during which event in the judicial process?
   A. Pretrial hearing
   B. Preliminary hearing
   C. Omnibus hearing
   D. 3.5 hearing

6. If a defendant is currently in jail and defense counsel enters a *not guilty* plea at arraignment, how long does the court technically have to set a trial date?
   A. Twenty-four hours
   B. Three and a half days
   C. Sixty days
   D. Ninety days

7. According to the reading, how long does a magistrate have to sentence a person convicted in superior court?
   A. Sixty days
   B. Ninety days
   C. Four to six weeks
   D. None of the above

8. What was the legal term given that describes the exchange of information pertinent to the case between defense and prosecution attorneys?
   A. Discovery
   B. *Voir dire*
   C. Omnibus
   D. Plea bargaining

9. What was mentioned within the narrative to be of primary importance prior to charges being formally filed?

    A. Investigators furnishing complete details of the crime involved

    B. Defendant identification

    C. An appropriate magistrate signature

    D. The assignment of a court case number for information and records

10. How many jurors must reach a guilty verdict before a person can be convicted in superior court?

    A. A simple majority

    B. A two-thirds majority

    C. A three-quarters majority

    D. It must be a unanimous decision.

11. If a defendant was well aware of his or her constitutional rights and offered authorities a confession (incriminating evidence) and then later decided that the confession should not be used, which of the following hearings determines admissibility of such evidence in superior court?

    A. Omnibus hearing

    B. Plea bargaining hearing

    C. 3.5 hearing

    D. Arraignment hearing

12. According to the narrative, what is another term for *released without bail*?

    A. Personal recognizance

    B. Probation

    C. *Voir dire*

    D. Court rule 3.5

13. All of the following statements from the reading are true except

    A. The state must prove its charges beyond a reasonable doubt before a person can be convicted in superior court.

    B. Magistrate precedence normally dictates the punishment appropriate for the crime.

    C. Another term for a delayed trial is *continued*.

    D. Final statements for a trial are rendered first by the prosecuting attorney.

14. After the filing-unit clerk logs in the case and assigns a case number to it, who was mentioned as having discretion at this point to either file formal charges against the defendant or to drop the case?

    A. Superior court magistrate

    B. Information and records department

    C. Senior deputy prosecuting attorney

    D. Superior court clerk

15. What kind of hearing was said to be held in the event that there is some question about the legality of evidence seizure and possible infringement of a defendant's constitutional rights?

    A. Omnibus hearing

    B. Preliminary hearing

    C. Deferment hearing

    D. Suppression hearing

Study the following sketch for five minutes. Again, do not exceed the time allowed because otherwise you will forfeit the true sense of how these exams are actually conducted. When your time is up, turn to questions 16–25 without making further references to the sketch.

16. How many prisoners were shown in the sketch to be engaging in weight-lifting exercises?

    A. 1

    B. 2

    C. 3

    D. None of the above

17. What was the total count of inmates visible in the exercise yard?

    A. 16

    B. 18

    C. 20

    D. 22

18. How many armed guards were positioned in the most distant tower seen in the sketch?

    A. 1

    B. 2

    C. 3

    D. None of the above

19. There were four inmates shown to be participating in what kind of sports activity?

    A. Baseball

    B. Horseshoes

    C. Football

    D. Basketball

20. How many inmates were depicted in the sketch as doing push-ups as part of a calisthenics regimen?

    A. 1

    B. 2

    C. 3

    D. More than 3

21. What was the name of the correctional facility in question?

    A. Piedmont Corrections

    B. Hastings State Prison

    C. Winston Adult Detention

    D. Wilmington Corrections

22. How many rows of bleachers were apparent in the sketch?

    A. 6

    B. 5

    C. 4

    D. Bleachers were not shown in the sketch.

23. How many inmates were depicted in the sketch as apparently choosing to jog as a form of exercise?

    A. 1

    B. 2

    C. 3

    D. No inmates were shown running in the sketch.

24. Directionally speaking, the guard tower in full view was in which corner of the exercise yard?

    A. Northeast

    B. Southeast

    C. Southwest

    D. Northwest

25. Which inmates are presently using the facilities depicted in the sketch? (Assume for the question that all schedules are strictly followed.)

    A. Cell blocks A and B inmates

    B. Only cell block C inmates

    C. Only cell block D inmates

    D. No time references were provided to determine such information.

Answer questions 26–27 on the basis of the following information.

Despite stringent regulations within a correctional facility to control overtly dangerous contraband, inmates, with little ingenuity, can combine readily accessible ingredients to manufacture a crude explosive device. Bleach, ammonia, peroxide, baking soda, match heads, etc., by themselves are relatively harmless. However, under certain conditions, they have the potential to be used as explosives. When a Corrections Officer has reasonable suspicion that such material or devices have been discovered, it is imperative that the immediate area be cleared of any personnel and sealed, a floor supervisor be promptly notified, and qualified personnel be summoned to properly handle the situation.

26. Officer McNeil was conducting a standard cell search when he noticed a cigarette lighter inconspicuously placed on a bookshelf as having the appearance that it had been tampered with. Traces of a dry, white-colored paste were apparent on the exterior of the lighter in addition to the presence of a small coiled wire attached to the side. Under the circumstances, which of the following actions taken by Officer McNeil would be considered contrary to established guidelines?

    A. Promptly removing any inmate in the immediate area to another secure location

    B. Transferring the suspected article discovered to a more isolated area for further scrutiny

    C. Summoning authorities with explosives expertise to either remove, disarm, or detonate the suspected device

    D. Notifying his immediate on-duty floor supervisor of what had been discovered during a routine search

27. Which of the following statements would be considered true with regard to the information provided?

    A. Bleach, ammonia, peroxide, baking soda, match heads, etc., are all considered to be dangerous contraband.

    B. Correctional facilities have very little difficulty restricting dangerous contraband.

    C. The household products described in the question are always dangerous when mixed.

    D. None of the above

28. Regular inmate counts are prerequisite to security maintenance. However, surprise nighttime counts are conducted on occasion. During such proceedings, inmates are told to stand facing the walkways while gripping the bars to their cells. The most probable reason for such a policy would be which of the following?

    A. It serves as some form of exercise for those inmates who are not physically active.

    B. It thwarts any deceptive practice that may play a part in an escape attempt.

    C. It represents a legitimate (i.e., nonharassing) means of reprimanding prisoners in general.

    D. General cell searches may be conducted without the prospect of purposeful distraction or intervention by inmates.

29. If two words had to be chosen to best describe the kind of relationship that should exist between a professional Corrections Officer and the inmate population in general, what would they most likely be?

    A. Forceful and disinterested

    B. Personable and courteous

    C. Civil and impersonal

    D. Attentive and caring

30. Officer Jenkins received a directive from Captain Dillon to immediately implement a new technique that was intended to expedite the intake-booking process. Officer Jenkins complied with the directive, but later decided that it was costing the department more time and money than it was worth. The most reasonable way for Officer Jenkins to handle the situation would be which of the following?

    A. Continue using the new procedure, but inform Captain Dillon of his appraisal

    B. Immediately revert to the old procedures and inform Captain Dillon later

    C. Continue using the new procedure and not say anything

    D. Scrap the entire system and try something truly innovative

Answer questions 31–33 on the basis of the following passage:

Evidence is essentially a means of proof or the establishment of facts in a trial. Evidence may be manifested in trial in one of several forms. According to *Black's Law Dictionary,*

Direct evidence is a form of testimony from a witness who actually saw, heard, or touched the subject of interrogation.

Opinion evidence is a form of testimony from a witness describing what he or she thinks, believes, or infers in regard to facts in dispute, as distinguished from his or her personal knowledge of the facts themselves.

Circumstantial evidence is a form of testimony not based on actual personal knowledge or observation of the facts in controversy, but of other facts from which deductions are drawn, indirectly showing the facts sought to be proved.

Real evidence are objects or items furnished for view or inspection, as distinguished from a description furnished by a witness.

31. During a murder trial, a forensics expert testified that the fatal wound inflicted upon inmate Carr was consistent with the kind of shank (i.e., sharp metal object) found on inmate Smith at the time of his arrest. In addition, blood residue found on the weapon in question was, in fact, found to be the same type as that of the victim. What form of evidence would both of these testimonies be considered?

    A. Direct evidence

    B. Opinion evidence

    C. Circumstantial evidence

    D. Real evidence

32. The alleged weapon discovered to be in inmate Smith's possession at the time of his arrest would be considered what form of evidence?

    A. Direct evidence

    B. Opinion evidence

    C. Circumstantial evidence

    D. Real evidence

33. An inmate who was assigned to the same cell block as Smith testified that he did not see or hear of any struggle per se, but did corroborate with one other inmate witness that Smith was seen running from Carr's cell shortly after 6:00 P.M. According to the reading, this form of testimony would best be considered as:

    A. Direct evidence

    B. Opinion evidence

    C. Circumstantial evidence

    D. Real evidence

Answer questions 34–36 on the basis of the following reading:

Homicide is defined in *Black's Law Dictionary* as "the act of a human being taking the life of another human being either through felonious, excusable, or justifiable means."

First-degree murder involves causing the death of another with premeditated intent; or, through indifference to life, causing circumstances that create a grave risk and actually result in the death of another; or causing the death of another, whether the victim or a third party, in the commission of or attempt to commit rape, robbery, arson, burglary, or kidnapping, or in flight therefrom. First-degree murder is considered a Class A felony.

Second-degree murder involves intentionally causing the death of another without premeditation, or during the commission of or attempt to commit offenses not specifically mentioned under first-degree murder or flight therefrom. Second-degree murder is considered a Class A felony.

First-degree manslaughter involves a person recklessly causing the death of another or the intentional and unlawful killing of a fetus by causing injury to the mother. First-degree manslaughter is considered a Class B felony.

Second-degree manslaughter involves criminal negligence that results in the death of another. Second-degree manslaughter is considered a Class C felony.

Homicide by abuse involves causing the death of either a child under the age of fifteen or a dependent adult suffering from severe developmental disabilities through a pattern of extreme indifference to life. Homicide by abuse is considered a Class A felony.

34. Bill Adams had just been released from a special sex offenders unit at a state reformatory. Two weeks later, he attempted to rape at knifepoint a local resident by the name of Marlene Wilson. Despite the threat, Ms. Wilson was not compliant with Adams's demands. She was not raped; however, her resistive efforts toward Adams resulted in her being fatally stabbed to death. Adams was later arrested, and shortly thereafter he confessed to authorities that he was responsible for the crime. According to the reading, under the circumstances Adams should be charged with which of the following crimes?

    A. Class A felony

    B. Class B felony

    C. Class C felony

    D. Second-degree murder

35. Ricky Matthews, a recently paroled convict, was driving his 1991 Ford Taurus west on Interstate 80 when he made an improper lane change that forced another vehicle off the road. The driver of that vehicle, Tracy Cummings, was killed instantly when her car collided with an oak tree. Mr. Matthews's blood-alcohol level registered far above what was legally tolerated by the state. In this instance, according to the reading, Mr. Matthews should be charged with which offense?

    A. Class A felony

    B. Class C felony

    C. First-degree manslaughter

    D. He should not be charged with anything besides driving while under the influence of alcohol (DUI).

36. Inmate Comstock was permitted a rare conjugal visit from his wife in Crestwood Prison. However, upon learning during the visit that she was four months pregnant by another man, inmate Comstock knocked his wife to the floor. Authorities immediately responded to her cries for help, but not before her husband forcefully kicked her in the stomach. She suffered severe abdominal pain following the incident and, shortly thereafter, was transported to the Madison County emergency unit for medical assistance. Despite the efforts of hospital personnel, she miscarried four hours later. According to the reading, under the circumstances inmate Comstock should be charged with which of the following crimes?

    A. Class A felony

    B. First-degree murder

    C. Homicide by abuse

    D. Class B felony

Answer questions 37–40 on the basis of the following reading:

Extortion is defined as the obtaining of property or services from another by wrongful use or actual or threatened force, violence, or fear.

First-degree extortion involves the direct or indirect threat to cause future bodily injury or physical damage to the property of another or to subject the person threatened to restraint or confinement. First-degree extortion is a Class B felony punishable by up to ten years in prison.

Second-degree extortion involves the direct or indirect threat to expose a secret, whether true or not, that instills contempt or hatred toward another; to withhold crucial testimony or to disseminate false testimony that affects another person's legal defense or claim; to perpetuate a strike or boycott to obtain property unrelated to the event itself; or to act in a way harmful to another person's safety, health, business, or personal relationships. Second-degree extortion is a Class C felony punishable by up to seven years in prison.

Bribery is defined as the offering, giving, receiving, or soliciting of anything of value to influence action as an official or in the discharge of legal or public duty. Any person whose official conduct is connected with the administration of government is subject to this legal provision. Bribery is a Class A felony punishable by up to fifteen years in prison.

37. Ann Compton, a convicted extortionist, threatened a neighbor currently standing trial for first-degree theft that she would make a materially false statement against her defense in court if she did not receive $500. Under these circumstances and according to the preceding narrative, which of the following could Ms. Compton be charged with?

    A. Class A felony

    B. Perjury

    C. Class C felony

    D. The narrative is not applicable to this situation.

38. Harold Russell, a recently furloughed convict, telephones one of the witnesses who had testified against him in court ten years earlier. He explains that the streets are unsafe these days and that the witness or his wife may have an unfortunate "accident" if they are not careful. At this point, Mr. Russell hangs up. Accordingly, Mr. Russell could be prosecuted under which of the following statutes if the witness in question was the Mayor?

    A. Bribery

    B. First-degree extortion

    C. Second-degree extortion

    D. None of the above

39. Barb Waterhouse threatened to expose a local warden's extramarital affair if he failed to render harsher treatment for repeat sex offenders. If the warden made local authorities aware of the threat, Ms. Waterhouse could be prosecuted under which of the following statutes?

    A. Bribery

    B. First-degree extortion

    C. Second-degree extortion

    D. None of the above

40. Dan Evans, a person twice convicted for the collection of unlawful debt, calls Charlie McKay and explains in no uncertain terms that if he does not pay the $1800 owed as interest from an earlier gambling activity, Mr. Evans and some "friends" would break both of Mr. McKay's legs later in the week. On the presumption that Mr. Evans is arrested and prosecuted for the offense, how much prison time could Mr. Evans potentially face?

    A. Seven years

    B. Ten years

    C. Fifteen years

    D. None of the above

Answer questions 41–47 on the basis of the following scheduled inmate work assignments.

ARLINGTON CORRECTIONS PRISON WORK DETAIL
FOR THE MONTH OF JUNE

Inmate ID #	Sunday	Monday	Tuesday	Wednesday	Thursday	Friday	Saturday
670	T	K-2				T	
			E-6	L-5	L-3		Q-5 I-7
470		I-2		O-2			T
	L-3		I-6		E-5	L-5	
372	K-1		T				
		L-3		Q-3	I-4	Q-3	L-3
512				T		E-2	
	L-5	E-5	L-3		I-4		K-5
463	T	F-1	I-1	E-1		E-2	
		L-5			B-3	F-4	L-5
521					T	E-1	K-1
	I-7	E-7	L-5	L-3			
718		T	O-1				
	O-4		E-6	B-5 K-6	L-3	L-3	O-7

Inmate Identification Reference	Work Detail Reference Codes	Numerical Time Slot Assignments
Barker - 463	Laundry - B	8:00 A.M.–Noon = 1
Lomax - 670	Metal Shop - E	10:00 A.M.–Noon = 2
Jankowski - 372	GED Studies - F	Noon–1:00 P.M. = 3
Faulkner - 470	Librarian Assistant - I	Noon–4:00 P.M. = 4
Bonner - 512	Mop cell block walkways - K	Noon–2:00 P.M. = 5
Peyton - 718	Kitchen cleanup - L	2:00 P.M.–4:00 P.M. = 6
Voight - 521	Shower area cleanup - O	2:00 P.M.–6:00 P.M. = 7
	Visitor's area cleanup - Q	
	Designated day off - T	

41. According to the work schedule provided, which inmate was granted the most time off for apparent good behavior?

    A. Jankowski

    B. Voight

    C. Lomax

    D. Bonner

42. Who, among the group of inmates listed, was pursuing high school equivalency studies?

    A. Peyton

    B. Bonner and Faulkner

    C. Voight and Lomax

    D. Barker

43. Who had apparent trustee status permitting assigned details in the visitor area?

    A. Lomax

    B. Both Faulkner and Barker

    C. Both Jankowski and Lomax

    D. Peyton

44. Which of the following inmates was assigned the most hours during the course of the week to perform kitchen cleanup duty?

    A. Voight

    B. Barker

    C. Peyton

    D. Jankowski

45. Which inmate had a designated weekday assignment of mopping the prison walkways during the afternoon?

    A. Bonner

    B. Peyton

    C. Voight

    D. Faulkner

46. Which of the inmates, perhaps for disciplinary action, was scheduled the largest share of cleanup duty in general?

    A. Peyton

    B. Lomax

    C. Bonner

    D. Jankowski

47. According to the work schedule provided, which of the following statements is true?

    A. Jankowski was scheduled to work as a library assistant twice a week.

    B. Barker was assigned to work one hour on Wednesdays doing laundry.

    C. Bonner was scheduled to work two hours on Saturday afternoon mopping prison walkways.

    D. Voight was scheduled to receive a total of eight hours of classroom instruction in metal shop over a period of three different days during the week.

48. Assume that you have just been given a directive from a high level administrator to implement a new policy that you are certain will cause additional tension between inmates and yourself. Your best means to handle such a situation would be to do which of the following?

    A. Try to explain to inmates that none of the changes to go into effect are of your doing

    B. Make it obvious to inmates that you are in complete disagreement with what has been handed down

    C. Circumvent the new directives as much as possible to reduce potential tensions

    D. Act as directed without reservation, but convey your concerns to your immediate supervisor

49. While conducting your rounds, you notice inmate Winters talking to inmate Perkins. Within the span of a couple of minutes, inmate Winters leaves, but not before visually upsetting inmate Perkins. After finding out from Perkins that Winters wanted a homosexual relationship, your best means to handle this situation would be to do which of the following?

    A. Leave the matter to be settled between themselves

    B. Inform Winters to desist in compliance with regulations or face disciplinary action

    C. Immediately isolate both prisoners in separate cells

    D. Tell inmate Winters to show some respect and decency to other inmates

50. Inmate Mussman had aspirations of becoming an attorney immediately following his release from prison. All things considered, inmate Mussman was a model prisoner. On occasion, though, he would violate the lights-out policy by studying legal briefs one or two hours beyond what was permitted. His cell mate did not seem to object to his late night studies. Under the circumstances, which of the following actions should be taken by Corrections personnel?

    A. Directly inform Mussman that he must comply with the policy or face certain disciplinary action

    B. Allow the leniency to continue because of his future professional endeavors

    C. Ignore the practice altogether because it does not pose a problem for his cell mate

    D. Allow inmate Mussman greater daytime access to the library to do his necessary research

51. While supervising a group of inmates on work furlough, Officer Jasper noticed that one of the prisoner's restraints had become quite loose. Under the circumstances, he should do which of the following?

    A. At the conclusion of the scheduled furlough, report that a coworker failed to do his or her job

    B. Leave the group temporarily to file a report with an immediate superior

    C. Properly secure the restraint immediately

    D. Ignore the matter because most inmates in work furlough programs can be trusted

52. Corrections Officer Seals observes two inmates in the recreation room shouting at each other and posturing to begin a fistfight. Officer Seals's best approach to handle the matter would be which of the following?

    A. Yell at the prisoners to stop their bickering

    B. Immediately report the altercation to a floor supervisor

    C. Confront the two inmates in a calm manner and explain the potential discipline for such behavior

    D. Allow the situation to work itself out

53. Inmate Daniels has a cousin, who lives out of state, who decided to pay an impromptu visit because she was in the area on business. Visitor policy, however, prohibits any visit without prior written notification and subsequent approval by Lieutenant James Marston. Under the circumstances, which of the following actions would be appropriate?

    A. Daniels should be permitted the visit because his cousin, after all, is from out of state.

    B. An immediate supervisor should be contacted.

    C. Daniels's cousin should not be permitted the visit.

    D. Daniels should be consulted to see if some kind of mistake occurred with the required paperwork.

54. Mrs. Claymore claims that she had sent her husband, an inmate at Torrington Corrections, $150 cash, but later was told by him that he only received $50. The most appropriate way for Corrections personnel to initially handle such a discrepancy would be which of the following?

    A. Ignore the problem because Mr. Claymore, in all likelihood, lied to his wife

    B. Take up a collection to make up the difference owed

    C. Initiate an internal investigation of those suspected of being responsible

    D. Check the receipt log

Answer questions 55–58 on the basis of the following code format. Select the code that most accurately defines the key given for the question.

Key	A	D	E	I	G	T	O	R	C	H
Code	1	5	3	4	8	7	2	6	9	0

55. Trade

    A. 76153

    B. 71653

    C. 76281

    D. 78204

56. Garage

    A. 861813

    B. 816183

    C. 811683

    D. 868113

57. Theater

    A. 7031376

    B. 7031736

    C. 7301736

    D. 7130763

58. Reached

    A. 6319053

    B. 6931056

    C. 6391035

    D. 6319036

Answer questions 59–62 on the basis of the following multiple code format.

Key	2	4	3	6	8	1	5
Alternate	J	A	V	D	O	L	U
Codes	R	I	B	K	F	S	M
	C	W	G	Y	Z	E	X
	H	T	N	C	Q	A	P

59. The code word *jailer* is an accurate translation of which of the following numbers?

    A. 214112

    B. 241412

    C. 244112

    D. Both choices A and C

60. The code word *convict* is an accurate translation of which of the following numbers?

    A. 2833444

    B. 6833424

    C. 2834344

    D. None of the above

61. According to the number-letter key provided, which of the following selections represents a code that is in alphabetical order?

    A. 3661548

    B. 2426185

    C. 2145345

    D. 4366814

62. Study the following codes in relation to the key provided. Select the answer that accounts for the number of coding errors found.

Code	Key
AJMOBCL	4258325
QPUXI	85554
RTHCDEZ	2422618
MQABHGJ	5813432
FWYLO	64618
BYZAIWX	3681345
KDOLN	66813

A. More than 5 errors

B. 5 errors

C. 4 errors

D. Less than 4 errors

Answer questions 63–65 on the basis of the following passage.

The number located at the top of a driver's license consists of the first five letters of the last name, the first letter of the first name, and the first letter of the middle name. The birth year when subtracted from one hundred produces the first two numerical digits. A check digit inserted by the computer produces the third numerical digit. A code for the month of birth and a code for the day of birth are inserted toward the end. Month and day codes are represented here:

Months	Days		
January - A	01 - A	13 - M	25 - Y
February - B	02 - B	14 - N	26 - Z
March - D	03 - C	15 - O	27 - 1
April - F	04 - D	16 - P	28 - 2
May - G	05 - E	17 - Q	29 - 3
June - H	06 - F	18 - R	30 - 4
July - J	07 - G	19 - S	31 - 5
August - L	08 - H	20 - T	
September - O	09 - I	21 - U	
October - P	10 - J	22 - V	
November - R	11 - K	23 - W	
December - T	12 - L	24 - X	

63. According to the formula prescribed, John Doe Smith, born 10-26-56, would be issued which of the following driver's license numbers?

A. JDSMITH44ZP9

B. SMITHJD449PZ

C. DJSMITH449PZ

D. SMITHJD44PZ

64. According to the formula prescribed, Jason Lowell Halvorson, born June 16, 1975, would be issued which of the following driver's license numbers?

   A. HALVOJL251HP

   B. HALVEJL523PH

   C. HALVOLJ25H1P

   D. HALVOJL521HP

65. According to the formula prescribed, Vicki Jean Bartenolli, born August 30, 1963, would be issued which of the following driver's license numbers?

   A. VJBARTE378L4

   B. JVBART837L4

   C. BARTEJV371L4

   D. BARTEVJ378L4

Questions 66–72 pertain to spelling. Each question has four numerically identified columns, each comprising various word sets. One of the word sets given will contain an intentionally misspelled word. Select the column number that represents the misspelled word and mark your answer sheet accordingly.

66.

I	II	III	IV
Penitentiary	Bulletin	Violation	Bureau
Mistaken	Contraband	Disciplin	Disappear
District	Attorney	Conspiracy	Security
Coroner	Commissary	Fighting	Committee

   A. I

   B. II

   C. III

   D. IV

67.

I	II	III	IV
Infraction	Mustache	Negligent	Intimidation
Miscellanious	Physical	Retaliate	Fracture
Patient	Obscene	Disagree	Incident
Grievance	Privilege	Jury	Felony

   A. I

   B. II

   C. III

   D. IV

68.

I	II	III	IV
Medical	Professional	Informant	Seize
Parole	Witness	Penalty	Proceedure
Statute	Vicinity	Personnel	Sincerity
Sergeant	Frequent	Suspicion	Testimony

A. I

B. II

C. III

D. IV

69.

I	II	III	IV
Transferred	Judicial	Delusion	Cigarette
Inquiry	Disoriented	Dangerous	Private
Hazard	Appoint	Weapon	Psychiatrist
Observed	Rehabilitate	Planetiff	Describe

A. I

B. II

C. III

D. IV

70.

I	II	III	IV
Lethal	Epileptic	Narcotics	Extortion
Beleive	Custody	Knife	Fugitive
Apprehend	Bail	Obnoxious	Investigate
Courteous	Molest	Incriminate	Laboratory

A. I

B. II

C. III

D. IV

71.

I	II	III	IV
Forfeit	Surveillance	Thorough	Muscle
Indecent	Realise	Receipt	Homicide
Loiter	Psychology	Preliminary	Forcibly
Version	Unconscious	Prejudiced	Opinion

A. I

B. II

C. III

D. IV

72.

I	II	III	IV
Negotiable	Insurance	Interview	Heroin
Offender	Metropolitan	Hemorrhage	Punitive
License	Parallel	Wednesday	Weight
Exercise	Lieutenent	Schedule	Subpoena

A. I

B. II

C. III

D. IV

Questions 73–83 pertain to vocabulary proficiency. Each question will pose a statement that will have a particular word in italics. You must determine from the four alternative choices given which one correctly defines the word in question and then mark your answer sheet accordingly.

73. Sergeant Bernstein's report was seemingly *redundant* in a couple of areas. *Redundant* most nearly means:

A. Incomprehensible

B. Repetitious

C. Concise

D. Easy to understand

74. Cliff's *facetiousness* with the law officer landed him a jail term. *Facetiousness* most nearly means:

A. Serious nature

B. Blitheness

C. Wisecracking

D. Stubborn attitude

75. Jurors were not permitted to *divulge* any information to a third party while sequestered. *Divulge* most nearly means:

A. Conceal

B. Distort

C. Expose

D. Disclose

76. The minor infraction was enough to warrant permanent *expulsion*. *Expulsion* most nearly means:

A. Displacement

B. Replacement

C. Disgrace

D. Subjugation

77. Many people are of the belief that the rights and privileges guaranteed by the Constitution are the main factor preventing total *anarchy* in this nation. *Anarchy* most nearly means:

 A. Compatibility

 B. Conformity

 C. Disorder

 D. Harmony

78. Jerry had nothing but *contempt* for the legal system once Judge Skyler refused to dismiss his speeding ticket. *Contempt* most nearly means:

 A. Disdain

 B. Praise

 C. Respect

 D. High regard

79. The suspect freely made her confession without *coercion* in the hope of gaining a lighter sentence. *Coercion* most nearly means:

 A. Reservations

 B. Assistance

 C. Stipulation

 D. Intimidation

80. It was an *alleged* accident that Ms. Phelps overdosed on sleeping pills. *Alleged* most nearly means:

 A. Guaranteed

 B. Credible

 C. Indisputable

 D. Purported

81. The defense attorney repeated the witness's statement *verbatim*. *Verbatim* most nearly means:

 A. Imprecisely

 B. Word for word

 C. Perfunctory

 D. Eloquently

82. Vice Detective Sid Morrissey is a *proficient* interrogator. *Proficient* most nearly means:

 A. Incompetent

 B. Prodigious

 C. Expert

 D. Amateur

83. Mr. Austin was a little *ambiguous* concerning his whereabouts at the time of the murder. *Ambiguous* most nearly means:

    A. Vague

    B. Explicit

    C. Recalcitrant

    D. Too relaxed

Questions 84–93 relate to grammar, punctuation, and spelling. Each question will provide a written statement that may or may not contain specific errors. Select, from the choices provided, the answer that represents an accurate assessment of the statement in question and then mark your answer sheet accordingly.

84. A person who desires to be a firefighter for example may set fire to a structure and endeavor to achieve a spectacular rescue in order to gain notoriety.

    The statement, in terms of English usage,

    A. Is structurally incorrect

    B. Contains one or more misspellings

    C. Lacks necessary punctuation and/or capitalization

    D. Is grammatically correct

85. The appropriate examination and correct evaluation of real evidence is a responsibility of the technician or expert, whom by reason of his training and experience is qualified in the specialty involved.

    The statement, in terms of English usage,

    A. Is structurally incorrect

    B. Contains one or more misspellings

    C. Lacks necessary punctuation and/or capitalization

    D. Is grammatically correct

86. The importance of the proceedure becomes apparent when consideration is given to the fact that an officer may be called to the witness stand several months after an investigation has been completed.

    The statement, in terms of English usage,

    A. Is structurally incorrect

    B. Contains one or more misspellings

    C. Lacks necessary punctuation and/or capitalization

    D. Is grammatically correct

87. The FBI, in the uniform crime reports, predicts that a total of 4,500,000 robbery offenses will be committed in the United States in 1993.

    The statement, in terms of English usage,

    A. Is structurally incorrect

    B. Contains one or more misspellings

    C. Lacks necessary punctuation and/or capitalization

    D. Is grammatically correct

88. Because Pete Mitchell was too young he was immediately disqualified from further consideration for employment.

    The statement, in terms of English usage,

    A. Is structurally incorrect

    B. Contains one or more misspellings

    C. Lacks necessary punctuation and/or capitalization

    D. Is grammatically correct

89. An incident report should be typewritten if possible; if not, it should be neatly and legibly written by pen in black or blue ink. Erasures and whiteout should be avoided; there should be no more than two to a page, and they should be neatly made and present no difficulty in reading and no possibility of misinterpretation.

    The statement, in terms of English usage,

    A. Is structurally incorrect

    B. Contains one or more misspellings

    C. Lacks necessary punctuation and/or capitalization

    D. Is grammatically correct

90. Forgery is committed by an individual who, with intent to defraud, knowingly makes or utters a false writing that apparently imposes a legal liability on another or affects his legal right or liability to his prejudice.

    The statement, in terms of English usage,

    A. Is structurally incorrect

    B. Contains one or more misspellings

    C. Lacks necessary punctuation and/or capitalization

    D. Is grammatically correct

91. When officers take their lunch hour with Lieutenant Branstad, you usually end up talking about procedural policies.

    The statement, in terms of English usage,

    A. Is structurally incorrect

    B. Contains one or more misspellings

    C. Lacks necessary punctuation and/or capitalization

    D. Is grammatically correct

92. To judges and juries, few kinds of evidence are as persuasive as fingerprints; however, investigating officers often miss fingerprints that might help insure convictions.

    The statement, in terms of English usage,

    A. Is structurally incorrect

    B. Contains one or more misspellings

    C. Lacks necessary punctuation and/or capitalization

    D. Is grammatically correct

93. Containing a glove, pouch, handcuff case, mace holder, and penholder, an officer wears a belt that stores much more than a gun.

> The statement, in terms of English usage,

    A. Is structurally incorrect

    B. Contains one or more misspellings

    C. Lacks necessary punctuation and/or capitalization

    D. Is grammatically correct

Answer questions 94–96 on the basis of this flow chart.

State and Federal Court Systems

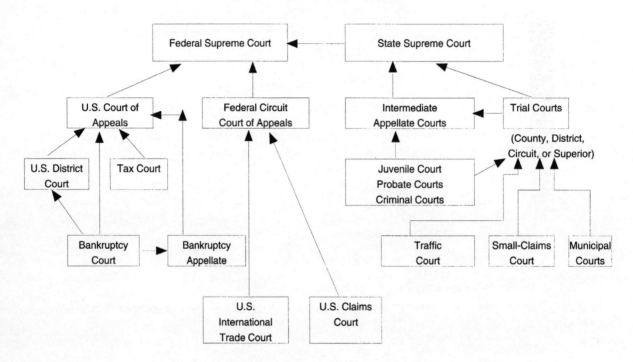

94. Which court may review a decision made by a Supreme Court?

    A. Intermediate Appellate Court

    B. Federal Supreme Court

    C. U.S. District Court

    D. None of the above

95. All of the following lower courts with limited jurisdictions have only one avenue of appeal except:

    A. Juvenile Court

    B. Small-claims Court

    C. Traffic Court

    D. Municipal Court

96. According to the flow chart, all of the following statements are true except:

    A. Only one court has three potential avenues of appealing a decision.

    B. Decisions arrived at in U.S. Claims Court can be appealed directly to the federal Circuit Court of Appeals.

    C. Decisions heard in the federal Supreme Court can originate from only three different venues.

    D. All of the above are correct.

Following are bar graphs that represent various demographics of state prison admissions. Answer questions 97–100 on the basis of the information provided.

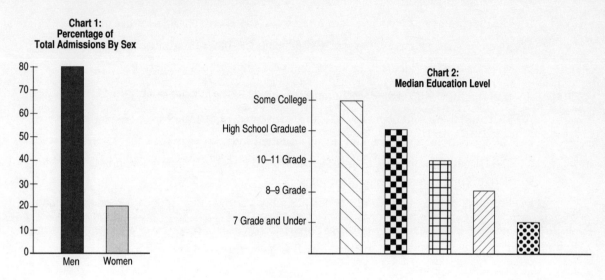

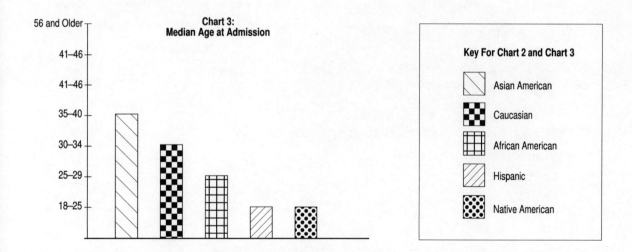

97. According to the prison admission statistics provided, which ethnic groups would be considered the least educated?

    A. Asian American

    B. Native American

    C. Hispanic

    D. Caucasian

98. The median age of Asian American inmates admitted to prison is shown to be which of the following?

    A. 30–34 years of age

    B. 18–25 years of age

    C. 35–40 years of age

    D. 25–29 years of age

99. All of the following statements are true except?

    A. There are disproportionately more men than women admitted into prison.

    B. The median age of Hispanics admitted to prison is comparable to that of Native Americans.

    C. Asian Americans are among the best educated of inmates admitted.

    D. Most Caucasians incarcerated have had post-high-school education.

100. Which of the following statements would be considered the least accurate?

    A. There are higher numbers of African Americans incarcerated than Hispanics.

    B. The median age of Asian Americans admitted into prison is between 25 and 29 years of age.

    C. The Hispanic inmate population demonstrated higher educational standards than those of the Native American inmate population.

    D. The median age of Hispanics is considerably younger than that of Asian Americans.

The following pie chart represents a proportional breakdown of sentenced prisoners released from Bedford Corrections in 1995. Answer questions 101–103 on the basis of the data shown.

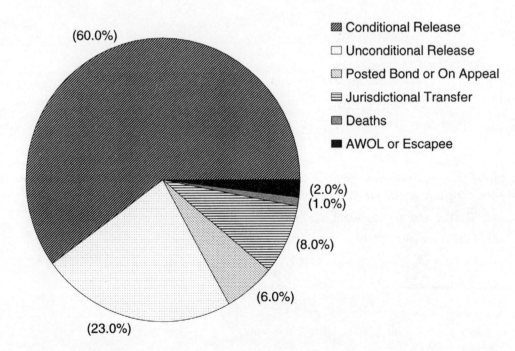

101. The third largest group of prisoners shown to be released was contingent on what basis?

    A. Posted bond

    B. Unconditional

    C. Appeal

    D. Jurisdictional transfer

102. The two smallest groups of prisoners released, not counting dead prisoners, would comprise what proportion of total releases?

    A. 3%

    B. 8%

    C. 10%

    D. 14%

103. The three largest groups of prisoners released, not counting jurisdictional transfers, would comprise what proportion of total releases?

    A. 91%

    B. 89%

    C. 83%

    D. 60%

Study the following uniform crime report to answer questions 104–107.

| | Males | | | | Females | | | |
| | Total | | Under 18 | | Total | | Under 18 | |
Criminal Offense	1985	1990	1985	1990	1985	1990	1985	1990
Murder & nonnegligent manslaughter	13,141	15,906	1,015	1,293	6,750	6,953	1,501	1,709
Robbery	49,192	46,702	2,950	2,893	23,471	23,405	2,090	2,740
Forcible rape	16,531	19,603	983	1,107	1,006	1,180	105	145
Burglary	67,985	82,996	13,580	14,012	9,706	11,340	936	1,050
Arson	9,512	10,759	235	257	123	137	13	29
Motor vehicle theft	72,503	73,415	12,509	12,703	24,600	24,807	1,326	1,349
Larceny	426,719	503,971	29,601	35,803	290,439	312,482	18,901	18,996
Aggravated assault	232,500	256,319	18,900	23,752	137,506	145,990	15,403	18,901

104. In the five-year period indicated in the survey, which criminal offense committed by male juveniles experienced the greatest percentage increase?

    A. Murder and nonnegligent manslaughter

    B. Forcible rape

    C. Larceny

    D. Aggravated assault

105. According to the most recent statistics, how many more times is a man likely to commit murder or nonnegligent manslaughter than a woman?

    A. 3:1

    B. 2.67:1

    C. 2.29:1

    D. 2.2:1

106. Motor vehicle theft accounts for what percentage of the total crimes committed by female juveniles?

    A. 1%

    B. 3%

    C. 5%

    D. 7%

107. Which category of offenders demonstrates the largest percentage decrease in robbery?

    A. Adult males

    B. Juvenile males

    C. Adult females

    D. Juvenile females

108. If a new prison van can be driven 115 miles in town on 5 gallons of gas, how many miles could it be driven under the same conditions with a full tank of gas? (Consider the vehicle to have a 30-gallon capacity for the purpose of the question.)

    A. 720

    B. 690

    C. 675

    D. 650

109. Suppose a county correctional facility has enough emergency provisions on hand to sustain 240 prisoners (its capacity) for 14 days. If the current inmate populations were at 140 percent of the prison's capacity, how long would the same provisions last?

    A. 23.5 days

    B. 19.6 days

    C. 15.3 days

    D. 10 days

110. Suppose an investigator needed to protect a crime scene in an outdoor area against rain or other natural contaminants that could hinder an investigation. If the area of concern was circular, with a radius of 6.5 feet, how wide would a square tarp have to be to sufficiently cover the area described?

    A. 6.5 feet

    B. 13 feet

    C. 14.5 feet

    D. 16 feet

111. Assume Officer Bill McPherson and Officer Terry Henderson are next-door neighbors and coincidentally work in the same department. If Officer McPherson can commute to work in 45 minutes doing an average speed of 30 mph, how fast could Officer Henderson get to work driving at an average speed of 35 mph, assuming the same route is taken and all other factors remain constant?

    A. 52.5 minutes

    B. 42.13 minutes

    C. 38.57 minutes

    D. 36.79 minutes

112. If a Corrections applicant scored 80%, 82%, 90%, and 87% on her first four exams, what kind of grade would be required on the fifth exam to acquire an overall average of 87%?

    A. 87%

    B. 89%

    C. 96%

    D. 98%

113. A rectangular area of 47.5 feet by 13.2 feet was roped off for a murder investigation. How many square feet does that encompass?

    A. 627

    B. 593

    C. 572.5

    D. 402

Read the narrative below and then refer to the blank fingerprint processing report that immediately follows to answer questions 114–125.

Mr. James Emery Hall was arrested November 13, 1996, by State Patrol Officer Lt. Pete Kendrick, badge number 1515, on charges of aggravated assault of an officer (NCIC Code 13501-A) and resisting arrest (NCIC Code 13721-B). Mr. Hall's erratic driving pattern on Interstate 199 prompted Officer Kendrick to pull him over to conduct a field sobriety check. Pursuant to Officer Kendrick's request to submit to a breathalyzer test, Mr. Hall became agitated and struck the officer in the face. There was a brief struggle, but Mr. Hall was subdued, handcuffed, and Mirandized (i.e., read his rights). During the course of his arrest, Mr. Hall (the suspect in question) maintained that his name was Jeffery T. Beaumont. A computer-records search of what apparently was a forged ID indicated that no such person existed. However, his physical description—Caucasian, 6', 2", approximately 215 pounds, black hair, and brown eyes—matched that of a Mr. James Emery Hall, who was the legally registered owner of the vehicle pulled over. There was also an existing warrant out for his arrest for failure to appear in court over two unrelated misdemeanor charges. Lakeview Police Officer Harry M. Stevens, badge number 503, took custodial responsibility of transporting Mr. Hall to Lewis County Detention for booking and intake. Corrections Officer John Cornwall, badge number 181, received Mr. Hall at 0937 hours on the same day of his arrest and inventoried his personal effects for property storage. Mr. Hall was issued receipt number 1517 for his personal belongings. Mr. Hall was much more compliant during the booking and intake process than he was during his arrest. Not only was he cooperative with being finger-printed, he additionally provided Officer Cornwall his true identity, including his Social Security number (555-22-0557), place of birth (Cedar Rapids, IA), and birthdate (October 3, 1957). He remains in detention pending an arraignment hearing scheduled on November 19, 1996, in Lewis County Superior Court. Mr. Hall's case file reference number is 26-07A.

Fingerprint Processing Report

Name of Suspect ① Last Name ② Middle Initial ③ First Name	⑭ Processing Date and Time	⑱ Signature of Processing Officer
④ Aliases	⑮ Date Arrested	⑲ Arresting Agency
⑤ Date of Birth ⑥ Place of Birth	⑯ Offense(s) Charged	⑳ Custodial Officer's Name and Badge #
⑦ Social Security Number		㉑ Property Inventory Log Number
⑧ Sex ⑨ Race ⑩ Eyes ⑪ Hair ⑫ Height ⑬ Weight	⑰ Applicable NCIC Codes for Respective Offenses	㉒ Case File Reference Number
㉓ L.Thumb ㉔ L.Index ㉕ L.Middle	㉖ L.Ring	㉗ L.Little
㉘ R.Thumb ㉙ R.Index ㉚ R.Middle	㉛ R.Ring	㉜ R.Little

114. According to the narrative, what information concerning Mr. Hall should be placed in Box 9 of this report?

    A. Male

    B. Brown

    C. Caucasian

    D. 6'2"

115. What information concerning Mr. Hall should be placed in Box 7 of this report?

    A. 525-22-0557

    B. NCIC Code 13721-B

    C. 503

    D. None of the above

116. The name of Lt. Pete Kendrick would be appropriately inserted where on the fingerprint processing report?

    A. Box 20

    B. Box 19

    C. Box 18

    D. None of the above

117. With regard to Mr. Hall's arrest, whose name should be inserted in Box 18?

    A. John Cornwall

    B. Lt. Pete Kendrick

    C. Harry Stevens

    D. None of the above

118. What would be the appropriate report code(s) to indicate Mr. Hall's offenses?

    A. NCIC Code 13721-B

    B. NCIC Code 13151-A

    C. NCIC Code 13501-A

    D. Both selections A and C

119. During the actual fingerprinting, where would Mr. Hall's right index and right middle fingerprint impressions be respectively placed?

    A. Boxes 29 and 30

    B. Boxes 24 and 25

    C. Boxes 23 and 30

    D. Boxes 31 and 32

120. Which of the following selections would be the correct entry for Box 19?

    A. Sheriff's Department

    B. Lakeview Police Department

    C. State Patrol

    D. Lewis County Corrections

121. What would be the correct respective information to be placed in Box 20?

    A. Lt. Pete Kendrick / 1515

    B. 503 / Harry M. Stevens

    C. Harry M. Stevens / 503

    D. 1515 / Lt. Pete Kendrick

122. The proper information to insert in Box 14 is which of the following selections?

    A. 11-13-96 / 0937 hours

    B. 10-03-57 / 0931 hours

    C. 11-19-96 / 0937 hours

    D. None of the above

123. The name of Jeff T. Beaumont would be appropriately inserted where on the fingerprint processing report?

    A. Box 1

    B. Box 3

    C. Box 4

    D. Box 18

124. All of the following selections are true with respect to the fingerprint report prepared on Mr. Hall except?

    A. *215 pounds* would be inserted in Box 13.

    B. *Black* and *brown* would be inserted in Boxes 11 and 10 respectively.

    C. *Male* would be inserted in Box 8.

    D. All of the above are correct.

125. What information concerning Mr. Hall should be inserted in Box 22 of the report?

    A. 13501-A

    B. 555-22-0557

    C. 26-07B

    D. None of the above

ANSWER SHEET TO PRACTICE EXAM 1

1.	Ⓐ Ⓑ Ⓒ Ⓓ	31. Ⓐ Ⓑ Ⓒ Ⓓ	61. Ⓐ Ⓑ Ⓒ Ⓓ
2.	Ⓐ Ⓑ Ⓒ Ⓓ	32. Ⓐ Ⓑ Ⓒ Ⓓ	62. Ⓐ Ⓑ Ⓒ Ⓓ
3.	Ⓐ Ⓑ Ⓒ Ⓓ	33. Ⓐ Ⓑ Ⓒ Ⓓ	63. Ⓐ Ⓑ Ⓒ Ⓓ
4.	Ⓐ Ⓑ Ⓒ Ⓓ	34. Ⓐ Ⓑ Ⓒ Ⓓ	64. Ⓐ Ⓑ Ⓒ Ⓓ
5.	Ⓐ Ⓑ Ⓒ Ⓓ	35. Ⓐ Ⓑ Ⓒ Ⓓ	65. Ⓐ Ⓑ Ⓒ Ⓓ
6.	Ⓐ Ⓑ Ⓒ Ⓓ	36. Ⓐ Ⓑ Ⓒ Ⓓ	66. Ⓐ Ⓑ Ⓒ Ⓓ
7.	Ⓐ Ⓑ Ⓒ Ⓓ	37. Ⓐ Ⓑ Ⓒ Ⓓ	67. Ⓐ Ⓑ Ⓒ Ⓓ
8.	Ⓐ Ⓑ Ⓒ Ⓓ	38. Ⓐ Ⓑ Ⓒ Ⓓ	68. Ⓐ Ⓑ Ⓒ Ⓓ
9.	Ⓐ Ⓑ Ⓒ Ⓓ	39. Ⓐ Ⓑ Ⓒ Ⓓ	69. Ⓐ Ⓑ Ⓒ Ⓓ
10.	Ⓐ Ⓑ Ⓒ Ⓓ	40. Ⓐ Ⓑ Ⓒ Ⓓ	70. Ⓐ Ⓑ Ⓒ Ⓓ
11.	Ⓐ Ⓑ Ⓒ Ⓓ	41. Ⓐ Ⓑ Ⓒ Ⓓ	71. Ⓐ Ⓑ Ⓒ Ⓓ
12.	Ⓐ Ⓑ Ⓒ Ⓓ	42. Ⓐ Ⓑ Ⓒ Ⓓ	72. Ⓐ Ⓑ Ⓒ Ⓓ
13.	Ⓐ Ⓑ Ⓒ Ⓓ	43. Ⓐ Ⓑ Ⓒ Ⓓ	73. Ⓐ Ⓑ Ⓒ Ⓓ
14.	Ⓐ Ⓑ Ⓒ Ⓓ	44. Ⓐ Ⓑ Ⓒ Ⓓ	74. Ⓐ Ⓑ Ⓒ Ⓓ
15.	Ⓐ Ⓑ Ⓒ Ⓓ	45. Ⓐ Ⓑ Ⓒ Ⓓ	75. Ⓐ Ⓑ Ⓒ Ⓓ
16.	Ⓐ Ⓑ Ⓒ Ⓓ	46. Ⓐ Ⓑ Ⓒ Ⓓ	76. Ⓐ Ⓑ Ⓒ Ⓓ
17.	Ⓐ Ⓑ Ⓒ Ⓓ	47. Ⓐ Ⓑ Ⓒ Ⓓ	77. Ⓐ Ⓑ Ⓒ Ⓓ
18.	Ⓐ Ⓑ Ⓒ Ⓓ	48. Ⓐ Ⓑ Ⓒ Ⓓ	78. Ⓐ Ⓑ Ⓒ Ⓓ
19.	Ⓐ Ⓑ Ⓒ Ⓓ	49. Ⓐ Ⓑ Ⓒ Ⓓ	79. Ⓐ Ⓑ Ⓒ Ⓓ
20.	Ⓐ Ⓑ Ⓒ Ⓓ	50. Ⓐ Ⓑ Ⓒ Ⓓ	80. Ⓐ Ⓑ Ⓒ Ⓓ
21.	Ⓐ Ⓑ Ⓒ Ⓓ	51. Ⓐ Ⓑ Ⓒ Ⓓ	81. Ⓐ Ⓑ Ⓒ Ⓓ
22.	Ⓐ Ⓑ Ⓒ Ⓓ	52. Ⓐ Ⓑ Ⓒ Ⓓ	82. Ⓐ Ⓑ Ⓒ Ⓓ
23.	Ⓐ Ⓑ Ⓒ Ⓓ	53. Ⓐ Ⓑ Ⓒ Ⓓ	83. Ⓐ Ⓑ Ⓒ Ⓓ
24.	Ⓐ Ⓑ Ⓒ Ⓓ	54. Ⓐ Ⓑ Ⓒ Ⓓ	84. Ⓐ Ⓑ Ⓒ Ⓓ
25.	Ⓐ Ⓑ Ⓒ Ⓓ	55. Ⓐ Ⓑ Ⓒ Ⓓ	85. Ⓐ Ⓑ Ⓒ Ⓓ
26.	Ⓐ Ⓑ Ⓒ Ⓓ	56. Ⓐ Ⓑ Ⓒ Ⓓ	86. Ⓐ Ⓑ Ⓒ Ⓓ
27.	Ⓐ Ⓑ Ⓒ Ⓓ	57. Ⓐ Ⓑ Ⓒ Ⓓ	87. Ⓐ Ⓑ Ⓒ Ⓓ
28.	Ⓐ Ⓑ Ⓒ Ⓓ	58. Ⓐ Ⓑ Ⓒ Ⓓ	88. Ⓐ Ⓑ Ⓒ Ⓓ
29.	Ⓐ Ⓑ Ⓒ Ⓓ	59. Ⓐ Ⓑ Ⓒ Ⓓ	89. Ⓐ Ⓑ Ⓒ Ⓓ
30.	Ⓐ Ⓑ Ⓒ Ⓓ	60. Ⓐ Ⓑ Ⓒ Ⓓ	90. Ⓐ Ⓑ Ⓒ Ⓓ

91. Ⓐ Ⓑ Ⓒ Ⓓ
92. Ⓐ Ⓑ Ⓒ Ⓓ
93. Ⓐ Ⓑ Ⓒ Ⓓ
94. Ⓐ Ⓑ Ⓒ Ⓓ
95. Ⓐ Ⓑ Ⓒ Ⓓ
96. Ⓐ Ⓑ Ⓒ Ⓓ
97. Ⓐ Ⓑ Ⓒ Ⓓ
98. Ⓐ Ⓑ Ⓒ Ⓓ
99. Ⓐ Ⓑ Ⓒ Ⓓ
100. Ⓐ Ⓑ Ⓒ Ⓓ
101. Ⓐ Ⓑ Ⓒ Ⓓ
102. Ⓐ Ⓑ Ⓒ Ⓓ

103. Ⓐ Ⓑ Ⓒ Ⓓ
104. Ⓐ Ⓑ Ⓒ Ⓓ
105. Ⓐ Ⓑ Ⓒ Ⓓ
106. Ⓐ Ⓑ Ⓒ Ⓓ
107. Ⓐ Ⓑ Ⓒ Ⓓ
108. Ⓐ Ⓑ Ⓒ Ⓓ
109. Ⓐ Ⓑ Ⓒ Ⓓ
110. Ⓐ Ⓑ Ⓒ Ⓓ
111. Ⓐ Ⓑ Ⓒ Ⓓ
112. Ⓐ Ⓑ Ⓒ Ⓓ
113. Ⓐ Ⓑ Ⓒ Ⓓ
114. Ⓐ Ⓑ Ⓒ Ⓓ

115. Ⓐ Ⓑ Ⓒ Ⓓ
116. Ⓐ Ⓑ Ⓒ Ⓓ
117. Ⓐ Ⓑ Ⓒ Ⓓ
118. Ⓐ Ⓑ Ⓒ Ⓓ
119. Ⓐ Ⓑ Ⓒ Ⓓ
120. Ⓐ Ⓑ Ⓒ Ⓓ
121. Ⓐ Ⓑ Ⓒ Ⓓ
122. Ⓐ Ⓑ Ⓒ Ⓓ
123. Ⓐ Ⓑ Ⓒ Ⓓ
124. Ⓐ Ⓑ Ⓒ Ⓓ
125. Ⓐ Ⓑ Ⓒ Ⓓ

Answers can be found on pages 215–222.

ANSWERS TO PRACTICE EXAM 1

Refer to narrative for any clarification of questions 1 through 15.

1. *C*   Judicial Summary of a Criminal case in Superior Court

2. *D*   The reading discusses how serious criminal charges — namely, felonies — are handled in superior court. However, there were no direct references within the narrative.

3. *A*   *Voir dire*

4. *B*   Administrative Recognizance Release Program (ARRP)

5. *C*   Plea-bargaining agreements must be heard prior to or during an omnibus hearing.

6. *C*   According to the reading, a person currently in custody must be given a trial date within sixty days of arraignment to be assured the right to a speedy trial.

7. *C*   Four to six weeks was the time given in which a judge has to sentence a convicted person.

8. *A*   Discovery

9. *B*   The reading emphasized that a defendant, whether in custody or not, must be identified prior to charges being formally filed.

10. *D*   Jurors must be unanimous; otherwise, the jury is considered hung and the charges are either dismissed or retried later.

11. *C*   Court rule 3.5 establishes the admissibility of such evidence.

12. *A*   *Personal recognizance* means the same thing as *release without bail*.

13. *B*   State sentencing guidelines, not the judge, were mentioned near the end of the narrative as being the determining factor.

14. *C*   It was pointed out that C is the person responsible.

15. *D*   A pretrial suppression hearing would determine evidence admissibility in this case.

16. *C*   One prisoner was bench-pressing while another was serving as his spotter. A third inmate was shown doing curls.

17. *B*   There was a total of eighteen inmates shown in the sketch.

18. *A*   There was only one armed guard in the location described.

19. *D*   Four inmates were shown to be playing basketball.

20. *B*   Only two inmates were conducting push-up exercises.

21. *D*   Wilmington Corrections

22. *A*   There were six rows of bleachers provided for the inmates.

23. *B*   There were two inmates shown to be jogging as a means of exercise.

24. *C*   Southwest corner

25. *C*   Since the clock in the sketch indicates it is 3:45 P.M., it can be assumed that inmates from cell block D are presently using the facilities shown. That assumption is based on the recreational rotation schedule provided and the fact that such arrangements are strictly applied.

26. *B*   Despite Officer McNeil's good intentions in selection B, his actions could lead to an accidental detonation. The suspected article should be left untouched until qualified personnel can decide how it should be handled.

27. *D*   Selection A is false because the reading made the distinction that each of the products listed, in an individual sense, does not pose an immediate threat. Consequently, such items remain readily available within a correctional facility. Selection B is false because it was

stated that, even under strict regulations, the goal of restricting all dangerous contraband remains an elusive endeavor. Selection C is incorrect by broadly defining that all products, when mixed, can be considered dangerous. According to the reading, only certain combinations of such products warrant concern.

28. **B** This kind of policy, as opposed to conventional bed checks, precludes the possibility of blankets and pillows being made up as though someone were present in an assigned cell while, in fact, he or she was elsewhere. Selection D might have some merit, but facility-wide cell searches conducted in this manner are tantamount to harassment, particularly if reasonable suspicion, for whatever the case, is nonexistent.

29. **C** While selections B and D are, of course, commendable qualities, both would actually be a deterrent to an officer working within a correctional environment. Such behavior is viewed with contempt, not to mention weakness, by most inmates. An officer who makes a regular effort of being nice toward inmates unintentionally sets himself up to be a future target of manipulation. There is no use riding roughshod over inmates either, as implied by selection A, because there is enough tension in a prison setting to begin with.

30. **A** It is imperative that all supervisory directives are followed *unless* they pose an obvious safety risk to either inmates or staff. In this case, the procedure should be carried out, but Officer Jenkins should make his concerns known to his superior officer; remaining mute over such a matter, as suggested in selection C, would only foster frustration. Both selections B and D would constitute justifiable grounds for getting Officer Jenkins fired.

31. **B** The forensics specialist is considered to be an expert witness who gives an opinion on matters he or she is qualified to testify about by virtue of his or her knowledge, special skill, or other abilities.

32. **D** The shank recovered can be considered real or physical evidence.

33. **C** Since the witness in question was not aware of the murder and simply corroborated the fact that the defendant was seen fleeing the scene of the crime, the evidence can be considered circumstantial, in that it indirectly ties the defendant to the murder. Selection A would be more in line if the witness involved actually saw the murder take place.

34. **A** Mr. Adams murdered Ms. Wilson during a rape attempt. Accordingly, Mr. Adams should be charged with first-degree murder, which is a Class A felony.

35. **C** Mr. Matthews's actions would be considered reckless, especially with alcohol involved. Ms. Cummings's death should be treated as first-degree manslaughter. Selection D is incorrect because no act committed by anyone in a state of intoxication is deemed less criminal as a result of his or her condition.

36. **D** Specifically, inmate Comstock should be charged with first-degree manslaughter, a Class B felony.

37. **C** Ms. Compton has committed second-degree extortion, a Class C felony.

38. **D** Even though Mr. Russell had implied the threat of physical harm to either the witness or his wife, it cannot be classified as either bribery or extortion because he did not ask to receive anything in the way of property or services. This is more along the lines of malicious harassment, which was not discussed in the narrative.

39. **A** Since Ms. Waterhouse stood to gain a favor from a public servant because of the threat, she could be prosecuted for bribery.

40. **B** Under the circumstances, Mr. Evans can be prosecuted for first-degree extortion, which carries a maximum sentence of ten years in prison.

41.   *C*   Inmate #670 (i.e., Lomax) received two days off instead of just one day, as the other inmates were shown to have been granted.

42.   *D*   Only inmate #463 (Barker) had scheduled GED studies.

43.   *C*   Both inmates #670 (Lomax) and #372 (Jankowski) were designated as being responsible for visitor area cleanup.

44.   *B*   Barker (inmate #463) was scheduled for four hours of kitchen cleanup duty during the week. Everyone else was scheduled either two or three hours per week to do the same.

45.   *B*   Peyton (inmate #718) had such responsibility on Wednesday afternoons. Bonner, on the other hand, cannot be considered because his duty fell on a Saturday instead of a weekday.

46.   *A*   Inmate #718 (Peyton) was assigned some form of cleanup duty every day of the week, including some double shifting on Tuesdays and Wednesdays, with the exception of Monday, which was his assigned day off.

47.   *C*   Jankowski was only scheduled to be a library assistant on Thursdays. Barker was scheduled to do laundry duty on Thursday afternoons. Voight was scheduled for eight hours of shop class, but only on Mondays and Fridays for four hours, respectively.

48.   *D*   All directives from higher level personnel should be followed regardless of potential inconvenience or perceptions of how well they will be received by inmates in general. Constructive feedback in the form of suggestions to an immediate superior would be an appropriate method of expressing one's concerns. However, demonstrating any misgivings about procedural changes among inmates is a sure invitation to future problems. If inmates perceive division within the ranks, you can be assured they will attempt to exploit the situation for personal gain.

49.   *B*   It can be presupposed for the question that homosexual relations in a prison setting are, in fact, an infraction of established regulations. Selection B best surmises the chain of events that should follow. Selection A would be tantamount to condoning future fights and/or survival-of-the-fittest mentality. Selection C, on the other hand, is too extreme for such an incident; that form of disciplinary action is usually reserved for prisoners that commit serious infractions such as possession of weapons, illegal drugs, etc. Choice D would accomplish very little.

50.   *A*   All rules should be equally applied and enforced—*no exceptions.* Anything less would be considered either harassment or favoritism, both of which are a prelude to inmate tension and contempt for authority.

51.   *C*   All other selections do not address the immediate concerns for a potential escape attempt. If necessary, reports can be filed at a later time.

52.   *C*   Shouting or harsh words used to control such a situation would only escalate tensions and increase the chance of physical violence to occur. Selections B and D, in the immediate sense, would allow inmates too much autonomy. In all likelihood, the fight would occur anyway and someone would inevitably get hurt.

53.   *C*   Despite the appearance of extenuating circumstances, visitor policy must be followed without exception.

54.   *D*   All money, regardless of its later disposition, is logged on a receipt book. Typically, anything over $100 requires two parties to verify the count. Such measures preclude the possibility of mishandling inmate property and consequent embarrassment to the department, not to mention potential civil liability.

55.   *A*   76153 accurately represents the key word *trade.*

56. *B*   816183 accurately represents the key word *garage.*

57. *B*   7031736 accurately represents the key word *theater.*

58. *D*   The first six numbers of selection D have been correctly coded. All other selections have fewer first numbers accurately transposed.

59. *D*   214112 and 244112 both translate into the code word *jailer.*

60. *B*   6833424 translates into the code word *convict.*

61. *C*   RSTUVWX or 2145345

62. *C*   Four errors are given:
AJMOBCL should be (4 or 1), 2, 5, 8, 3, (2 or 6)
MQABHGJ should be 5, 8, (4 or 1), 3, 2, 3, 2
FWYLO should be 8, 4, 6, 1, 8
BYZAIWX should be 3, 6, 8, (4 or 1), 4, 4, 5

63. *B*   SMITH: First five letters of last name
J: First letter of first name
D: First letter of middle name
100 − 56 = 44: Birth year calculation
9: Check digit (could be any single number)
P: Month of birth
Z: Day of birth

64. *A*   HALVO: First five letters of last name
J: First letter of first name
L: First letter of middle name
100 − 75 = 25: Birth year calculation
1: Check digit (could be any single number)
H: Month of birth
P: Day of birth

65. *D*   BARTE: First five letters of last name
V: First letter of first name
J: First letter of middle name
100 − 63 = 37: Birth year calculation
8: Check digit (could be any single number)
L: Month of birth
4: Day of birth

66. *C*   Discipline

67. *A*   Miscellaneous

68. *D*   Procedure

69. *C*   Plaintiff

70. *A*   Believe

71. *B*   Realize

72. *B*   Lieutenant

73. *B*   Repetitious

74. *C*   Wisecracking

75. *D*   Disclose

76. *A*   Displacement

77. *C*   Disorder

78. *A*   Disdain

79. *D*   Intimidation

80. *D*   Purported

81. *B*   Word for word

82. *C*   Expert

83. *A*   Vague

84. *C*   The words *for example* are nonrestrictive modifiers that should be preceded and followed by commas.

85. *A*   When the relative or interrogative pronoun is the subject of the verb, the nominative form *who* is used, not *whom,* even when the subject is separated from its verb by other words.

86. *B*   *Proceedure* is misspelled. It should be spelled *procedure.*

87. *C*   *Uniform Crime Reports* is a proper noun, requiring capitalization.

88. *C*   The independent clause *he was immediately disqualified* should have been preceded by a comma.

89. *D*   Grammatically correct

90. *B*   *Commited* is misspelled. It should be spelled *committed.*

91. *A*   The antecedent, *officers*, fails to agree with the pronoun *you*. It would be correctly written by using *they* in place of *you*.

92. *B*   The word *insure* is an inappropriate homonym that means "to guarantee against loss or harm." *Ensure* means "to secure or guarantee." This is a subtle kind of misspelling that many people tend to overlook.

93. *A*   The sentence contains a misplaced participial phrase. A better way to say the same thing is, "Containing a glove, pouch, handcuff case, mace holder, and penholder, an officer's belt stores much more than a gun."

94. *B*   According to the flow chart presented, only the U.S. Supreme Court can review a state Supreme Court decision.

95. *A*   Juvenile Court can appeal either directly to a trial court or to an intermediate Appellate Court.

96. *D*   Selection A refers to Bankruptcy Court. Selection C refers to the U.S. Court of Appeals, the federal Circuit Court of Appeals, and the state Supreme Court.

97. *B*   Native Americans demonstrated an educational level of 7th grade and under.

98. *C*   The median age for the Asian American inmate population was shown to be 35–40 years.

99. *D*   Caucasians were shown to have a median education level of high-school graduation. However, the key word to pay attention to is *median*. That indicates that there are some offenders that had post-secondary education, but that is equally offset by some that dropped out of high school prior to graduation. Some, but not most, Caucasians had college-level training.

100. *A*   From the data provided, it is impossible to draw conclusions about specific ethnic inmate populations. Only the median age and median educational levels of those admitted into prison were given.

101. *D*   Largest group — Conditional release (60%)
Second largest group — Unconditional release (23%)
Third largest group — Jurisdictional transfer (8%)

102.　*B*　2% (AWOL or escapees) + 6% (Posted bond or on appeal) = 8% of total given

103.　*B*　60% (Conditional release) + 23% (Unconditional release) + 6% (Posted bond or on appeal) = 89% of total given

104.　*A*　A. Murder/manslaughter: 1,293 - 1,015 = 278 additional cases

$$\frac{278 \text{ additional cases}}{1,015 \text{ reference caseload}} \times 100 = 27.39\% \text{ increase}$$

B. Forcible rape: 1,107 − 983 = 124 additional cases

$$\frac{124 \text{ additional cases}}{983 \text{ reference caseload}} \times 100 = 12.6\% \text{ increase}$$

C. Larceny: 35,803 − 29,601 = 6,202 additional cases

$$\frac{6,202 \text{ additional cases}}{29,601 \text{ reference caseload}} \times 100 = 20.95\% \text{ increase}$$

D. Aggravated assault: 23,752 − 18,900 = 4,852 additional cases

$$\frac{4,852 \text{ additional cases}}{18,900 \text{ reference caseload}} \times 100 = 25.67\% \text{ increase}$$

105.　*C*　From the most recent figures (1990), men committed 15,906 homicides, while women committed 6,953, which when divided (i.e., 15,906 divided by 6,953) reflects a 2.29:1 relationship.

106.　*B*　There were 44,919 crimes committed by female juveniles in 1990. 1,349 of those cases constituted motor vehicle theft. To determine the annual caseload percentage for this crime, we simply divide 1,349 by 44,919 and then multiple the quotient by 100. The answer is 3%.

107.　*A*　Adult male

A.　49,192 − 46,702 = 2,490

$$\frac{2,490}{49,192} \times 100 = 5\% \text{ decrease in robbery cases for adult males}$$

B.　2,950 − 2,893 = 57

$$\frac{57}{2,950} \times 100 = 2\% \text{ decrease in robbery cases for juvenile males}$$

C.　23,471 − 23,405 = 66

$$\frac{66}{23,471} \times 100 = .3\% \text{ decrease in robbery cases for adult females}$$

D.　2,740 − 2,090 = 650

$$\frac{650}{2,090} \times 100 = 31\% \text{ increase in robbery cases for juvenile females}$$

108. *B* This question simply requires a direct proportion:

$$\frac{5 \text{ gallons}}{30 \text{ gallons}} = \frac{115 \text{ miles}}{X \text{ miles}}$$

Therefore,

$$5X = 3,450$$
$$X = 690 \text{ miles}$$

109. *D* This is basically a two-part question involving an inverse proportion. First, it must be determined how many inmates are in the overcrowded correctional facility: 1.40 (i.e., 140%) × 140 (facility capacity) = 336 inmates. The second step involves setting up an inverse proportion to determine the solution. (It is an inverse rather than a direct proportion because the more inmates incarcerated, the shorter the time that provisions will last.) Therefore,

$$\frac{336 \text{ inmates}}{240 \text{ inmates}} = \frac{14 \text{ days}}{X \text{ days}}$$

Therefore,

$$336X = 3,360$$
$$X = 10 \text{ days}$$

110. *B* Since the widest extent of a circle is its diameter (i.e., radius × 2), that would represent the minimum width required to sufficiently cover the area described. Therefore, a 13-foot square tarp would suffice.

111. *C* We realize that the faster someone drives to a given destination, the shorter the time it will require to get there. Therefore, an inverse proportion is needed to solve the problem.

$$\frac{45 \text{ minutes}}{X \text{ minutes}} = \frac{35 \text{ mph}}{30 \text{ mph}}$$

Therefore,

$$35X = 1,350$$
$$X = 38.57 \text{ minutes}$$

112. *C* When determining the average of test scores for an applicant, it is necessary to add all test scores together and divide by the number of tests taken. Therefore, if we know what were the four previous test scores and the desired overall average, we can find the percent required for the last exam:

$$\frac{80\% + 82\% + 90\% + 87\% + X}{5} = 87\%$$

$$\frac{3.39 + X\%}{5} = 0.87$$

Therefore,

$$3.39 + X\% = 4.35$$
$$X\% = 0.96; X = 96\%$$

113. *A* The square footage of a rectangular area is found by multiplying its length by its width. In this case, 47.5 ft. × 13.2 ft. = 627 square feet.

114. *C* The narrative described Mr. Hall as being Caucasian.

115. *D*   Selection A is in error due to an incorrect number. Mr. Hall's Social Security number was stated toward the end of the reading as being 555-22-0557.

116. *D*   Lt. Pete Kendrick was the arresting officer in question. His name is not required on the fingerprint processing report.

117. *A*   John Cornwall is the officer in charge of booking and intake.

118. *D*   The reading stipulated that Mr. Hall was charged with aggravated assault of an officer (NCIC Code 13501-A) and resisting arrest (NCIC Code 13721-B).

119. *A*   Boxes 29 and 30

120. *C*   Lt. Pete Kendrick was the arresting officer of concern. It was stated in the first part of the narrative that he worked for the State Patrol. Selection A was never mentioned.

121. *C*   Lakeview Police Officer Harry M. Stevens (badge 503) had custodial responsibility of transporting Mr. Hall to Lewis County Detention for booking and intake. Selection B is incorrect because the respective information is reversed.

122. *A*   The reading stated that Mr. Hall was processed in Lewis County Detention on the same day that he was arrested, which in this case was November 13, 1996. He was actually received for processing at 9:37 A.M., or 0937 hours.

123. *C*   *Jeff T. Beaumont* was an alias used by Mr. Hall to deceive authorities.

124. *D*   All selections represent accurate information.

125. *D*   Mr. Hall's case file reference number was given toward the end of the narrative as being 26-07A, not 26-07B as provided by selection C.

TEST RATINGS ARE AS FOLLOWS:

120–125 correct — Excellent
113–119 correct — Very good
106–112 correct — Good
100–105 correct — Fair
99 or fewer correct — Unsatisfactory

Go back to each question you missed and determine if the question was just misinterpreted for one reason or another, or if your response reflects a weakness in subject matter. If it is a matter of misinterpretation, try reading the question slower while paying particular attention to key words such as *not, least, except* or *without.* If, on the other hand, you determine a weakness in a certain area, do not despair, because that is what this study guide is for: to identify any area of weakness before you take the actual exam. Reread the material on the area of concern in this study guide. If you still feel a need for supplemental material, your local library is an excellent source.

Chapter 9

Practice Exam 2

The time allowed for the entire examination is two and a half hours. Each question has four answers, lettered A, B, C and D. Choose the best answer and then, on the answer sheet provided on pages 271–272 (which you can remove from the study guide), find the corresponding question number and darken the circle corresponding to the answer you have selected.

Assume that you are a Detention Officer working for the local county jail. At the beginning of working the weekend swing shift, your immediate supervisor tells you that you will have custodial responsibility of six people who were booked earlier in the morning. Before starting your rounds, you have been given exactly twenty minutes to glance over the individual case files to gain some familiarity with the inmates in question. Study the information provided below while making sure not to exceed the time specified. Then proceed to answer questions 1–15 without making further reference to the material just looked over.

Case file: J-30

Name: Howard K. Stevens

DOB: September 22, 1978

Height: 5'11"

Weight: 165 pounds

Hair: Brown

Eyes: Green

Race: Caucasian

Sex: Male

Offense(s) charged: Operation of a motor vehicle under the influence of a controlled substance

Cell assignment: A Wing, number 11

Case file: N-04

Name: Christy R. Ballard

DOB: January 14, 1972

Height: 5'6"

Weight: 185 pounds

Hair: Red

Eyes: Brown

Race: African American

Sex: Female

Offense(s) charged: Second-degree assault and extortion

Cell assignment: B Wing, number 5

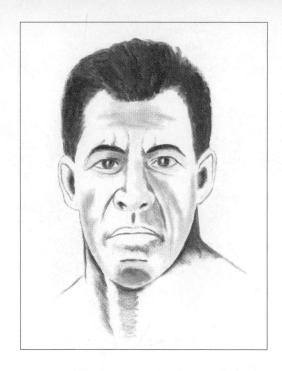

Case file:	K-72
Name:	Mark P. Elroy
DOB:	December 5, 1970
Height:	6'3"
Weight:	260 pounds
Hair:	Black
Eyes:	Hazel
Race:	Caucasian
Sex:	Male
Offense(s) charged:	Involuntary manslaughter and operation of a motor vehicle while under the influence of alcohol
Cell assignment:	A Wing, number 13

Case file:	L-07
Name:	Lisa G. Potter
DOB:	March 25, 1972
Height:	5'3"
Weight:	115 pounds
Hair:	Black
Eyes:	Green
Race:	African American
Sex:	Female
Offense(s) charged:	First-degree assault of an officer
Cell assignment:	B Wing, number 13

Case file: A-17

Name: Brian L. Thompson

DOB: July 17, 1975

Height: 6'

Weight: 215 pounds

Hair: Brown

Eyes: Brown

Race: Caucasian

Sex: Male

Offense(s) charged: Second-degree child molestation and communicating with a minor for immoral purposes

Cell assignment: C Wing, number 02

Case file:	H-18
Name:	Walter B. Phelps
DOB:	December 17, 1965
Height:	6'5"
Weight:	250 pounds
Hair:	Black
Eyes:	Brown
Race:	African American
Sex:	Male
Offense(s) charged:	First-degree murder, possession of an unlawful weapon, and resisting arrest
Cell assignment:	A Wing, number 08

Answer questions 1–15 on the basis of the case files just studied. *Do not refer back to the information given.*

1. What was Mr. Elroy specifically incarcerated for?

   A. First-degree manslaughter

   B. Extortion and first-degree assault

   C. Operation of a motor vehicle while under the influence of alcohol and involuntary manslaughter

   D. Second-degree assault of an officer

2. What did Ms. Ballard's file indicate that her height and weight were, respectively?

   A. 5'3" and 185 pounds

   B. 5'6" and 115 pounds

   C. 5'6" and 185 pounds

   D. 5'4" and 110 pounds

3. *Case file number A-17* pertains to whom?

   A. Brian Elroy

   B. Christy Potter

   C. Howard Stevens

   D. Brian Thompson

4. Case file number K-72 received which of the following cell assignments?

   A. A Wing, number 13

   B. C Wing, number 13

   C. B Wing, number 5

   D. None of the above

5. Which of the dates given below represent Walter Phelps's date of birth?

   A. 6-17-75

   B. 3-25-71

   C. 1-14-72

   D. 12-17-65

6. Select from the following composite sketches that which pertains to case file number N-04.

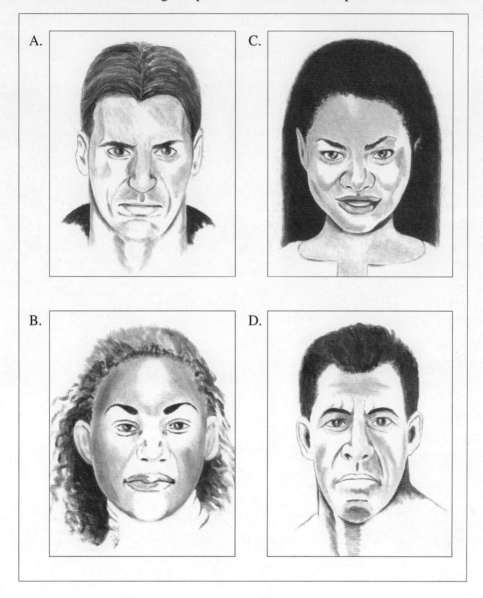

A. A

B. B

C. C

D. D

7. Which of the following composite sketches is representative of the individual who was charged with second-degree child molestation and communicating with a minor for immoral purposes?

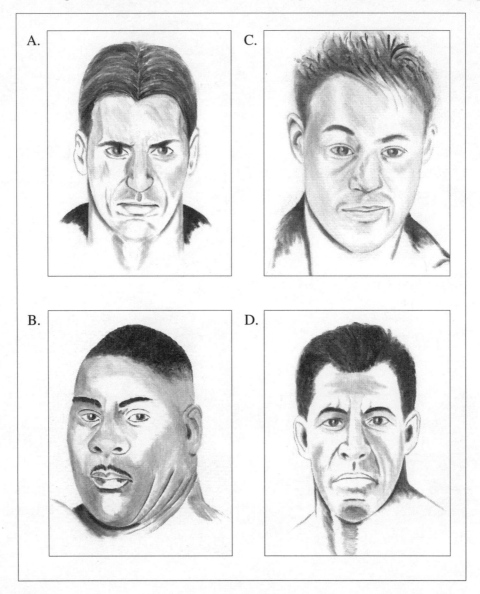

A. A

B. B

C. C

D. D

8. The following individual pictured received which of the following cell assignments?

   A. A Wing, number 13

   B. B Wing, number 4

   C. B Wing, number 13

   D. B Wing, number 8

9. Which of the following individuals shown was described as being 6'5" tall and weighing 250 pounds?

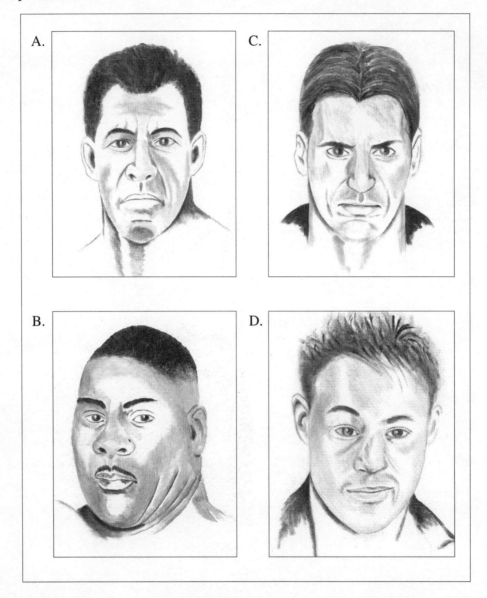

A. A

B. B

C. C

D. D

10. Howard K. Stevens has which of the following assigned case file numbers?

A. J-30

B. A-17

C. H-18

D. K-72

11. Which of the following composite sketches is representative of the individual who was charged with first-degree assault of an officer?

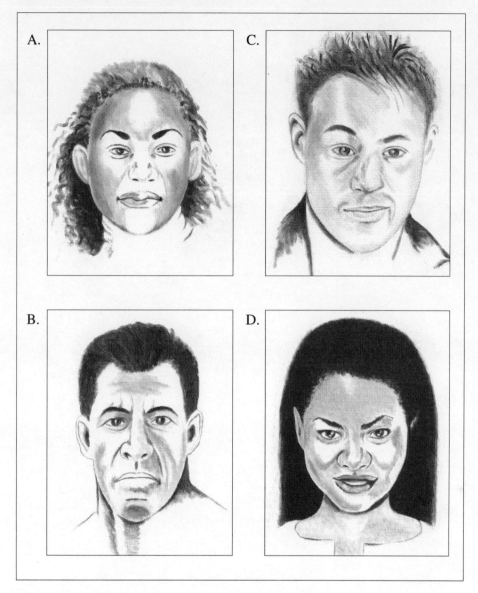

A. A

B. B

C. C

D. D

12. Which of the following individuals, according to the case files provided, was born on December 5, 1970?

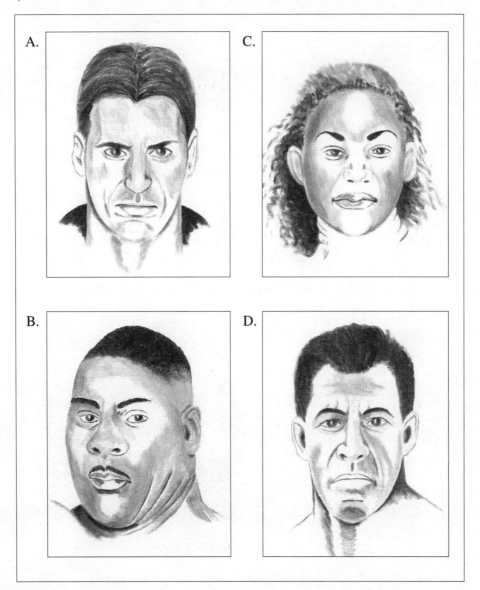

A. A

B. B

C. C

D. D

13. All of the following case files numbers pertained to individuals described as being Caucasian except?

A. K-72

B. J-30

C. L-07

D. A-17

14. The individual depicted in the following sketch was charged with which of the following offenses?

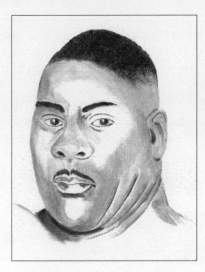

    A. Operation of a motor vehicle under the influence of a controlled substance

    B. First-degree murder, possession of an unlawful weapon, and resisting arrest

    C. Second-degree assault and extortion

    D. Involuntary manslaughter

15. Who was the only individual described in the case files provided as having hazel-colored eyes?

    A. Mark P. Elroy

    B. Christy R. Ballard

    C. Lisa G. Potter

    D. Brian L. Thompson

On March 3, 1995, Corrections Officers Jim Blaine, badge number 12, and Kevin Holt, badge number 17, were transporting three medium-security-risk inmates from Dover State Prison to Compton Superior Court for various arraignment hearings. Halfway to their destination, one of the inmates managed to overwhelm Officer Holt and confiscated his service revolver to effect their escape. Neither of the officers was hurt during the incident, and local law enforcement was immediately notified of the escape. Transportation officers provided the police with the following descriptions to aid in the follow-up search.

Study the details shared with local law enforcement agencies for fifteen minutes, including the events that led up to the incident. Then proceed to answer questions 16–25 without making further reference to the information just studied.

Leonard P. Schmidt

Inmate # A-215

Caucasian male

5'10"

Approximately 150 pounds

Black hair

Brown eyes

C-shaped scar near right eye

39 years of age

Serving 12–20 years for armed robbery and first-degree assault

Andrea L. Haynes

Inmate # C-015

African American female

5'4"

Approximately 125 pounds

Black hair

Green eyes

U-shaped scar on right cheek

31 years of age

Serving 5–10 years for possession of a controlled substances with the intent to deliver

Richard B. Lathrop

Inmate # A-171

African American male

5'6"

Approximately 140 pounds

Brown hair

Hazel eyes

Pronounced acne scars on both cheeks

42 years of age

Serving 13–18 years for first-degree arson and grand theft

16. Which of the composite sketches provided below is representative of the inmate serving 12–20 years for armed robbery and first-degree assault?

A.    B. 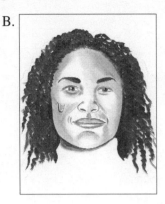   C.

A. A

B. B

C. C

D. None of the above

17. Which of the following numbers given correctly identifies Corrections Officer Kevin Holt?

A. Badge number A-17

B. Badge number C-12

C. Badge number B-11

D. Badge number 17

18. Which of the following composite sketches provided is representative of the inmate serving 13–18 years for possession of a controlled substance with the intent to deliver?

A. 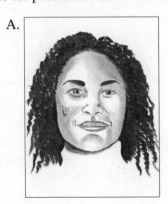   B.    C.

A. A

B. B

C. C

D. None of the above

19. The individual pictured to the right was stated as being how old?

    A. 22 years of age

    B. 31 years of age

    C. 39 years of age

    D. 52 years of age

20. The intended destination of the prison escort was given to be which of the following?

    A. Dover State Prison

    B. Compton Superior Court

    C. Comstock District Court

    D. Dover Adult Detention

21. Which of the inmates was described as weighing approximately 150 pounds?

    A. Inmate number A-711

    B. Inmate number C-015

    C. Inmate number A-215

    D. None of the above

22. Which of the following inmates did not have black hair?

    A.    B.    C.

    A. A

    B. B

    C. C

    D. All of the inmates were described as having black hair.

23. Without taking the aspect of escape into consideration, the prisoners were originally designated as being which of the following?

    A. Medium security risk

    B. Low security risk

    C. High security risk

    D. None of the above

24. The inmate to the right was described as having what color eyes?

   A. Blue

   B. Brown

   C. Green

   D. Hazel

25. Inmate number A-215 was described as being how tall?

   A. 5'7"

   B. 5'9"

   C. 5'10"

   D. 6'2"

Most states have adopted some form of sentencing guidelines to fairly administer sentence ranges for various offenses committed. Too many times in the past, similar offenses drew inconsistent penalties that some viewed as having to do with one's ethnicity, religious beliefs, economic background, etc. The implementation of such guidelines is intended to eliminate the prospect of arbitrary penalty decisions and provide a standard by which all crimes can be fairly assessed.

Following are hypothetical ratings and guidelines applied toward various offenses. Glance through the format provided to answer questions 26–29.

Crime Severity Ratings

A	B	C	D	E
First-degree murder	Second-degree murder	Involuntary manslaughter	First-degree assault	Second-degree malicious mischief
Kidnapping	First-degree arson	Vehicular homicide	First-degree malicious mischief	Indecent liberties
First-degree rape	Manufacture of a controlled substance with intent to deliver	Bribery	Possession of stolen property	Second-degree assault
Racketeering		Extortion	Unlawful possession of a firearm	Possession of a controlled substance
Homicide by abuse	Second-degree rape	Unlawful imprisonment	Motor vehicle theft	Malicious harassment
First-degree robbery	First-degree burglary	Second-degree arson	Prostitution	Second-degree assault
	Second-degree robbery	Second-degree burglary	Forgery	

Offense assessment ratings are determined by using the following equation. Insert all information applicable to the criminal in question and multiply each consideration by the factor given. The sum of the resulting products amounts to a Preliminary Offense Assessment rating (i.e., P.O.A.). After adjustments (if any) are made for the aggravated or mitigating circumstances mentioned, a final offense assessment rating can be determined. This figure, in conjunction with a crime severity rating, can then be used by the court to determine a fair and equitable penalty in accordance with established sentencing guidelines.

Offense Assessment Ratings Formula

Number of misdemeanor convictions   _____ × 0.5 = (_____) (+)

Number of previous violent felony convictions   _____ × 2.0 = (_____) (+)

Number of previous nonviolent felony convictions   _____ × 1.0 = (_____) (+)

Number of current convictions   _____ × 1.0 = (_____) (+)

(Subtotal and round up to the nearest whole number)

(Note: Juvenile history does not have relevance   P.O.A. (_____) (=)
in preliminary offense assessment ratings.)

If the offender utilized a firearm in the commission of the crime specified—add 2 points

If the offender was, at the time of the offense, on community-placement time—add 1 point

If the offender committed the crime on correctional facility property—add 1 point

Final offense assessment rating (_____)

Sentencing Guidelines

Severity Ratings		A	B	C	D	E
	1	25 yrs 6 mos	7 yrs 4 mos	6 yrs 3 mos	3 mos	30 days
	2	27 yrs 6 mos	9 yrs 4 mos	6 yrs 6 mos	6 mos	45 days
Offense	3	31 yrs 6 mos	11 yrs 4 mos	7 yrs 4 mos	1 yr 6 mos	2 mos
Assessment	4	35 yrs 6 mos	13 yrs 4 mos	8 yrs 4 mos	2 yrs 3 mos	3 mos
	5	39 yrs 6 mos	15 yrs 6 mos	9 yrs 4 mos	2 yrs 8 mos	6 mos
	6	44 yrs 6 mos	17 yrs 4 mos	10 yrs 6 mos	3 yrs 6 mos	1 yr
	7	49 yrs 6 mos	19 yrs 6 mos	11 yrs 6 mos	4 yrs 3 mos	1 yr 6 mos
	8	55 yrs–Life	20 yrs 4 mos	12 yrs 3 mos	5 yrs	2 yrs

26. Pete Millhouse has three misdemeanor convictions of third-degree assault, stemming from a failed marriage, and two previous violent felonies, including second-degree rape and unlawful imprisonment. He was just convicted of second-degree murder. According to sentencing guidelines, inmate Millhouse can expect to serve how much time?

    A. 11 years and 4 months

    B. 19 years and 6 months

    C. 49 years and 6 months

    D. 55 years to life

27. Bill Compton has two previous violent convictions of second-degree robbery as a juvenile, and a current conviction as an adult for first-degree robbery involving the use of a firearm. According to sentencing guidelines, inmate Compton can expect to serve how much time?

    A. 55 years to life

    B. 31 years and 6 months

    C. 25 years and 6 months

    D. 11 years and 4 months

28. Brenda Clark has four earlier misdemeanor convictions for possession of a controlled substance and two prior nonviolent felony convictions of possession of stolen property. She was just convicted of manufacturing of a controlled substance with the intent to deliver. According to sentencing guidelines, inmate Clark can expect to serve how much time?

    A. 7 years and 4 months

    B. 9 years and 4 months

    C. 13 years and 4 months

    D. 15 years and 6 months

29. Inmate James Nichols has a prior record of two violent felonies, including kidnapping and first-degree robbery. He was just convicted of second-degree murder for killing a fellow inmate after an argument in the prison recreation room. Inmate Nichols can expect to serve how much additional time according to the sentencing guidelines?

    A. 7 years and 4 months

    B. 9 years and 4 months

    C. 15 years and 6 months

    D. 17 years and 4 months

Monitoring prisoner movement within correctional facilities is a regular task Corrections Officers undertake. This is particularly important when prisoners move from any given cell block to another part of the prison. Regular tabulation of head counts are forwarded to a central control room and can be checked against records kept of total inmate populations, including new admissions and releases. In the event of a count discrepancy, recounts are immediately taken for verification. From the standpoint of security maintenance, it is obviously imperative that inmate counts be done correctly.

Study the following schedule and answer questions 30–34 on the basis of the information provided.

STATUS (IN / OUT)		Initial Inmate Count at 6:00 A.M.	10:30 A.M. Count	Noon Count	3:00 P.M. Count	Final Count Prior to Lockdown
Admissions into Facility		0	8	0	3	0
Jurisdictional Transfers Out of Facility		0	5	1	2	0
Releases		0	1	0	1	0
Wing I	IN	37	6	13	14	28
	OUT	0	33	18	12	0
Wing II	IN	45	17	1	16	35
	OUT	0	44	2	23	0
Medical Appointments Outside of Facility	IN	0	0	0	0	0
	OUT	0	2	0	0	0
Medical Appointments In-House Sick Calls	IN	9	0	1	2	5
	OUT	0	6	2	2	0
Recreation Room	IN	0	22	4	12	13
	OUT	0	6	19	7	19
Exercise Yard	IN	0	18	3	35	13
	OUT	0	0	16	5	48
Visitor Room	IN	0	10	8	12	2
	OUT	0	9	5	2	16
Cafeteria	IN	0	4	43	0	0
	OUT	0	1	3	40	2
Judicial Hearings Off-Premises	IN	0	0	0	5	0
	OUT	0	7	0	0	0
Library	IN	0	15	4	10	0
	OUT	0	0	13	5	11

30. What was the total inmate population according to the 10:30 A.M. count?

    A. 91

    B. 87

    C. 84

    D. 79

31. How many inmates were in Wing II during the 3:00 P.M. count?

    A. 10 inmates

    B. 23 inmates

    C. 33 inmates

    D. 44 inmates

32. Which of the following areas had the fewest number of inmates present and accounted for during the noontime count?

    A. Recreation room

    B. Exercise yard

    C. Visitor room

    D. Library

33. According to the schedule shown, approximately what percentage of inmates returned the same day from judicial hearings?

    A. 62%

    B. 71%

    C. 75%

    D. 81%

34. According to the final count, how many inmates were admitted into the prison's infirmary for at least an overnight stay?

    A. 4 inmates

    B. 5 inmates

    C. 6 inmates

    D. 7 inmates

Answer questions 35–37 on the basis of the following reading:

According to Webster's dictionary, *duress* is defined as

> *(1) compulsion by threat or force; coercion. (2) constraint or coercion of a degree sufficient to void any legal agreement entered into or any act performed under its influence. (3) forcible restraint, especially imprisonment.*

In other words, *duress* implies that an individual is not acting of his or her free will. Specifically, under duress, someone may act wrongfully without criminal intent. However, whoever dictates the wrongful behavior of another by duress is responsible for the criminal intent.

Therefore, someone who commits a crime under a threat against his or her person will not be held accountable for the criminal act (murder being the exception). In the courts' view of the matter, the conduct of the person actually committing the crime is justifiable under such circumstances. However, once the threat ceases to exist, any further acts contributing to the commission of a crime can no longer be justifiable. The courts further point out that the threat perceived by anyone forced into conducting criminal activity must be in the present, not the future. The prospect of the threat of force being carried out at some future time if the individual in question doesn't cooperate is not reason enough for criminal behavior to continue. Any criminal act under such circumstances is committed with intent and is therefore subject to prosecution.

35. What would be an appropriate title for this passage?

    A. The complete definition of *duress* according to *Webster's*

    B. Duress: the perfect defense

    C. The definition and legal parameters of duress

    D. Duress: a synonym for criminal immunity

36. A person can commit most forms of criminal activity under duress without being guilty *except*:

    A. Robbery

    B. Burglary

    C. Libel

    D. Murder

37. Inmate Fred Wilson was approached by two members of the "Convict Brotherhood" and told, in no uncertain terms, that if he did not severely rough up a suspected "snitch" in his cell block, he, himself, would be subjected to the same treatment at a later time. The Convict Brotherhood was known to Fred as a group that was very capable of carrying out such threats. Assuming that inmate Wilson carries out its request by assaulting the person in question and the entire scheme of events becomes known to the authorities, it would be considered that

    A. Inmate Wilson would not be viewed by the courts as acting under duress.

    B. Inmate Wilson was, indeed, acting under duress and would be exempt from prosecution for first-degree assault.

    C. Inmate Wilson did not murder the person in question; therefore, the use of duress as a defense would be legitimate.

    D. None of the above

Answer questions 38–40 on the basis of the following narrative.

Robbery, by definition, is not a crime against property; rather, it is considered a crime against a person. If someone illegally takes the property of another by means of force or the threat of force, the law prescribes that a robbery has been committed. On the other hand, if property of some value is stolen from a person directly and the aspect of force is absent in the crime, the incident is then considered larceny. Whether it is petty or grand larceny is dependent upon the value of the property stolen.

This definition by itself may seem fairly straightforward. However, several factors need to be taken into consideration when determining if, indeed, a robbery did take place or if, instead, the crime was larceny. If intimidation such as libel, extortion, or blackmail precludes the use of force and is used to obtain property from another person, this is not considered robbery. Additionally, if an individual is unaware that property is being stolen from his or her person because he or she is either inattentive or unconscious, the action constitutes larceny, not robbery.

Finally, the use of force must be preliminary in the commission of the theft for it to be considered a robbery. If force takes place after the perpetrator has committed the crime, it cannot be considered a robbery. Both the timing and circumstances of a theft can make a crucial difference in how that crime will be charged according to common law.

38. All of the following were mentioned in the reading as forms of intimidation that preclude the use of force *except*:

    A. Extortion

    B. Bribery

    C. Libel

    D. Blackmail

39. Having spent most of his life behind bars, Ben Harris was no stranger to violence. One evening, after visiting a corner grocery store, Mr. Harris was confronted by two juveniles who demanded his wallet. Rather than risk the potential of one of the offenders producing a weapon, Mr. Harris complied with their demands. A minute later, however, Mr. Harris decided he had all he was going to take. He pursued the two offenders and a fistfight quickly ensued. Mr. Harris was beaten badly and required immediate medical attention. In this case, what should the two juveniles be charged with?

    A. Larceny, because the aspect of force was not a precondition to Mr. Harris handing over his wallet.

    B. Robbery, because the two juveniles had an altercation with Mr. Harris in connection with the theft of the wallet.

    C. Larceny, because the two offenders were juveniles.

    D. Robbery, because Mr. Harris thought that one or both of the juveniles may have been armed.

40. Corrections Officer Jack Arnold was riding the bus as part of his daily routine in commuting to work. This particular Monday morning, however, a larger-than-usual crowd took the bus downtown. Officer Arnold elected to stand in the aisle to provide a seat for a mother and her infant. A few stops later, there was standing room only. This was, in Tom Bessinger's mind, the perfect opportunity to pick someone's pocket. Tom was a real pro at lifting wallets and not getting caught. The stop-and-go action of the bus allowed Mr. Bessinger to "accidentally" bump into his victim (in this case, Officer Arnold) and create the minor distraction needed to pick the wallet. Consequently, it was only when Officer Arnold went to lunch that he discovered his wallet was missing. In this case, it can be said that Tom Bessinger committed

    A. Robbery, because his bumping into the victim constitutes force.

    B. Larceny, because the victim was totally unaware of the theft.

    C. Robbery, because cash and credit cards were taken from the person of another.

    D. No crime was committed because Mr. Arnold didn't report the incident to the authorities.

Following are hypothetical codes established by a statute law committee to address various prisoner infractions. Each code has three parts: a title, a chapter, and a section, in that order. Review each of these before proceeding with questions 41–50.

RCO 57.41.089 concerns the refusal to obey any lawful order issued by correctional staff.

RCO 41.57.011 concerns any unexcused absences from work detail.

RCO 16.92.705 concerns smoking in prohibited areas.

RCO 13.62.895 concerns any form of bribery used toward correctional staff for the intended gain of unauthorized services or favors.

RCO 17.05.669 concerns aiding and abetting another inmate to commit an infraction of established rules.

RCO 14.64.142 concerns the manufacture of controlled substances, intoxicants, or narcotics on facility premises.

CORRECTIONS OFFICER EXAM PREPARATION BOOK

RCO 09.59.041 concerns willful misrepresentation of facts with the intention of falsely impli-
cating another inmate.

RCO 71.83.611 concerns abusive language directed toward correctional staff.

RCO 18.60.807 concerns refusal to submit to medically supervised urinalysis or blood tests.

RCO 71.50.888 concerns attempted escape.

RCO 97.42.123 concerns attempted or actual assault and battery between inmates, self-defense
being the exception.

RCO 07.49.712 concerns attempted or actual assault and battery of any correctional staff or visitors by an inmate.

RCO 19.04.971 concerns inmates found to be in unauthorized areas.

RCO 01.59.017 concerns possession of any medically prescribed drugs without a doctor's pre-
scription.

RCO 06.15.777 concerns any form of gambling.

RCO 09.49.991 concerns forgery of any official document.

RCO 18.80.692 concerns the failure of an inmate to keep his or her quarters in a condition
acceptable to established regulations.

RCO 01.96.870 concerns verbal threats made between inmates.

RCO 80.86.040 concerns theft and possession of stolen property belonging to another inmate.

RCO 69.50.125 concerns the possession of any object or tool that has the obvious appearance of
being used as a potential weapon.

RCO 58.55.119 concerns riot instigation.

RCO 17.65.766 concerns arson or reckless burning of flammable material.

Note: Chapter numbers greater than 40 but less than 70 are considered to be serious prison infractions.
All other infractions are to be considered misdemeanors.

41. Inmate John Halverson was assigned to scrub the mess hall floor between 1:00 P.M. and 2:00 P.M.
However, inmate Halverson was observed by Corrections Officer McClary to be visiting with
other inmates in the TV room at 1:45 P.M. When Officer McClary clearly pointed out the violation
to inmate Halverson and ordered him to get back to his assigned detail, inmate Halverson refused
to comply and cursed him for not minding his own business. Pursuant to inmate Halverson's
immediate lockup, which of the following code infractions could be considered by an Adjustment
Committee Hearing for determining disciplinary action to be taken?

    A. Only RCO 57.41.089

    B. Only RCO 01.96.870 and RCO 57.41.089

    C. RCO 13.62.895, RCO 41.57.011, and RCO 17.05.669

    D. RCO 41.57.011, RCO 57.41.089, and RCO 71.83.611

42. "Longtimers" Jacob and Preston were playing a game of five-card stud poker for cigarettes when
inmate Preston adamantly accused his partner of bold-faced cheating. The two immediately
became embroiled in a fistfight, which was started by inmate Preston. Were it not for the timely
intervention of two floor supervisors, the injuries sustained by both inmates, in all likelihood,
would have been much worse. Pursuant to receiving medical attention and subsequent relegation
to separate isolation cells, inmate Preston could be comprehensively charged with which of the
following code infractions?

    A. RCO 17.05.669

    B. RCO 07.49.712 and RCO 06.15.777

    C. RCO 58.55.119

    D. RCO 06.15.777 and RCO 97.42.123

43. On the basis of the previous question, inmate Jacobs should be charged with which of the following code infractions?

    A. RCO 07.49.712

    B. RCO 97.42.123 and RCO 06.15.777

    C. RCO 06.15.777

    D. RCO 18.60.807 and RCO 17.05.669

44. Immediately following morning count, Officer Peterson noticed inmate Kessler walking down an aisle with an uncoordinated and unsteady gait. When Officer Peterson confronted inmate Kessler to check and see if he was all right, inmate Kessler appeared lethargic and was unresponsive to his questioning. Inmate Kessler was a known drug addict, so Officer Peterson had reasonable suspicion that he was on some sort of controlled substance apparently smuggled into the facility. When Officer Peterson ordered inmate Kessler to accompany him to the prison infirmary for medically supervised drug screening, inmate Kessler immediately became belligerent, telling him to "screw off," and then attempted to slug him. Other officers came to Officer Peterson's assistance and inmate Kessler was subdued and locked in segregation shortly thereafter. On the basis of this situation, inmate Kessler could be comprehensively charged with which of the following code infractions?

    A. RCO 01.59.017 and RCO 41.57.011

    B. RCO 57.41.089, RCO 71.83.611, RCO 07.49.712, and RCO 18.60.807

    C. RCO 09.59.041 and RCO 14.64.142

    D. RCO 18.60.807 and RCO 07.49.712

45. Inmate Matt Charles is confined to an isolation unit pending an Adjustment Committee Hearing review of his alleged infractions. He stands accused of instigating a riot in cell block B, trashing his own quarters before setting fire to his cell mate's bunk bed mattress as well as his own, and verbally threatening and assaulting three other inmates for not participating in the ensuing melee. From what has been described, which of the following selections would account for all infractions, serious as well as misdemeanor, allegedly committed by inmate Charles?

    A. RCO 58.55.119, RCO 18.80.692, RCO 01.96.870, RCO 97.42.123, and RCO 17.65.766

    B. RCO 97.42.123, RCO 01.96.870, RCO 18.80.692, RCO 80.86.040, and RCO 09.49.991

    C. RCO 17.65.766, RCO 58.55.119, RCO 01.96.870, RCO 19.04.971, and RCO 09.59.041

    D. RCO 18.80.692, RCO 71.50.888, RCO 13.62.895, RCO 16.92.705, and RCO 07.49.712

46. On the basis of the previous question, which of the alleged offenses committed by inmate Charles would be considered misdemeanor by an Adjustment Committee Hearing?

    A. Only RCO 18.80.692

    B. Both RCO 97.42.123 and RCO 58.55.119

    C. Only RCO 01.96.870

    D. Both RCO 18.80.692 and RCO 01.96.870

47. Inmate Zimmerman, a relative newcomer to Colcott Corrections, was persuaded by cell mate Branstad that if he offered $20 to Officer Winston, who was posted in the prisoner infirmary, he would "look the other way" when extra over-the-counter medication mysteriously disappeared. Inmate Zimmerman acted on the advice given by his cell mate, but instead of getting Officer Winston's anticipated cooperation, he found himself promptly put on report. Under the circumstances, Zimmerman can be charged with which of the following code infractions?

  A. RCO 17.05.669

  B. RCO 09.59.041

  C. RCO 13.62.895

  D. RCO 14.64.142

48. Referring to the previous question, which of the following code infractions, if any, would apply to inmate Branstad's actions?

  A. RCO 57.41.089

  B. RCO 13.62.895 and RCO 17.05.669

  C. RCO 17.05.669

  D. Inmate Branstad did not commit any infractions.

49. Inmate trustee Jim Rodgers was assigned regular work detail in the food-service division of Arlington Corrections. Inmate Rodgers learned earlier from inmate Clyde Austin that certain ingredients such as yeast, sugar, raisins, fruit juice, etc., when combined and heated, promoted a fermentation process conducive to producing a crude form of alcoholic beverage. Inmate Rodgers exploited his position by providing the necessary resources, and both he and Austin regularly conspired in making the illicit brew. This went on for some time before security received an anonymous tip, and both were placed in segregation. In an initial effort to preserve his trustee status, inmate Rodgers professed his innocence and blamed a neighboring inmate for "setting him up." However, a follow-up investigation disproved the assertion. Under the circumstances, which of the following code infractions would apply toward inmate Rodgers for disciplinary consideration?

  A. RCO 80.86.040 and RCO 18.80.692

  B. RCO 14.64.142, RCO 17.05.669, and RCO 09.59.041

  C. RCO 17.05.669 and RCO 14.64.142

  D. RCO 41.57.011

50. On the basis of the previous question, inmate Austin is guilty of which of the following serious code infractions?

  A. RCO 17.05.669 and RCO 09.59.041

  B. RCO 14.64.142

  C. RCO 09.59.041, RCO 17.05.669, and RCO 14.64.142

  D. RCO 07.49.712, RCO 69.50.125, and RCO 09.49.991

51. Assume you are a Corrections Officer working the graveyard shift, and on two separate occasions you observe Officer Pratt sound asleep at his post. The best immediate means to handle such a situation would be to do which of the following?

    A. Take a photograph of Officer Pratt dozing and then threaten him later with the prospect of turning such evidence over to an immediate supervisor if he is caught sleeping on the job again

    B. Malign Officer Pratt in front of inmates to get back at him

    C. Drop subtle hints to coworkers regarding Officer Pratt's blatant incompetence

    D. Confront Officer Pratt directly about your immediate security concerns

52. Inmate Russell approaches you on Monday and explains that he believes he was overcharged on his commissary account for the month of October. He supports his reasoning by pointing out two specific deductions made for items he never purchased. Your reply at this point is that you would look into the matter immediately. However, in your attempt to stay ahead of the paperwork on some recent transfers, you neglect to follow up on inmate Russell's request before the week's end. At this point, your most appropriate means of handling the matter would be which of the following?

    A. Ignore the request altogether

    B. Tell inmate Russell to get someone else to investigate the matter

    C. Explain to inmate Russell that you have been busy, but you will look into the problem as soon as possible

    D. Tell inmate Russell that you have more important things to do than investigate every trivial matter that is of concern to inmates

53. Corrections Officer Hadley happens to observe a coworker who has obvious intentions of taking office supplies (i.e., departmental property) home with him. Under the circumstances, Officer Hadley should do what?

    A. Notify the warden of the impending theft

    B. Confront the officer directly and enquire the reason behind it

    C. Ignore the obvious because, after all, they are only office supplies

    D. Share your suspicions with other coworkers

54. Corrections Officer Hendricks can easily identify with inmates who are serving time for alcohol-related offenses. Having been an alcoholic himself at one time prior to working for Corrections, he knows full well the struggles that face such individuals. Sometimes, out of sympathy, he would share his past experiences with certain inmates, primarily trying to instill some degree of hope. From a departmental standpoint, Officer Hendricks's actions should be considered which of the following?

    A. Good policy, because it fosters better communication between Corrections personnel and inmates.

    B. Bad policy, because prisoners may conclude that he is weak and prone to err, which undermines his supervisory authority.

    C. Good policy, because honesty is the best policy in all circumstances.

    D. Bad policy, because his time can be better spent on other administrative functions than in assuming the role of counselor.

55. Inmate John Oliver's wife has just been through a serious surgical procedure. Assume that you are a Corrections Officer. As a personal favor, he asks you directly if you could go to the hospital and check on her condition for him. Considering the fact that Oliver is a model prisoner, you would best handle the situation by doing which of the following:

    A. Assure him that you will do so immediately after you get off of your shift

    B. Personally call the hospital information desk and inquire about her condition on inmate Oliver's behalf

    C. Explain to him that prison policy prohibits you from acting on such a request

    D. Arrange for him to be transported to the hospital to see her himself

56. Assume for the question that you are a Corrections Officer who has just given a directive to an inmate to move from one unit to another. However, the inmate in question has other ideas about being moved and becomes verbally defiant. Your best approach to handle this situation would be which of the following?

    A. If you are armed, shoot the inmate and be done with the matter.

    B. Attempt to reason with the inmate and, if necessary, offer an alternative course of action

    C. Directly state the consequences for not following a directive and then leave to notify a supervisor about the situation

    D. Physically restrain him on the spot and escort him to segregation for initially not acting on the request

57. A relatively new prisoner threatens a Corrections Officer with the prospect of his committing suicide if he does not receive certain privileges. How would this kind of situation best be handled by the officer in question?

    A. Treat his threat seriously and, upon notifying an immediate superior, place him in a suicide-watch unit until changes dictate otherwise

    B. Ignore his demands because inmates constantly conjure up schemes to manipulate officers for personal gain

    C. Give in to his demands so he will not hurt or kill himself

    D. Dare him to follow up on his threat

58. Officer Wilmont observes Officer Benning, a new hire, accepting nonmonetary gifts, which really do not amount to much, as small tokens of appreciation for his friendliness. Under the circumstances, Officer Wilmont should do what?

    A. Allow the practice to continue unabated because the acceptance of such gifts does not constitute bribery

    B. Point out to Officer Benning the fallibilities of such practices and request that he desist immediately

    C. Immediately inform his supervisor of what is going on

    D. Talk to other staff members and get their opinions on the matter

59. Assume, for the question, that you are a Corrections Officer who witnesses a superior officer, one who has the admiration and respect of fellow officers, verbally abusing a particular inmate. Assume, too, that you know it is against prison guidelines to treat any prisoner in such a manner. Your best means to handle this situation would be which of the following?

    A. Considering the officer's rank and reputation, you would best let the incident pass without expressing your misgivings to anyone.

    B. Immediately relay your concerns to the warden

    C. Send an anonymous memo to him that underscores the prison regulation he is guilty of violating

    D. Confront the officer directly and insist that such treatment stop

60. As a strange coincidence, you learn that a very close friend of yours was just admitted into the same cell block that you supervise. Under the circumstances, how should you treat this situation?

    A. Try to make your friend as comfortable as possible by omitting him from the less desirable work details assigned to other inmates

    B. Make it a point to avoid him entirely during your rounds

    C. Explain your relationship to your immediate superior and ask that either he or you be transferred to another area

    D. Tell other inmates that he is a good friend of yours and he is not to be bothered

Questions 61–71 pertain to vocabulary proficiency. Each question will pose a statement that will have a particular word in italics. You must determine from the four choices given which one correctly defines the word in question and then mark your answer accordingly.

61. There were some *controversial* topics in the governor's State of the State address. *Controversial* most nearly means:

    A. Arguable

    B. Prejudicial

    C. Unbelievable

    D. Boring

62. Mr. Miller was subject to arrest for *advocating* civil disobedience. *Advocating* most nearly means:

    A. Supporting

    B. Conducting

    C. Abhorring

    D. Repressing

63. The defendant was *jubilant* over the verdict. *Jubilant* most nearly means:

    A. Dejected

    B. Elated

    C. Exonerated

    D. Indifferent

64. In order to protect the *integrity* of this department, a high standard of ethical conduct is expected of all officers. *Integrity* most nearly means:

   A. Name

   B. Uprightness

   C. Cohesiveness

   D. Suitability

65. Every Corrections Officer should *endeavor* to identify the needs of the community within his or her jurisdiction. *Endeavor* most nearly means:

   A. Persevere

   B. Strive

   C. Refuse

   D. Reconcile

66. His actions were considered *flagrant* violations of departmental rules and regulations. *Flagrant* most nearly means:

   A. Glaring

   B. Minor

   C. Inadvertent

   D. Significant

67. Burglary and larceny are considered to be the most *pervasive* of all the major crimes. *Pervasive* most nearly means:

   A. Costly

   B. Violent

   C. Elusive

   D. Widespread

68. In general, attorneys seem to have a more *pessimistic* view of government leadership than others. *Pessimistic* most nearly means:

   A. Gloomy

   B. Positive

   C. Reserved

   D. Enlightened

69. The suspect was *petulant* when asked about his past drug and alcohol abuse. *Petulant* most nearly means:

   A. Cooperative

   B. Querulous

   C. Apathetic

   D. Offended

70. Assault and battery is commonplace among the *indigent. Indigent* most nearly means:

    A. Affluent

    B. Neglected

    C. Destitute

    D. Wealthy

71. The evidence submitted in the hearing was ruled *irrelevant* to the case. *Irrelevant* most nearly means:

    A. Pertinent

    B. Immaterial

    C. Important

    D. Applicable

Questions 72–80 pertain to spelling. Each question has four numerically identified columns, each comprising various word sets. One of the word sets given will contain an intentionally misspelled word. Select the column number that represents the word in question and mark your answer sheet accordingly.

72.

I	II	III	IV
Escape	Judge	Policies	Combative
Retribution	Aggressive	Maximum	Frequently
Instinct	Excellant	Institutional	History
Accurate	Gambling	Disabled	Lawyer

    A. I

    B. II

    C. III

    D. IV

73.

I	II	III	IV
Riot	Theft	Holster	Ingest
Tier	Insulted	Uniform	Dispense
Tacticol	Sheriff	Escorted	Grabbed
Reliable	Provoke	Frisk	Academy

    A. I

    B. II

    C. III

    D. IV

74.

I	II	III	IV
Inhaled	Detached	Schizophrenic	Public
Organized	Deterrent	React	Diabetic
Prisoner	Superior	Request	Promotional
Exclude	Manipulate	Confusian	Threaten

A. I

B. II

C. III

D. IV

75.

I	II	III	IV
Pursue	Prosecutor	Perimeter	Gymnasium
Search	Grazed	Extradite	Eliminate
Original	Borderline	Consistent	Coordinate
Beaton	Purpose	Educational	Suffocate

A. I

B. II

C. III

D. IV

76.

I	II	III	IV
Telephone	Interrogate	Premises	Evidence
Resistance	Sanitary	Illegel	Tamper
Notify	Trespassing	Religious	Vehicle
Liaison	Victim	Immediately	Tattoo

A. I

B. II

C. III

D. IV

77.

I	II	III	IV
Sodomy	Administrative	Leisure	Proceded
Occurred	Relevant	Prosecute	Reckless
Expression	Profane	Recurrence	Hostage
Belligerent	Mischief	Malicious	Captain

A. I

B. II

C. III

D. IV

78.

I	II	III	IV
Asphyxiated	Insufficient	Polygraph	Larceny
Conscious	Probation	Strangulate	Experience
Comply	Recieve	Tuesday	Quite
Marijuana	Noisy	Warrant	Intelligent

A. I

B. II

C. III

D. IV

79.

I	II	III	IV
Urgent	Exceed	Committed	Behavior
Opposite	Beginning	Similarity	Coherent
Indigent	Coerce	Prejudice	Possession
Forgery	Depression	Municipal	Superviser

A. I

B. II

C. III

D. IV

80.

I	II	III	IV
Sprain	Minor	Reference	Robery
Mileage	Legal	Questionnaire	Refuse
Government	Prescription	Liquor	Patience
Illiterate	Secretary	Occasion	Juvenile

A. I

B. II

C. III

D. IV

Questions 81–92 relate to grammar, punctuation, and spelling. Each question will provide a written statement that may or may not contain specific errors. Select, from the choices provided, the answer that represents an accurate assessment of the statement in question and then mark your answer sheet accordingly.

81. Police personnel in most jurisdictions are percieved by the general public as being spread too thin to fulfill all the responsibilities that come with serving the community.

      The statement, in terms of English usage,

  A. Is structurally incorrect

  B. Contains one or more misspellings

  C. Lacks necessary punctuation and/or capitalization

  D. Is correct in all aspects

82. One of the areas that has been affected by budgetary constraint is job training.

      The statement, in terms of English usage,

  A. Is structurally incorrect

  B. Contains one or more misspellings

  C. Lacks necessary punctuation and/or capitalization

  D. Is correct in all aspects

83. Drug Awareness and Resistance Education programs are designed for juveniles contemplating the use of drugs and their parents.

      The statement, in terms of English usage,

  A. Is structurally incorrect

  B. Contains one or more misspellings

  C. Lacks necessary punctuation and/or capitalization

  D. Is correct in all aspects

84. Undercover investigators must exercise a great deal of caution in planning and affecting communication with supervisory personnel.

      The statement, in terms of English usage,

  A. Is structurally incorrect

  B. Contains one or more misspellings

  C. Lacks necessary punctuation and/or capitalization

  D. Is correct in all aspects

85. It is recommended that, when at all possible, apparent suicides should be handled with the same degree of attention given a homicide.

      The statement, in terms of English usage,

  A. Is structurally incorrect

  B. Contains one or more misspellings

  C. Lacks necessary punctuation and/or capitalization

  D. Is correct in all aspects

86. Police Officer Harris eluded to the hazards of joining a gang when he referred to a list of juveniles who have been killed in gang-related incidents.

    The statement, in terms of English usage,

    A. Is structurally incorrect

    B. Contains one or more misspellings

    C. Lacks necessary punctuation and/or capitalization

    D. Is correct in all aspects

87. Involuntary commitment is possible through a mental health professional when the suspect refuses appropriate treatment, is a danger to him or herself or others and can be detained for 14 to 60 days.

    The statement, in terms of English usage,

    A. Is structurally incorrect

    B. Contains one or more misspellings

    C. Lacks necessary punctuation and/or capitalization

    D. Is correct in all aspects

88. The evidentiary value of labratory tests on fibers varies greatly depending on the quantity of fibers collected and the uniqueness of the characteristics found during the examination.

    The statement, in terms of English usage,

    A. Is structurally incorrect

    B. Contains one or more misspellings

    C. Lacks necessary punctuation and/or capitalization

    D. Is correct in all aspects

89. It is not uncommon in many jurisdictions for felony cases to be referred by the district attorneys office to a city attorneys office for the purpose of reducing the charges to a misdemeanor.

    The statement, in terms of English usage,

    A. Is structurally incorrect

    B. Contains one or more misspellings

    C. Lacks necessary punctuation and/or capitalization

    D. Is correct in all aspects

90. Larceny is defined as the felonious taking and carrying away of someone else's personal property, without they're consent, with the intention of permanently depriving that person of its use or possession.

    The statement, in terms of English usage,

    A. Is structurally incorrect

    B. Contains one or more misspellings

    C. Lacks necessary punctuation and/or capitalization

    D. Is correct in all aspects

91. Many states explicitly prohibit the placement of some or all types of juveniles in adult institutions.

    The statement, in terms of English usage,

    A. Is structurally incorrect

    B. Contains one or more misspellings

    C. Lacks necessary punctuation and/or capitalization

    D. Is correct in all aspects

92. A legal obligation against the state is an obligation that would form the basis of a judgement against the state in a court of competant jurisdiction should the legislature permit the state to be sued.

    The statement, in terms of English usage,

    A. Is structurally incorrect

    B. Contains one or more misspellings

    C. Lacks necessary punctuation and/or capitalization

    D. Is correct in all aspects

Answer question 93 on the basis of the following chart.

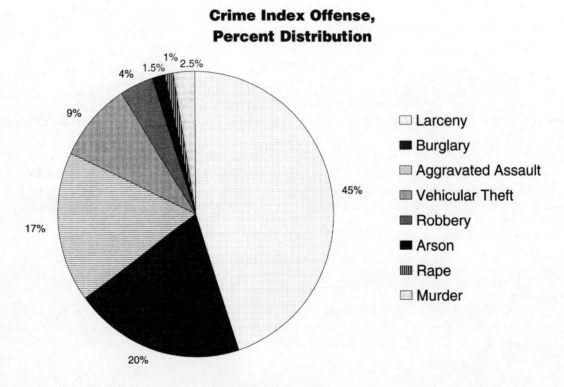

Crime Index Offense, Percent Distribution

93. If there were a total of 10,000 offenses reported and the percent distribution of the crimes was as indicated in the chart, how many actual aggravated assault cases would there be?

    A. 2000

    B. 1850

    C. 1700

    D. None of the above

94. If it is reported that one robbery is committed every 45 seconds, one burglary every 10 seconds, and one aggravated assault every 27 seconds, how many of each crime would be committed per hour?

    A. 90, 200, 270, respectively

    B. 80, 360, 133, respectively

    C. 75, 400, 230, respectively

    D. None of the above

95. If the Sheriff's Department responded to 245 traffic accidents for the month and the other 8% of its calls were attributed to stranded motorists, how many calls did the Sheriff's Department receive altogether?

    A. 248

    B. 253

    C. 266

    D. 275

96. A superior court judge recently told a board of commissioners that for the year, domestic filings increased 32% and juvenile filings increased 41%. Assuming the superior court's annual caseload for both kinds of filings was 231 and 163, respectively, what had been the number of filings in the previous year?

    A. 192 and 123, respectively

    B. 175 and 116, respectively

    C. 182 and 119, respectively

    D. 205 and 131, respectively

Answer questions 97–99 on the basis of the following statistics compiled from a hypothetical municipality.

Type of crime	Number of cases	Average number of man-hours assigned per case	Estimated total economic impact (loss in dollars)
Aggravated assault	117	1.5	NA
Arson	14	4.0	720,000
Auto theft	62	2.75	1,100,000
Burglary	312	3.75	925,000
Embezzlement	32	2.5	700,000
Fraud	79	1.5	1,250,000
Gambling	43	1.0	NA
Larceny	1,320	3.5	3,750,000
Murder	42	17.0	NA
Narcotics	981	1.0	NA
Forcible rape	52	10.5	NA
Robbery	674	4.0	2,600,000
Shoplifting	520	1.5	1,300,000
Vandalism	720	0.5	125,000

97. Assuming that crime against property includes arson, burglary, vandalism, larceny, robbery, embezzlement, auto theft, and shoplifting, what percentage of the total annual caseload would these crimes constitute?

    A. 71%

    B. 74%

    C. 76%

    D. None of the above

98. The Commission on Law Enforcement and Administration of Justice set a goal of reducing the homicide rate by at least fifteen percent within the next two years. Approximately how much would this trim the number of deaths per year indicated in this study?

    A. 7

    B. 4

    C. 3

    D. 2

99. The crime that requires the second-highest number of man-hours per case constitutes what percentage of the total crimes committed?

    A. 1%

    B. 2%

    C. 3%

    D. 4%

Answer questions 100–102 on the basis of the following chart.

	No. of reported cases of contraband possession	No. of reported cases of violence between inmates	No. of reported cases that involved trustee-status revocation
1995			
Compton Prison	252	25	32
Fullerton Corrections	137	14	14
Ridgeview Adult Detention	16	1	1
1996			
Compton Prison	213	12	17
Fullerton Corrections	149	7	18
Ridgeview Adult Detention	27	2	3

100. Compton Prison is shown to have had fewer reported cases of contraband possession in 1996 than in 1995. This reflects what percentage decrease?

    A. 13.2%

    B. 15.5%

    C. 16.7%

    D. 18.3%

101. Which correctional institution experienced the largest percentage increase in inmate trustee-status revocations?

    A. Ridgeview Adult Detention

    B. Compton Prison

    C. Fullerton Corrections

    D. Information in the survey is insufficient to make this determination.

102. If Fullerton Corrections experienced a 450 percent increase in the number of reported cases of violence between inmates from 1995 to 1997, how many cases were there in 1997?

    A. 57

    B. 58

    C. 63

    D. 77

The following graph represents a five-year study of recidivism rates (i.e., post-release resumption of criminal activity by inmates) in relation to the various forms of rehabilitation inmates received prior to being reincarcerated. The figures shown reflect median numbers compiled by twenty midwestern state correctional facilities over the five-year period. Examine the information shown and answer questions 103–105 on the basis of the data contained therein.

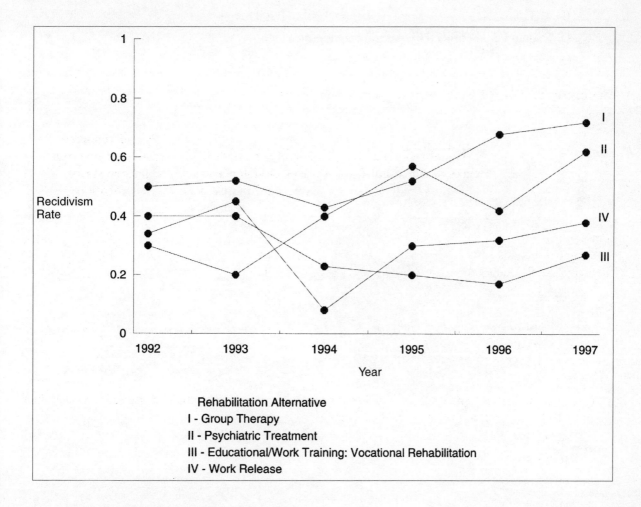

Rehabilitation Alternative
I - Group Therapy
II - Psychiatric Treatment
III - Educational/Work Training: Vocational Rehabilitation
IV - Work Release

103. Judging by the statistics shown, which form of rehabilitative measure used within Corrections is demonstrative of having the least effect on recidivism?

    A. Psychiatric Treatment

    B. Work Release

    C. Group Therapy

    D. Vocational Rehabilitation

104. Which form of rehabilitation had the most effective impact on recidivism rates according to the five-year study?

    A. Group Therapy

    B. Vocational Rehabilitation

    C. Work Release

    D. Psychiatric Treatment

105. Assume there were 840 inmates released during 1994 who had participated in some form of psychiatric treatment as a contingency to their release. According to the study, how many were back in the "establishment" at year's end because of reoffending?

    A. 275 inmates

    B. 336 inmates

    C. 423 inmates

    D. Cannot be determined by the information provided

The following pie chart represents a hypothetical caseload handled by medical personnel during the month of July in a municipal Corrections facility. Answer questions 106–108 on the basis of what is shown.

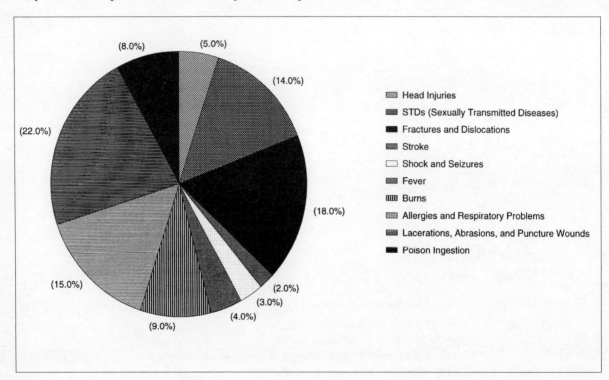

106. The three largest classifications of problems requiring medical attention cumulatively represent what percentage of the total caseload given?

   A. 35%

   B. 47%

   C. 54%

   D. 55%

107. Assuming the study was centered on an inmate patient count of 100 and half of the STD cases involved AIDS (Acquired Immune Deficiency Syndrome) complications, how many inmates would that account for?

   A. 3 inmates

   B. 6 inmates

   C. 7 inmates

   D. 14 inmates

108. Again, assume the study was centered on an inmate patient count of 100 and approximately 33%, 44%, and 22% of the burn cases accounted for were first-, second-, and third-degree burns, respectively. That being the situation, how many inmates actually suffered second-degree burns?

   A. 2 inmates

   B. 3 inmates

   C. 4 inmates

   D. 5 inmates

Key	1	7	3	6	5	4	2
Code	Z	Y	X	W	V	U	T

109. According to the number-letter key above, which of the following codes is considered inaccurate?

   A. 527   VTY

   B. 1654   ZWVU

   C. 726   YTV

   D. 31642   XZWUT

Key	12	15	18	21	24	27	30
Code	A	D	G	J	M	P	S

110. According to the number-letter key above, which of the following codes is considered the most accurate?

   A. 12, 24, 18, 30, 15, 15, 21   AMGPDDM

   B. 15, 30, 12, 24, 27, 30, 24   DSAMPJM

   C. 30, 21, 18, 15, 24, 12, 27   SJGDPAP

   D. 27, 21, 12, 18, 24, 24, 15   MJAJGGA

Key	I	S	C	E	N	O	T	R
Code	6	12	18	24	30	36	42	48

111. Which of the following codes represents the word *Corrections* according to the letter-number key given?

   A. 18, 36, 48, 48, 24, 18, 42, 6, 36, 30, 12

   B. 18, 36, 36, 48, 24, 18, 6, 42, 36, 30, 12

   C. 18, 36, 42, 42, 24, 18, 48, 6, 36, 30, 12

   D. 18, 36, 48, 48, 18, 24, 6, 42, 36, 12, 30

Key	D	T	C	J	I	S	N	O	U	R
Code	11	12	13	14	15	16	17	18	19	20

112. Which of the following codes represents the word *jurisdiction* according to the letter-number key given?

   A. 14, 19, 20, 15, 16, 15, 11, 13, 12, 18, 15, 17

   B. 14, 19, 20, 15, 16, 11, 15, 13, 15, 15, 17, 18

   C. 14, 20, 19, 16, 15, 11, 15, 13, 12, 15, 17, 17

   D. 14, 19, 20, 15, 16, 11, 15, 13, 12, 15, 18, 17

Key	01	05	02	04	09	12	03	06	11	07	08	10
Code	10	30	20	25	35	80	40	60	15	5	55	45

113. Assuming the key represents the calendar months for the year in no particular order, what would be the correct coding sequence for the months of July, August, January, March, December, September, February, and May, respectively?

   A. 5, 55, 10, 40, 80, 35, 20, 30

   B. 60, 5, 10, 40, 80, 55, 20, 5

   C. 07, 08, 01, 03, 12, 09, 02, 05

   D. 5, 55, 01, 03, 80, 35, 02, 25

114. With the same assumptions prescribed in the previous question, which of the following codes accurately reflects the months of November, April, October, June, and March, respectively?

   A. 11, 25, 45, 60, 40

   B. 20, 25, 60, 40, 45

   C. 15, 25, 45, 60, 40

   D. 11, 04, 15, 40, 80

Key	N	P	R	S	Q	O
	1	7	12	19	4	10
Alternate	14	9	18	2	13	20
Codes	6	15	24	8	22	5
	11	3	21	17	23	16

Answer questions 115 and 116 on the basis of the following multiple code format.

115. According to the letter-number key provided, which of the following codes represents the key arranged in alphabetical order?

 A. 1, 10, 15, 18, 12, 4

 B. 14, 16, 7, 22, 21, 8

 C. 6, 20, 22, 24, 7, 16

 D. 11, 5, 3, 12, 2, 17

116. Study the codes given below in relation to the key provided. Choose the selection that accounts for the number of coding errors found.

Code	Key
1, 23, 17, 15, 9, 3, 20	N, Q, S, P, P, P, O
12, 2, 10, 22, 16, 5, 8	R, S, O, Q, P, O, S
6, 13, 14, 21, 3	N, Q, N, R, P
16, 23, 4, 9, 1, 10, 13, 7	O, Q, Q, P, N, S, N, P
12, 2, 19, 18, 15, 16	R, S, S, R, P, O
3, 4, 5, 21, 24, 15, 11	P, Q, O, R, R, P, N
13, 17, 21, 6, 4, 2, 1	Q, S, R, N, Q, S, N
19, 2, 16, 7, 20, 5, 21, 14	S, S, O, P, O, O, R, N

 A. 6 errors

 B. 4 errors

 C. 3 errors

 D. 2 errors

Look over the following completed Notice of Infraction (NOI) court docket. Answer questions 117–125 on the basis of the information provided in this report.

117. According to the court docket, what was the defendant cited for?

 A. Traffic infraction

 B. Non-traffic infraction

 C. Criminal traffic

 D. Criminal non-traffic

118. According to the citation, the vehicle driven by the defendant was which of the following?

 A. State exempt vehicle

 B. Commercial vehicle

 C. Recreational vehicle

 D. Rental vehicle

UNIFORM COURT DOCKET

☐ TRAFFIC INFRACTION	☑ CRIMINAL TRAFFIC
☐ NON-TRAFFIC INFRACTION	☐ CRIMINAL NON-TRAFFIC

☐ CITY/TOWN OF **ANKENY**

PLAINTIFF VS. NAMED DEFENDANT

IN THE ☑ DISTRICT ☐ MUNICIPAL COURT OF **DES MOINES**
STATE OF
IOWA
COUNTY OF

THE UNDERSIGNED CERTIFIES AND SAYS THAT IN THE STATE OF IOWA

DRIVER'S LICENSE NO.		STATE	EXPIRES	SOCIAL SECURITY NUMBER
SANCHEZ 5214IP		NE	98	108-59-4832

NAME	LAST	FIRST	MIDDLE	☐ INTERPRETER NEEDED
	SANCHEZ	MICHAEL	P.	

ADDRESS ☐ IF NEW ADDRESS
423 CRESTVIEW DR.

CITY	STATE	ZIP CODE	EMPLOYER
GRAND ISLAND	NE	65721	COMTRONICS LTD

SEX	RACE	DATE OF BIRTH	HEIGHT	WEIGHT	EYES	HAIR	RESIDENTIAL PHONE NUMBER
M	W	* 03-15-68	601	190	GR	BLK	(308) 513-1480

VIOLATION DATE	MONTH	DAY	YEAR	TIME (24 HRS)
ON OR ABOUT	MARCH	16	1996	2345 HRS

AT LOCATION	M.P.	CITY/COUNTY OF
INTERSTATE 35	162	POLK

DID OPERATE THE FOLLOWING VEHICLE/MOTOR VEHICLE ON A PUBLIC HIGHWAY AND

VEHICLE LICENSE NO.	STATE	EXPIRES	VEH. YR.	MAKE	MODEL	STYLE	COLOR
BLO 745	NE	97	94	FORD	2 DR	THUNDERBIRD	SIL/BLK

TRAILER #1 LICENSE NO.	STATE	EXPIRES	TR. YR.	TRAILER#2 LICENSE NO.	STATE	EXPIRES	TR. YR.

OWNER/COMPANY IF OTHER THAN DRIVER	ADDRESS	CITY	STATE	ZIP CODE
BUDGET RENTAL	1890 172ND ST.	OMAHA	NE	60711

ACCIDENT	BAC	COMMERCIAL	RENTAL	HAZARD	EXEMPT	FARM	FIRE
NO PD I F	READING	VEHICLE ☐ YES ☑ NO	VEHICLE ☑ YES ☐ NO	PLACARD ☐ YES ☐ NO	VEHICLE	R.V.	OTHER

DID THEN AND THERE COMMIT EACH OF THE FOLLOWING OFFENSES/INFRACTIONS

1. VIOLATION/STATUTE CODE	DESCRIPTION	VEHICLE SPEED	IN A	ZONE	☑ RADAR
7.81.699	D.U.I.	92	65		☐ PACE
					☐ AIRCRAFT

2. VIOLATION/STATUTE CODE	DESCRIPTION
19.13.672	FIRST DEGREE RECKLESS DRIVING

PENALTY/BAIL
U.S. FUNDS $ 25,000

DATE NOTICE ISSUED	BOOKING DATE	TIME	APPEARANCE DATE	MO	DAY	YR.
03-16-96	03-17-96	0250 HRS		03	19	96

WITHOUT ADMITTING HAVING COMMITTED EACH OF THE ABOVE INFRACTIONS/OFFENSES, I PROMISE TO RESPOND AS DIRECTED ON THIS NOTICE

I CERTIFY (OR DECLARE) UNDER PENALTY OF PERJURY UNDER THE LAWS OF THE STATE OF IOWA THAT I HAVE REASONABLE GROUNDS/PROBABLE CAUSE TO BELIEVE AND DO BELIEVE THE ABOVE NAMED PERSON COMMITTED THE ABOVE INFRACTION(S) AND/OR OFFENSE(S) CONTRARY TO LAW.

OFFICER(S)	NUMBER
BEN WHITE	175
JILL FOSTER	189

X _Michael Sanchez_
DEFENDANT'S SIGNATURE

DATE	PLACE
03-16-96	ANKENY, IA

	INF	RESPONSE	DISPOSITION	CRG	PLEA	CNG	FINDING	FINE	SUSPENDED	SUB-TOTAL
ABSTRACT OF JUDGMENT	1	C NC	C N D P	1	G NG		G NG D BF	$ 4700.00	$	$ 4700.00
	2	C NC	C N D P	2	G NG		G NG D BF	$	$	$
								$	$	$

FINDING/ JUDGMENT DATE	03-19-96	TO SERVE	90 DAYS	WITH	60	DAYS SUSPENDED	CREDIT FOR TIME SERVE 2 DAYS	OTHER COSTS	$ 375.00
ABSTRACT MAILED TO ANKENY	03-21-96	RECOMMENDED NONEXTENSION OF SUSPENSION					LICENSE SURRENDER DATE 03-19-96	TOTAL COSTS	$5075.00

119. When and where was the Notice of Infraction issued?

    A. March 3, 1996 / Polk County

    B. March 15, 1968 / Omaha, NE

    C. March 16, 1996 / Polk County

    D. March 17, 1996 / Des Moines, IA

120. The defendant was caught exceeding the posted speed limits by how much?

    A. 92 miles per hour

    B. 27 miles per hour

    C. 65 miles per hour

    D. 60 miles per hour

121. In which state was the defendant's license issued?

    A. Nebraska

    B. New Hampshire

    C. New Mexico

    D. Iowa

122. The defendant's date of birth was shown to be which of the following?

    A. March 21, 1996

    B. March 16, 1968

    C. March 15, 1968

    D. March 17, 1996

123. According to the NOI judgment abstract, Mr. Sanchez had how much time left to serve in lieu of posting bail?

    A. 28 days

    B. 30 days

    C. 60 days

    D. 90 days

124. When is the license of the vehicle in question due to expire?

    A. 1994

    B. 1998

    C. 1996

    D. 1997

125. All of the following statements are true except:

    A. The defendant was 28 years old at the time of his arrest.

    B. The defendant was a white male who was 6'1" tall and weighed 190 pounds.

    C. Milepost marker 162 on Interstate 35 is located in Polk County, IA.

    D. Sanchez's given home address is 1890 172nd St., Omaha, NE 60711.

ANSWER SHEET TO PRACTICE EXAM 2

1. Ⓐ Ⓑ Ⓒ Ⓓ
2. Ⓐ Ⓑ Ⓒ Ⓓ
3. Ⓐ Ⓑ Ⓒ Ⓓ
4. Ⓐ Ⓑ Ⓒ Ⓓ
5. Ⓐ Ⓑ Ⓒ Ⓓ
6. Ⓐ Ⓑ Ⓒ Ⓓ
7. Ⓐ Ⓑ Ⓒ Ⓓ
8. Ⓐ Ⓑ Ⓒ Ⓓ
9. Ⓐ Ⓑ Ⓒ Ⓓ
10. Ⓐ Ⓑ Ⓒ Ⓓ
11. Ⓐ Ⓑ Ⓒ Ⓓ
12. Ⓐ Ⓑ Ⓒ Ⓓ
13. Ⓐ Ⓑ Ⓒ Ⓓ
14. Ⓐ Ⓑ Ⓒ Ⓓ
15. Ⓐ Ⓑ Ⓒ Ⓓ
16. Ⓐ Ⓑ Ⓒ Ⓓ
17. Ⓐ Ⓑ Ⓒ Ⓓ
18. Ⓐ Ⓑ Ⓒ Ⓓ
19. Ⓐ Ⓑ Ⓒ Ⓓ
20. Ⓐ Ⓑ Ⓒ Ⓓ
21. Ⓐ Ⓑ Ⓒ Ⓓ
22. Ⓐ Ⓑ Ⓒ Ⓓ
23. Ⓐ Ⓑ Ⓒ Ⓓ
24. Ⓐ Ⓑ Ⓒ Ⓓ
25. Ⓐ Ⓑ Ⓒ Ⓓ
26. Ⓐ Ⓑ Ⓒ Ⓓ
27. Ⓐ Ⓑ Ⓒ Ⓓ
28. Ⓐ Ⓑ Ⓒ Ⓓ
29. Ⓐ Ⓑ Ⓒ Ⓓ
30. Ⓐ Ⓑ Ⓒ Ⓓ
31. Ⓐ Ⓑ Ⓒ Ⓓ
32. Ⓐ Ⓑ Ⓒ Ⓓ
33. Ⓐ Ⓑ Ⓒ Ⓓ
34. Ⓐ Ⓑ Ⓒ Ⓓ
35. Ⓐ Ⓑ Ⓒ Ⓓ
36. Ⓐ Ⓑ Ⓒ Ⓓ
37. Ⓐ Ⓑ Ⓒ Ⓓ
38. Ⓐ Ⓑ Ⓒ Ⓓ
39. Ⓐ Ⓑ Ⓒ Ⓓ
40. Ⓐ Ⓑ Ⓒ Ⓓ
41. Ⓐ Ⓑ Ⓒ Ⓓ
42. Ⓐ Ⓑ Ⓒ Ⓓ
43. Ⓐ Ⓑ Ⓒ Ⓓ
44. Ⓐ Ⓑ Ⓒ Ⓓ
45. Ⓐ Ⓑ Ⓒ Ⓓ
46. Ⓐ Ⓑ Ⓒ Ⓓ
47. Ⓐ Ⓑ Ⓒ Ⓓ
48. Ⓐ Ⓑ Ⓒ Ⓓ
49. Ⓐ Ⓑ Ⓒ Ⓓ
50. Ⓐ Ⓑ Ⓒ Ⓓ
51. Ⓐ Ⓑ Ⓒ Ⓓ
52. Ⓐ Ⓑ Ⓒ Ⓓ
53. Ⓐ Ⓑ Ⓒ Ⓓ
54. Ⓐ Ⓑ Ⓒ Ⓓ
55. Ⓐ Ⓑ Ⓒ Ⓓ
56. Ⓐ Ⓑ Ⓒ Ⓓ
57. Ⓐ Ⓑ Ⓒ Ⓓ
58. Ⓐ Ⓑ Ⓒ Ⓓ
59. Ⓐ Ⓑ Ⓒ Ⓓ
60. Ⓐ Ⓑ Ⓒ Ⓓ
61. Ⓐ Ⓑ Ⓒ Ⓓ
62. Ⓐ Ⓑ Ⓒ Ⓓ
63. Ⓐ Ⓑ Ⓒ Ⓓ
64. Ⓐ Ⓑ Ⓒ Ⓓ
65. Ⓐ Ⓑ Ⓒ Ⓓ
66. Ⓐ Ⓑ Ⓒ Ⓓ
67. Ⓐ Ⓑ Ⓒ Ⓓ
68. Ⓐ Ⓑ Ⓒ Ⓓ
69. Ⓐ Ⓑ Ⓒ Ⓓ
70. Ⓐ Ⓑ Ⓒ Ⓓ
71. Ⓐ Ⓑ Ⓒ Ⓓ
72. Ⓐ Ⓑ Ⓒ Ⓓ
73. Ⓐ Ⓑ Ⓒ Ⓓ
74. Ⓐ Ⓑ Ⓒ Ⓓ
75. Ⓐ Ⓑ Ⓒ Ⓓ
76. Ⓐ Ⓑ Ⓒ Ⓓ
77. Ⓐ Ⓑ Ⓒ Ⓓ
78. Ⓐ Ⓑ Ⓒ Ⓓ
79. Ⓐ Ⓑ Ⓒ Ⓓ
80. Ⓐ Ⓑ Ⓒ Ⓓ
81. Ⓐ Ⓑ Ⓒ Ⓓ
82. Ⓐ Ⓑ Ⓒ Ⓓ
83. Ⓐ Ⓑ Ⓒ Ⓓ
84. Ⓐ Ⓑ Ⓒ Ⓓ
85. Ⓐ Ⓑ Ⓒ Ⓓ
86. Ⓐ Ⓑ Ⓒ Ⓓ
87. Ⓐ Ⓑ Ⓒ Ⓓ
88. Ⓐ Ⓑ Ⓒ Ⓓ
89. Ⓐ Ⓑ Ⓒ Ⓓ
90. Ⓐ Ⓑ Ⓒ Ⓓ
91. Ⓐ Ⓑ Ⓒ Ⓓ
92. Ⓐ Ⓑ Ⓒ Ⓓ
93. Ⓐ Ⓑ Ⓒ Ⓓ

94. (A) (B) (C) (D)
95. (A) (B) (C) (D)
96. (A) (B) (C) (D)
97. (A) (B) (C) (D)
98. (A) (B) (C) (D)
99. (A) (B) (C) (D)
100. (A) (B) (C) (D)
101. (A) (B) (C) (D)
102. (A) (B) (C) (D)
103. (A) (B) (C) (D)
104. (A) (B) (C) (D)

105. (A) (B) (C) (D)
106. (A) (B) (C) (D)
107. (A) (B) (C) (D)
108. (A) (B) (C) (D)
109. (A) (B) (C) (D)
110. (A) (B) (C) (D)
111. (A) (B) (C) (D)
112. (A) (B) (C) (D)
113. (A) (B) (C) (D)
114. (A) (B) (C) (D)
115. (A) (B) (C) (D)

116. (A) (B) (C) (D)
117. (A) (B) (C) (D)
118. (A) (B) (C) (D)
119. (A) (B) (C) (D)
120. (A) (B) (C) (D)
121. (A) (B) (C) (D)
122. (A) (B) (C) (D)
123. (A) (B) (C) (D)
124. (A) (B) (C) (D)
125. (A) (B) (C) (D)

Answers can be found on pages 273–282.

ANSWERS TO PRACTICE EXAM 2

Refer to the case files provided for any clarification of questions 1–25.

1. C   Mark P. Elroy was charged for the offenses of involuntary manslaughter and operation of a motor vehicle while under the influence of alcohol.

2. C   Ms. Ballard was described in her file as being 5'6" and 185 pounds.

3. D   Case file A-17 was assigned to Brian L. Thompson.

4. A   Case file K-72 received a cell assignment in A Wing, number 13.

5. D   Mr. Phelps's DOB is 12-17-65.

6. B   Case file N-04 belongs to Ms. Christy Ballard.

7. A   The composite sketch of Brian L. Thompson is the correct selection.

8. C   The composite sketch is Lisa G. Potter, who received B Wing, number 13, for a cell assignment.

9. B   Walter Phelps

10. A   J-30

11. D   The composite sketch of Lisa G. Potter is the correct selection.

12. D   Mark P. Elroy's DOB is 12-5-70.

13. C   L-07 is Lisa G. Potter's assigned case file number. Her ethnicity is African American.

14. B   Selection B represents the charges brought against Mr. Phelps.

15. A   Only Mark P. Elroy was described as having hazel eyes.

16. C   The composite sketch of Leonard P. Schmidt would be the correct selection.

17. D   Corrections Officer Kevin Holt's badge number was stated in the reading as being number 17.

18. D   Andrea L. Haynes was convicted for the offense described in the question; however, she was sentenced to serve only 5-10 years.

19. B   Andrea L. Haynes was stated as being 31 years of age.

20. B   Selection B is the destination stated in the reading. Selection A is the given point of origin.

21. C   Inmate Leonard P. Schmidt was described as weighing approximately 150 pounds.

22. C   Inmate Richard B. Lathrop was described as having brown hair.

23. A   Medium security risk

24. D   Richard B. Lathrop was described as having hazel eyes.

25. C   Inmate Leonard P. Schmidt was described as being 5'10".

26. B

Number of misdemeanor convictions	3	× .5 =	1.5
Number of previous violent felony convictions	2	× 2 =	4
Number of previous nonviolent felony convictions	0	× 1 =	0
Number of current convictions	1	× 1 =	1
		POA = 6.5 rounded up to	7

Second-degree murder has a B severity rating.

An offense assessment of 7 as applied to a B severity crime rates 19 1/2 years.

27. *B*   Number of misdemeanor convictions $\underline{\quad 0 \quad} \times .5 = \quad 0$

              Number of previous violent felony convictions $\underline{\quad 0 \quad} \times 2 = \quad 0$

                 (Remember that juvenile offenses, regardless of their nature,

                   are not taken into consideration for sentence determination.)

              Number of previous nonviolent felony convictions $\underline{\quad 0 \quad} \times 1 = \quad 0$

              Number of current convictions $\underline{\quad 1 \quad} \times 1 = \quad 1$

                                                POA = $\underline{\quad 1 \quad}$

                    Aggravated circumstances of using a firearm, add 2 points =   2

                              Final offense assessment rating =   3

              First-degree robbery has an A severity rating.

              An offense assessment of 3 as applied to an A severity crime rates $31\frac{1}{2}$ years.

28. *D*   Number of misdemeanor convictions $\underline{\quad 4 \quad} \times .5 = \quad 2$

              Number of previous violent felony convictions $\underline{\quad 0 \quad} \times 2 = \quad 0$

              Number of previous nonviolent felony convictions $\underline{\quad 2 \quad} \times 1 = \quad 2$

              Number of current convictions $\underline{\quad 1 \quad} \times 1 = \quad 1$

                                                POA =   5

              Manufacturing of a controlled substance with the intent to deliver has a B severity rating.

              An offense assessment of 5 as applied to a B severity crime rates $15\frac{1}{2}$ years.

29. *D*   Number of misdemeanor convictions $\underline{\quad 0 \quad} \times .5 = \quad 0$

              Number of previous violent felony convictions $\underline{\quad 2 \quad} \times 2 = \quad 4$

              Number of previous nonviolent felony convictions $\underline{\quad 0 \quad} \times 1 = \quad 0$

              Number of current convictions $\underline{\quad 1 \quad} \times 1 = \quad 1$

                                                POA =   5

           Aggravated circumstances of the crime occurring on prison premises, add 1 point = $\underline{\quad 1 \quad}$

                              Final offense assessment rating =   6

              Second-degree murder has a B severity rating.

              An offense assessment of 6 as applied to a B severity crime rates $17\frac{1}{3}$ years.

30. *C*   Initial inmate count at 6:00 A.M. was 91 (i.e., 37 + 45 + 9). There were 8 admissions; however, there were also 5 transfers, 1 release, 2 outside-of-facility medical appointments, and 7 off-premises for various judicial hearings. Therefore, 91 + 8 - 5 - 1 - 2 - 7 = 84 total inmate count at 10:30 A.M.

31. *A*   45 inmates were initially in Wing II according to the 6:00 A.M. count.

              17 inmates checked in at 10:30 A.M., while 44 inmates checked out.

              1 inmate checked in at noon, while 2 inmates checked out.

              16 more inmates checked in at 3:00 P.M., while 23 more inmates checked out.

              Therefore, 45 + 17 - 44 + 1 - 2 + 16 - 23 = 10 inmates were present in Wing II during the 3:00 P.M. count.

32. *A*   No inmates were on any of the mentioned premises during the initial count at 6:00 A.M. Inmate movement thereafter would be as follows:

Recreation Room: 22 inmates checked in at 10:30 A.M., while 6 inmates checked out. 4 inmates checked in at noon, while 19 inmates checked out. Therefore, 22 - 6 + 4 - 19 leaves only 1 inmate on the premises.

Exercise Room: 18 inmates checked in at 10:30 A.M., while none checked out. 3 inmates checked in at noon, while 16 inmates checked out. Therefore, 18 + 3 - 16 leaves 5 inmates on the premises.

Visitor Room: 10 inmates checked in at 10:30 A.M., while 9 inmates checked out. 8 inmates checked in at noon, while 5 inmates checked out. Therefore, 10 - 9 + 8 - 5 leaves 4 inmates on the premises.

Library: 15 inmates checked in at 10:30 A.M., while none checked out. 4 inmates checked in at noon, while 13 inmates checked out. Therefore, 15 + 4 - 13 leaves 6 inmates on the premises.

33. *B*   At 10:30 A.M. 7 inmates were escorted off the premises to attend various judicial hearings. Only 5 inmates were returned by day's end. Therefore, $5 \div 7 \times 100 = 71.4\%$.

34. *D*   9 inmates were initially in the in-house infirmary, according to the 6:00 A.M. count. No inmate checked in at 10:30 A.M., while 6 inmates checked out. 1 inmate checked in at noon, while 2 inmates checked out. 2 inmates checked in at 3:00 P.M., while 2 inmates checked out. At the close of the day, 5 more inmates checked in without any further discharges. Therefore, 9 - 6 + 1 - 2 + 2 - 2 + 5 leaves 7 inmates in the infirmary prior to lockdown.

35. *C*   Selection A was mentioned in the reading, but it fails to describe the contents of the entire passage. Selections B and D were neither mentioned nor implied in this reading.

36. *D*   Murder was pointed out in the passage as being the one exception. In a court's view, it is necessary to put the life of another before one's own.

37. *A*   Selection B assumes that inmate Wilson, a future defendant in a court of law, could use duress as a defense against the charge of assault. While it is true that two other inmates with supposed gang affiliation did make a threat against him to coerce his cooperation in the intended assault, it was done so in future terms. In other words, they would be back at a later time to execute their threat in the event of his noncompliance. The courts would view that inmate Wilson had ample time to have contacted and involved Corrections staff to stop such a plot. Selection C is not an accurate assumption for the same reasons as described for selection B, despite the fact that no one was murdered.

38. *B*   Only bribery was not mentioned in the reading.

39. *A*   Selection A is correct. Despite what Mr. Harris may have perceived as being a threat (as suggested in selection C), the fact is that the pair did not use force or the threat of force to obtain his wallet; they merely demanded he hand it over without the predication of dire consequences if he did not comply. Selection B is incorrect because the altercation took place after the theft. The altercation itself was not a precondition to the juveniles' obtaining the wallet. Selection C is wrong because the age of the offenders has no bearing on whether a theft is considered a larceny or a robbery.

40. B   Selection A is incorrect because Tom Bessinger's method of operation is not considered force or the threat of force, particularly when the victim is unaware of the theft in the first place. Selection C is wrong because the reading didn't stipulate if there was cash or credit cards involved. Additionally, the taking of cash or credit cards from the person of another is, by itself, not a definition of robbery according to the passage. Selection D is incorrect because a crime did take place; it just wasn't discovered or reported immediately.

41. D   RCO 41.57.011 accounts for inmate Halverson's unexcused absence from his assigned work detail; RCO 57.41.089 accounts for his direct refusal to return to his assigned work detail; RCO 71.83.611 accounts for his cursing Officer McClary.

          Selection A is wrong in the respect that there were three code infractions, not just one, that could be considered by an Adjustment Committee Hearing in determining appropriate disciplinary measures.

42. D   Since inmate Preston initiated the assault, irrespective of the reasons given, he can be charged with code infraction RCO 97.42.123. He can also be charged for gambling, which is code infraction RCO 06.15.777.

43. C   Inmate Jacobs cannot be charged with code infraction RCO 97.42.123 because of the aspect of self-defense. However, he can still be charged for gambling, which is infraction code RCO 06.15.777.

44. B   Selection D is only half right by stating that inmate Kessler can be charged with refusing to submit to drug screening (RCO 18.60.807) in addition to the attempted assault on Officer Peterson (RCO 07.49.712). But the full extent to which inmate Kessler could be charged would also include the refusal to obey a lawful order (RCO 57.41.089) and the verbal abuse aspect directed toward Officer Peterson (RCO 71.83.611).

45. A   RCO 58.55.119, RCO 18.80.692, RCO 17.65.766, RCO 01.96.870, and RCO 97.42.123, respectively, represent the alleged offenses committed by inmate Charles. The remaining selections are only partially correct.

46. D   The notation was made that chapter numbers greater than 40 but less than 70 represented serious prison infractions. Therefore, the two infractions given in selection D would represent the misdemeanor offenses involved. Selections A and C are only half right.

47. C   Inmate Zimmerman can be charged with bribery, which is code infraction RCO 13.62.895.

48. C   Inmate Branstad is guilty of persuading inmate Zimmerman to bribe Officer Winston for illicit gain. However, he cannot be directly charged with attempted bribery as asserted by selection B. Only RCO 17.05.669 would be applicable.

49. B   Inmate Rodgers is guilty of aiding and abetting (i.e., conspiring with inmate Austin in the incident described), manufacturing an intoxicant, and falsely accusing another inmate of the crime. Selection C falls short by not including the charge of Rodgers's attempting to lay blame on another for his own actions.

50. B   The key word in this question is *serious*. Inmate Austin is guilty of both code infractions RCO 17.05.669 and RCO 14.64.142, but only the latter offense is considered to be serious.

51. *D* Officer Pratt's actions obviously jeopardize the safety and security of the facility. Initially confronting Officer Pratt about the problem in an unthreatening manner will most likely remedy the situation. If not, then an immediate supervisor should be appraised of the potential security breach. Selections A and C would only serve to create friction between those affected and, in all likelihood, make the problem worse than it already is. It is imperative that officers never resort to what is suggested in selection B. Such incidents are perceived by inmates as a flagrant sign of weakness and an erosion of supervisory capacity, a situation that is sure to be exploited by some.

52. *C* Keeping your word within the limits of your authority is important. If such a request is handled in any of the other ways suggested, apart from selection C, it can almost be assured that those affected would become resentful and angry. Managing such prisoners would, without doubt, become much more difficult.

53. *B* Selection B is the best approach because what may be perceived as an obvious theft may, in fact, be an authorized action. The coworker in question may have been given permission to take certain material home for a promotional exam or some other form of self-improvement study, just to name a couple of possibilities. Jumping to any such conclusions, without finding out the facts first, could lead to an embarrassing end.

54. *B* Selection B pretty much sums up the consequences for his sharing confidence with various inmates. Corrections Officers should be friendly toward inmates, but not familiar. That degree of impartiality maintains the supervisory relationship.

55. *C* Despite the fact that inmate Olson has been a model prisoner, any form of favoritism toward inmates is expressly forbidden. There are other social service workers within Corrections or the judicial system who can serve as appropriate liaisons for such information.

56. *C* Doing what is stated in selection C places the onus on the inmate as to how he or she prefers to have the situation handled. One way or another, he or she will be transferred to the other unit. Leaving the immediate area to notify a supervisor about the situation accomplishes one of two things. First, it provides a brief cooling-off period where tensions can subside a bit; and secondly, the involvement of a supervisor with necessary backup reinforces the fact that there will be consequences to pay for noncompliance. Handling the matters as suggested in selection B would, in effect, further reinforce negative behavior, thereby making future management particularly difficult. Selection D is relatively premature for the situation at hand, not to mention potentially hazardous without adequate backup. As much as it may be tempting for some Corrections Officers to do, selection A is an unrealistic notion.

57. *A* While selection B does have merit, all suicide threats need to be taken seriously. Second-guessing potential manipulation if, after the fact, an inmate commits suicide is on the same order as closing the barn door after the horse has already escaped. No amount of re-examining the situation will bring the inmate back to life. Therefore, all appropriate measures to reduce the likelihood of the inmate carrying out his threat should be taken. This, however, does not include the means suggested by selection C. If an inmate were to successfully coerce an officer under such circumstances, it would most assuredly open up the prospect for future manipulation. Selection D is tantamount to condoning suicide, which is obviously an unacceptable means of handling such threats.

58. *B* Contrary to what selection A implies, Officer Benning is, in fact, accepting bribes. Regardless of how innocent it may appear, such actions open potential avenues for future exploitation and manipulation by inmates. Officer Wilmont's intercession at this point is sufficient, providing the practice is no longer continued. Otherwise, selection C would be the next best step. Selection D essentially amounts to gossip, which, at best, would invariably tarnish the man's reputation among coworkers. The professional approach to handling such a matter is described in selection B.

59. *D* Regardless of your position and the apparent uneasiness of expressing a criticism toward a superior, prison rules are meant to be abided by everyone. You can tactfully remind the offending officer of that fact and then request that he immediately desist from such actions. Otherwise, a report of the continuing violations to his commanding officer would be in order.

60. *C* The relationship should be divulged to an immediate superior because of the potential conflict of interest. Transferring the friend to another area outside of your custodial responsibilities would be the most appropriate step taken. Selection A would be blatant favoritism, which other inmates would come to resent. Selection B would almost be impossible considering the close contact officers have with inmates. Selection D would, without question, be the biggest mistake, particularly if certain inmates did not like you personally. This frustration may carry over by your "taking it out" on your friend. Despite well-meaning intentions, you may very well have jeopardized his safety.

61. *A* Arguable

62. *A* Supporting

63. *B* Elated

64. *B* Uprightness

65. *B* Strive

66. *A* Glaring

67. *D* Widespread

68. *A* Gloomy

69. *B* Querulous

70. *C* Destitute

71. *B* Immaterial

72. *B* Excellent

73. *A* Tactical

74. *C* Confusion

75. *A* Beaten

76. *C* Illegal

77. *D* Proceeded

78. *B* Receive

79. *D* Supervisor

80. *D* Robbery

81. B   The word *to* that follows the word *spread* should be spelled *too,* which is an adverb indicating "in addition." *Percieved* is misspelled as well. It should be *perceived.* Remember the basic rule: *i* before *e* except after *c.*

82. A   Since *areas* is plural, it needs to be followed by *have been* instead of *has been.*

83. A   This statement is confusing due to a misplaced modifier. The statement would be better structured by placing *for* prior to *their parents.*

84. B   *Affect* is a verb that means "to act upon." *Effect* is a noun that means "something produced by an agency or cause."

85. D   This statement is grammatically correct in every way.

86. B   *Elude* means "to escape or avoid." *Allude* means to "refer to indirectly."

87. C   A comma should have been placed after *others.*

88. B   Labratory should be spelled *laboratory.*

89. C   Apostrophes need to be placed before an *s* in *attorneys* to indicate possession (*attorney's*).

90. A   *They're* is an improperly used contraction meaning "they are." *Their* is also wrong since it is plural where singular is needed. Replacing *they're* with *his* or *her* would render the statement grammatically correct.

91. D   This statement is grammatically correct in every way.

92. B   The words *judgement* and *competant* are both misspelled. The correct spellings are *judgment* and *competent.*

93. C   Since 10,000 total offenses were reported and, according to the Crime Index, aggravated assault accounts for 17% of the total cases, you should simply multiply 0.17 by 10,000 to get the answer: 1,700.

94. B   First, it is necessary to figure how many seconds there are in one hour. Since there are 60 seconds per minute and 60 minutes per hour, there are 3600 seconds per hour. Then, just divide the time factor given for each crime into 3600 to arrive at the answer. Therefore,

   3600 divided by 45 = 80 robberies
   3600 divided by 10 = 360 burglaries
   3600 divided by 27 = 133 aggravated assaults

95. C   Since it is known that 245 responses represent 92% of the total calls (i.e., 100% - 8% = 92%), we can set up the following proportion to determine how many calls were received for the month altogether:

   $92 \div 100 = 245 \div X$; $92X = 24,500$; $X = 266$ calls

96. B   If domestic filings were up 32% for the year, 132% = 231, and 100% = $100/132 \times 231 = 175$ cases. If the gain in juvenile filings was up 41% for the year, 141% = 163, and 100% = $100/141 \times 163 = 115.6$, or 116 cases.

97. B   To determine what the percentage of the total annual caseload is in crimes against property, the individual caseloads for each applicable crime must first be added together: 14 + 312 + 720 + 1320 + 674 + 32 + 62 + 520 = 3,654 cases involving crimes against property. This figure is then divided by the total number of all criminal cases handled for the year and then multiplied by 100 to express the number found as a percentage. Therefore,

$$\frac{3654 \text{ crimes against property cases}}{4968 \text{ total criminal cases handled}} \times 100 = 73.55$$

or approximately 74%.

98. *B* Since the goal is to trim the homicide rate by 15% over a 2-year period, this translates into a 7.5% annual reduction (i.e., 15% divided by 2 years = 7.5%). Therefore, since there were 42 murders for the year, 42 × .075 = 3.15, we can safely say the commission hopes for approximately 4 fewer murders per year. It is important to note that we should not round off to 3.0 because the .15 does represent a tangible amount that must be accounted for.

99. *A* Forcible rape would constitute the second highest number of man-hours used per case. Therefore, divide the number of forcible rape cases by the total annual caseload of all crimes and multiply the resulting number by 100 to express it as a percentage.

$$\frac{52 \text{ cases of forcible rape}}{4968 \text{ total cases handled for the year}} \times 100 = 1\%$$

100. *B* Compton Prison had 39 fewer reported cases of contraband possession in 1996 than in 1995. To figure what percentage this difference corresponds to, we need to divide 39 by 252 and then multiply it by 100. Therefore,

$$39 \div 252 = 0.15476$$
$$0.15476 \times 100 = 15.476\%, \text{ or } 15.5\% \text{ when rounded off.}$$

101. *A* Ridgeview Adult Detention

Fullerton Corrections had 4 more cases involving trustee-status revocations in 1996 when compared to 1995. Therefore, 4 ÷ 14 × 100 = 28.57% increase.

Compton Prison had 15 more cases involving trustee-status revocations in 1996 when compared to 1995. Therefore, 5 ÷ 32 × 100 = 46.87% increase.

Ridgeview Adult Detention had 2 more cases involving trustee-status revocation in 1996 when compared to 1995. Therefore, 2 ÷ 1 × 100 = 200% increase.

102. *D* Since there were 14 reported cases of violence between inmates in Fullerton Corrections during 1995, we can figure the number of reported cases of violence between inmates in 1997 by setting up the problem as shown. Assume reported cases of violence between inmates in 1997 = X.

$$\frac{X}{\text{Reported cases of violence between inmates in 1995}} = 450\% \text{ or } 4.5$$

Therefore,

$$\frac{X-14}{14} = 4.5$$
$$X - 14 = 63$$

$$X = 77 \text{ reported cases of violence between inmates in 1997.}$$

103. *C* Group Therapy (i.e., I) was apparently the least effective rehabilitative measure used by the prisons under study. Inmates who were "rehabilitated" through this means more often than not demonstrated a higher recidivism rate as opposed to the other therapeutic options given.

104. *B* Vocational Rehabilitation (III) represents a trend, particularly over the last three years of the study, which is indicative of having the most impact on recidivism rates. Work Release rehabilitation actually had a significant short-term improvement in 1994, but overall, Vocational Rehabilitation consistently demonstrated better (i.e., lower) recidivism rates.

105. *B*   336 inmates. According to the survey, there was a 40% recidivism rate for those inmates who received psychiatric treatment as a form of rehabilitation prior to release. Therefore, 840 × .40 = 336 inmates reoffended and were consequently convicted and returned to prison.

106. *D*   In descending order: Lacerations, abrasions, and puncture wounds account for 22% of the total caseload; fractures and dislocations account for 18% of the total caseload; and allergies and respiratory problems account for 15% of the total caseload. Taken together, these three classifications comprise 55% of the total caseload given (22% + 18% + 15% = 55%).

107. *C*   On the basis of a patient count of 100 inmates and the fact that 14% of those are suffering from a sexually transmitted disease, that would mean there are 14 inmates with STDs (i.e., 100 × .14 = 14). If half of those inmates are affected by AIDS, that would mean that 7 inmates are afflicted with the illness and its associated complications (i.e., 14 × .50 = 7).

108. *C*   On the basis of a patient count of 100 inmates and the fact that 9% of those are burn cases, that would mean there are 9 inmates with varying degrees of burns (100 × .09 = 9). If approximately 44% of those inmates are suffering from second-degree burns, that would mean 4 inmates are coping with burns of that severity (i.e., 9 × .44 = 3.96 or 4).

109. *C*   YTV is an inaccurate translation of 726 according to the number-letter key given. It should be 726 - YTW.

110. *B*   The first five numbers of selection B are accurately translated. The remaining choices have fewer first numbers that have been correctly coded.

111. *A*   18, 36, 48, 48, 24, 18, 42, 6, 36, 30, 12 represents the word *Corrections* according to the letter-number key provided.

112. *D*   14, 19, 20, 15, 16, 11, 15, 13, 12, 15, 18, 17 represents the word *jurisdiction* according to the letter-number key provided.

113. *A*   July, August, January, March, December, September, February, and May—or 07, 08, 01, 03, 12, 09, 02, and 05—would be properly coded as 5, 55, 10, 40, 80, 35, 20, 30, according to the key given. Selection C correctly identifies the months in question in numerical form, but fails to translate that into a coded sequence.

114. *C*   November, April, October, June, and March—or 11, 04, 10, 06, and 03—would be properly coded as 15, 25, 45, 60, 40, according to the key in the previous question.

115. *B*   N, O, P, Q, R, S can correctly be coded as 14, 16, 7, 22, 21, 8. There are, of course, other codes that would suffice as well; however, this was the only correct option provided.

116. *D*   12, 2, 10, 22, 16, 5, 8 correctly represents R, S, O, Q, O, O, S.

    16, 23, 4, 9, 1, 10, 13, 7 correctly represents O, Q, Q, P, N, O, Q, P.

    The remaining codes are properly translated.

117. *C*   Criminal traffic

118. *D*   Rental vehicle

119. *C*   March 16, 1996 / Polk County

120. *B*   Mr. Sanchez was clocked doing 92 miles per hour in a 65 mile-per-hour zone. Therefore, 92 − 65 = 27 miles per hour over and beyond the posted speed limit.

121. *A*   Nebraska

122. *C*   March 15, 1968

123. *A*   Mr. Sanchez was originally sentenced to 90 days for the pair of violations. Sixty days were suspended, and he was given credit for having already spent 2 days in jail. Therefore, the time remaining would be 28 days.

124. *D*   1997

125. *D*   The defendant's home address was shown to be 423 Crestview Drive, Grand Island, NE 65721. Selection D, on the other hand, is the business address for Budget Rental in Omaha, NE.

Test Ratings are as follows:

120–125 correct — Excellent
113–119 correct — Very good
106–112 correct — Good
100–105 correct — Fair
99 or fewer correct — Unsatisfactory

Go back to each question you missed and determine if the question was just misinterpreted for one reason or another, or if your response reflects a weakness in the subject matter. If it is a matter of misinterpretation, try reading the question slower while paying particular attention to key words such as *not, least, except, without,* etc. If, on the other hand, you determine a weakness in a certain area, do not despair, because that is what this study guide is for: to identify any area of weakness before you take the actual exam. Reread the material on the area of concern in this study guide. If you still feel a need for supplemental material, your local library is an excellent source.

Chapter 10

Physical Fitness

With the physical demands that law enforcement may entail, it is not hard to understand why Corrections Departments require employees to be in top physical shape. In-station tasks require little exertion; however, when Corrections Officers are called to active duty, the switch from a sedentary pace to substantial physical exertion is stressful. This is particularly true for someone who is out of shape. The job may demand running, climbing, jumping, twisting, pulling, and lifting. The difficulty is also compounded by the fact that work may be performed under extreme temperatures and/or in poor-quality air. A Corrections Officer must be physically able to respond to these conditions while always being careful of his or her own safety. This is the primary reason Corrections Departments/Academies place an emphasis on physical fitness exams.

As mentioned in the introduction, physical fitness exams can be quite varied. What one department considers suitable may be considered inadequate by another. The point of the matter is that all physical ability tests are designed specifically to measure strength, stamina, and flexibility. How these capabilities are determined lies solely with the department you have applied to, since there is no nationally recognized standard. Try to ascertain in advance what will be expected by the department you are interested in and then practice these events in trial runs as best you can prior to the actual exam. It is better to learn of potential weaknesses beforehand rather than to fall short during a timed event and perform poorly or, worse, fail the test altogether. There should be no reason to let this job opportunity slip away simply because of physical unpreparedness. Approach this part of the screening process in the same manner as you do the written exam. By practicing the following suggested workout schedule, not only will you get in better shape, but you will be able to approach the physical fitness exam with the same degree of confidence and sense of ease as you do the written exam.

Before charging into any fitness workout, however, it is suggested that you visit your family doctor and get a complete medical evaluation. This will be a precondition to your employment with Corrections, a way to determine if any disease or physical condition may impair your ability to perform. (For further reference, see the section on medical evaluation at the beginning of this guide.) If, in fact, you do have a condition that potentially warrants rejection from employment consideration, consult your doctor — he or she may be able to prescribe treatment through a change of diet, specialized workout, medication, or surgery to correct the problem.

Inform your physician of your intentions concerning any kind of physical workout. No two people are the same; workout schedules vary. The guidelines provided in this book are just that — guidelines. Your doctor is better able to tailor a training program that will benefit you. Keep your doctor's advice in mind while you prepare for the exam.

Prior to actually taking the physical abilities test, you will be asked to either sign a liability waiver or fill out some form of medical questionnaire. The latter involves a wide range of questions relating to your present state of health. This kind of information will allow examiners to make an educated decision as to whether such an exam poses a health risk to a test candidate. Be truthful in filling out such a questionnaire because this is one more element that is cross-checked in a routine background investigation. Falsifying any information is grounds enough to disqualify an applicant.

Despite the variation seen in physical fitness exams, it can be generally assumed that three kinds of physical attributes are being scrutinized during these exams: flexibility, cardiovascular fitness, and muscular strength and endurance. Each of these areas uses different groups of muscles, and the exercises suggested below for each will improve them. However, it is important to realize that prior to any exercise there are preliminaries that can help to prevent injury.

RELAXATION AND WARM-UP ROUTINE

The first thing to do before starting any rigorous exercise is a relaxation and warm-up routine, which involves the head roll, paced breathing, and shoulder shrugs.

For the head roll, you can either stand, sit, or kneel. Allow your head to go limp and roll it around your neck two or three times in one direction and then two or three times in the other direction. It helps to close your eyes during this exercise to prevent any dizziness or loss of balance. Try to conduct this exercise slowly and smoothly.

Paced breathing involves lying on your back and placing your hands on your stomach. Concentrate on your breathing by paying close attention to how far your chest rises during each inhalation. Breathe evenly and slowly, and relax for about one minute during this exercise.

The third relaxation exercise is shoulder shrugs. Again, lie on your back. Simply pull your shoulders upward and maintain that position for a few seconds before allowing your shoulders to return slowly to their original position. Try to coordinate your breathing so that you inhale while pulling your shoulders up and exhale when your shoulders drop. Perform this exercise for approximately one minute.

FLEXIBILITY EXERCISES

Stretching exercises are important, too, because they prepare tendons and ligaments for further stretching and increase the flow of fluid around various joints. The whole concept is based on smooth, even, and slow motion. This kind of exercise is not intended to be conducted in fast or jerky movements.

The back stretch or swivel is the first flexibility exercise to do. Stand and, with your arms at your sides, try to lean as far forward as possible. Then, lean as far backward as you can. Repeat this exercise at least four times in both directions. Now, to limber up your back for bending sideways, remain standing, turn your head to the right, and slide your right hand down the length of your right leg as far as possible. Do this exercise at least four times on the right side and then four times on the left side.

To stretch the quadriceps (thigh muscles), stand and lean against a wall using your left hand as support. Reach behind with your right hand and lift your right leg up so that you can grasp your toes. Slowly pull your heel closer to your buttocks until the thigh feels stretched. Maintain this position for approximately five seconds. Repeat this exercise four times with the right leg before doing the same with the left leg.

To stretch the calf muscles in your leg, remain standing within arm's length of the wall. While facing the wall, keep your feet flat on the ground (do not allow your heels to lift) and allow yourself to lean forward for a few seconds. Push off against the wall to return to the starting position. Repeat this exercise three or four times with each leg.

Now, while sitting on the floor with your legs spread apart and the back of your legs flat on the floor (your knees should not lift), slide both hands as far down the leg as possible. Hold this position for a few seconds before sitting erect again. Repeat this exercise three or four times and then do the same for the other leg. This exercise stretches both back and hamstring muscles.

Remain in the sitting position and cross your legs, putting the soles of your feet together. Now, lean forward as far as possible and hold this position for a few seconds before sitting erect again. Repeat this exercise three or four times. This exercise stretches the groin muscles.

To stretch the hips, remain in the sitting position with your legs straight. Now, take your right leg and cross it over the left leg. Take the knee of the right leg and slowly bring it up to your chest. Hold that position for three to four seconds and then repeat this exercise twice more. Do the same with the left leg.

The final exercise involves stretching chest, shoulder, and back muscles. While kneeling, place your palms on the floor and then slowly slide both hands forward until your elbows touch the floor. Keep your head and back straight during this exercise. Return to your starting position and repeat this exercise three or four times.

Remember, the whole point of these exercises is to stretch various muscles. If you force a muscle to extend too far, pulling or tearing can occur, defeating the purpose of stretching and, possibly, incurring injury. Stretch various muscles only to the point of mild sensation, hold for a few seconds, and then relax. This procedure has the effect of increasing flexibility and loosening muscles for other exercises.

The last preliminary needed before any exercise is a cardiorespiratory warm-up. This simply involves conducting an exercise that is not too stressful, such as brisk walking or slow jogging for a few minutes. This allows the heart rate to increase gradually and prepares the heart for vigorous exercise. To prevent potential injury, a warm-up routine should always be done before any stressful exercise.

CARDIOVASCULAR FITNESS

Cardiovascular fitness has to do with your heart and lung capacity. As both of these organs become more fit, your body's ability to transport oxygen to its cells improves. Another beneficial result is that the heart beats less quickly, but pumps with greater strength—or, in other words, works more efficiently. There is also a corresponding increase in the peripheral circulatory system, thereby making it easier for various cells to absorb oxygen.

The best way to achieve cardiovascular endurance is to employ what physiologists call *aerobic exercise*. This may come in one of four forms: running, swimming, bicycling, or walking. When any of these forms of exercise is conducted fairly rigorously for approximately twenty-five minutes three times a week, cardiovascular endurance will improve. The key point here is to exercise at a moderate intensity, nonstop, for the full twenty-five minutes. Less time makes the exercise much less useful. That is why sports such as baseball, tennis, or basketball do not suffice. These sports require tremendous energy output some of the time; however, there are breaks in between. To be effective, the exercise has to be conducted for twenty-five *consecutive* minutes, stopping only to check your pulse.

To calibrate your progress using aerobics, physiologists have come up with a pulse-rated system. Your pulse measures the number of times your heart beats per minute. As your cardiovascular endurance improves, your heart beats less quickly when subjected to stress. To measure your pulse, simply apply one or two of your fingers (not your thumb) to the front of your neck next to the larynx and feel for the carotid artery. The pulse should be fairly obvious there. Be careful not to press too hard on this artery because unconsciousness may result, particularly after exercise. Count the number of times your heart beats within ten seconds and then multiply that number by six. This will provide you with an accurate assessment of your pulse. When performing a rigorous exercise for twenty-five minutes, stop after the first ten minutes to briefly take your pulse (ten seconds) and then immediately resume the exercise.

Intermix the four events of running, swimming, bicycling, and walking in your training. This helps to alleviate boredom and perpetuates the desire to continue training. When your twenty-five minutes of exercise are completed, it is necessary to follow it with a cool-down period. Walk or jog slowly for five to ten minutes. The general idea is to permit your body to return to its normal condition gradually. This cool-down can be followed by a few stretching exercises as well.

MUSCULAR STRENGTH AND ENDURANCE

Strength development can be accomplished by weight training and calisthenics. Both improve muscular endurance through repetitive movement, but do so in different ways. Calisthenics essentially uses exercises that employ your own body weight to serve as resistance. On the other hand, weight training involves lifting progressively heavier weights or resistances in the form of barbells or variable-resistance weight-training equipment.

CALISTHENICS

Calisthenics, like cardiovascular endurance exercises, need to be preceded by relaxation, stretching, and warm-up exercises. A daily routine of push-ups, sit-ups, pull-ups, leg lifts, and squats should be conducted over a period of fifteen to twenty-five minutes. Start out doing fifteen repetitions of each exercise and then work your way up to thirty. Don't expect this to occur overnight. Regularity is the key. Your persistence will reward you with greater strength within three to four weeks. Descriptions of each exercise follow.

Push-ups

Lie on your abdomen on the floor and place your hands, palms down, beneath your chest. As you extend your arms and push off from the floor, be sure to keep your back and knees straight. Once your arms are fully extended, lower yourself to the floor slowly and repeat the exercise.

Sit-ups

Lie on your back on the floor and either place your feet beneath a sofa or other heavy object, or have someone restrain your feet from lifting. Your knees should be straight and flat. With your hands locked behind your head, sit up and attempt to touch your knees with your elbows without lifting your knees. Do not try to force yourself to extend beyond what is comfortable. Stretch as far as possible and then return to the starting position to repeat.

Pull-ups

Use a chinning bar that is just a few inches higher than your highest reach when you are standing up and your arms are extended overhead. Using an overhand grip on the bar, raise yourself to the point where you bring your chin level with the bar. Try not to kick or swing while raising yourself. Lower yourself slowly to the starting position and repeat.

Leg Lifts

Lie on the floor on your right side with your legs kept straight and in line with one another. Use your left arm to gain support from the floor to prevent rollover. Lift your left leg as far as possible before returning to the starting position. Repeat this exercise a minimum of fifteen times before changing sides and doing the same exercise with the other leg.

Squats

In the standing position, extend your arms forward and then squat until your thighs are parallel to the ground. Return to the standing position and repeat the exercise.

WEIGHT TRAINING

Weight training, when done correctly, significantly increases muscular strength and endurance. However, three things should always be kept in mind before starting any kind of weight-training routine. Supervision by either a professional weight-training assistant or someone to act as a safety person during your lifts is essential, which is particularly true while bench-pressing barbells. The second consideration is always to begin light and progressively increase the weight you lift as you become stronger. Starting heavy is an open invitation to injuring muscle tissue instead of building it. The third consideration is to conduct a weight-training routine only three times per week at the maximum. Keep the number of repetitions to only three sets of ten. Doing more will tend to increase bulk rather than strength. If the repetitions seem fairly easy initially, increase the weight load by five or ten pounds at a time. Continue this progressive addition of weight as your strength improves. Following are exercises that concentrate on developing muscles needed most for Corrections Officer fitness exams: chest, shoulder, arm, and back.

Bench Press

For safety reasons, it is better to use bench press equipment rather than free weights. Whichever is available, lie on your back and grip the bar with both hands at shoulder width. Begin with light weights, as mentioned earlier, and lift or press the bar in a direction directly perpendicular to the chest by extending your arms. Try not to lock your elbows when fully extended. Slowly lower the bar to your chest and repeat the exercise.

Arm Curls

While standing, preferably with your back to a wall, allow your arms to be fully extended downward. Grasp the barbell with an underhand grip, with hands spaced shoulder width. Raise the barbell to your chest without allowing your elbows to move from your side. Lower the barbell to the starting position and repeat.

Half Squats

This is similar to squat calisthenics. The difference is that a barbell rests on the back of your neck while it is supported by both hands at shoulder width. As the weight is steadied on your shoulders, conduct squat repetitions as described under calisthenics.

Bent-over Rows

Begin in the standing position with the weight bar on the floor directly in front of you. While keeping your legs straight, lean over the barbell in such a way that your back becomes parallel to the floor. With an overhand grip, grasp the weight bar with both hands spaced shoulder width apart and lift the weight to your chest. Try to keep your back straight (i.e., parallel to the floor) and your head up while attempting the lift. Return the weight to the floor and repeat the exercise.

Chapter 11

The Oral Board

Once you have reached this point in the selection process, you will want to bear a few things in mind about the oral board. You will be notified by mail of the time and place of the interview. Pay particular attention to the date and become familiar in advance with the location of the interview. One sure way to disqualify yourself from serious consideration is to show up late for the interview.

Appearance is also important. Most people are told not to judge others by outward appearance; however, interviewers gain a distinct impression from the manner in which a candidate dresses. If an applicant is not well groomed (e.g., unshaven, hair uncombed), interviewers perceive that candidate, before so much as asking one question, as inattentive and somewhat sloppy. Even though the candidate may be the most hardworking and concerned person among those being interviewed, he or she will, in all likelihood, be passed over for another with a better appearance. First impressions are just as important as how you respond to questions asked by the interviewers. Therefore, be well groomed for the occasion and dress neatly. For men, this would entail a nice shirt (tie is optional), slacks, and a pair of dress shoes. For women, an attractive blouse, dress pants (or suit, or skirt, or a conservative dress), and dress shoes would be appropriate.

Also avoid smoking or chewing gum prior to or during an oral board; habits like these can create a poor appearance. The whole idea is to put your best foot forward to indicate you are the most enthusiastic and best-qualified candidate for the job. Contrary to what some applicants may think, outward appearance is very important. For the limited amount of time an interview board spends with a test applicant, all things become relevant, including the smallest details.

The interview itself is normally conducted by a board of three to five people. Most interview panels consist of Corrections Department officials or Civil Service personnel. Occasionally, people outside the Corrections Department and Civil Service are brought in to avoid potential bias on the board.

Ideally, those conducting the interview and the applicant being interviewed are complete strangers to one another. This way, a candidate who is not hired cannot discredit the selection process on the basis of bias or favoritism. Board members are also made aware that race, sex, color, creed, and political background have no bearing on these proceedings. Each interviewer has a rating sheet listing specific qualifications. The series of questions provides the interviewers with enough insight to accurately gauge the applicant's potential capabilities. Usually the beginning of the interview will focus attention on your job application form. Such things as your educational background, past employment history, and references are examined. It would behoove you to review everything you listed on your application form and have supportive reasoning for any career changes. If you can somehow demonstrate that the direction you took was based on the underlying aspiration to work in criminal justice, so much the better. However, do not deceive the panel regarding past choices. Chances are that if you do, you may contradict yourself at one point or another, and this will become immediately evident to the interviewers. The best policy here is to answer all questions honestly, even if some past decisions were not necessarily the best ones. If you feel that you have made a questionable career move or have had a falling-out with one or more past employers, explain why. If you can also show that something was learned or gained from the experience, point that out as well. Interviewers will appreciate your honesty and sincerity. A history of frequently switching jobs or changing careers without just cause is usually reason enough not to be hired.

While you are being interviewed in these areas of concern, interviewers will be assessing your communications skills and how well you respond to the questioning. It is well understood that oral boards are stressful to applicants. However, if an applicant appears excessively fidgety or worried or perspires profusely, and such nervousness encumbers the applicant's ability to answer questions, it can detract from what otherwise would have been a good interview. Advance preparation for the interview should help in this regard. Knowing (in general) the kinds of questions interviewers most likely will ask enhances your confidence. Beside further expounding on information given on the application form, questions such as the following are equally important:

- Why do you want to become a Corrections Officer?

- Why should you be hired over other similarly qualified applicants?

- Now that we know your strong points, what are your weaknesses?

- If you had to do everything over, what would you do differently?

- Do you have any regrets for anything in the past?

- What, if anything, do you feel are major accomplishments or achievements in your life?

- How do you feel you can help the community by working in Corrections?

These and a myriad of other questions are thought provoking. If you are prepared for such questioning, you will be better able to answer these questions in a satisfactory manner, rather than pausing at length to think of something. Simply answering *yes* or *no* is not sufficient. Supportive reasoning, even if it is brief, is what interviewers want to hear.

The interview will also focus on what your interests or hobbies are, as well as your attitudes toward particular job requirements. For instance,

- Why do you like to hunt, swim, bike, camp, etc.?

- Couldn't you have used your leisure time for better purposes?

- Do you do any extracurricular reading? If so, what?

- Do you keep current with local events by reading the paper?

- How do you feel about working irregular hours?

- Do you respond to criticism in a positive manner?

- Have you ever displayed your temper with coworkers at past jobs?

- What do you think of drugs and alcohol, both in the workplace and at home?

- Are you afraid of dying, heights, or speaking in front of large groups of people?

- How do you feel about using lethal force against another person when necessary?

Having prepared answers to these questions and others of a similar nature will definitely give you an edge over those who aren't prepared. Try to think of as many questions about your life as possible and prepare some reasoning to support your answers. You may be caught off guard by a few questions, but overall your preparation will pay off.

One other form the interview may take may concern your reaction to hypothetical circumstances or emergencies. It is not expected that you will have advanced knowledge of any specialized law-enforcement training. However, this kind of question can give interviewers insight into how well you can quickly reason and solve a problem. You may be given certain conditions to work within and then be expected to show how you would bring the situation under control.

These kinds of questions are obviously more difficult to prepare for, but two things are important to keep in mind. First, the safety of both Corrections personnel and the victim or member of the public involved is a primary consideration. Second, nearly everything Corrections personnel do should be part of a team effort. Consider these two things during any questioning. Interviewers will describe some situation and may very well throw in some constraints that may make the situation worse. Whatever is given, think the question through as best you can and decide how you would handle the circumstances. Immediate answers to questions of this nature without much forethought are bound to be incomplete and show poor judgment. Interviewers will observe how well you can assimilate information and identify specific problem areas. Your initiative and leadership beyond what is minimally necessary are other factors assessed.

If your interview is more in line with this kind of questioning, answer to the best of your ability and see the exercise through to the end. Whatever you do, don't become exasperated with the situation given and give up. Remember, the interviewers know that they are placing you in a very stressful position. Reacting in an appropriate and confident manner bodes well for your employment consideration.

When the interview is winding to a close, one of the panel members will ask you if you have any questions or concerns regarding Corrections. If you feel that you have other positive qualities that were not discussed during the interview, now is the time to mention them briefly. If you have some specific concerns regarding the department, this is the appropriate time to ask. Since there are other candidates to be interviewed, do not protract your own interview beyond a few minutes after the interviewers ask you for any further comments. Rambling on about something longer than necessary is viewed with disdain. Be brief with your questions if you have any and then thank each interviewer for his or her time and consideration.

Don't loiter after the interview to see how well you did. It will be another week or two before all things are considered and decisions are made with regard to hiring.

If you later learn you did not fare as well in the interview as you expected, don't become upset and write the experience off as though the examiners made the mistake. Rather, find out where your weaknesses were and learn from the experience. That way, on a follow-up interview to another exam, you will not make the same mistakes. It can also be said that a candidate who goes through the testing and selection process more than once is very determined. That attribute is looked upon favorably by any department because it shows that the applicant is truly dedicated to becoming a Corrections Officer. More often than not, these are candidates that departments seek to hire. There may be a few disappointments along the way to being hired; however, hard work and persistence are two key virtues that are prerequisites to a fulfilling career in criminal justice.

Refund Policy

In the unlikely event that you use this book but score less than 80 percent on the Corrections Officer examination, your money will be refunded for the retail price printed on the book. This guarantee specifically applies to the written exam, not the physical agility test, if required; psychological test; medical exam; or oral board. If a test applicant scores above 80 percent on the written test, but fails the aforementioned portions of the exam, he or she will not be eligible for a refund.

The following conditions must be met before any refund will be made. All exercises in this guide must be completed to demonstrate that the applicant did make a real attempt to practice and prepare to score 80 percent or better. Any refund must be claimed within ninety days of the date of purchase shown on your sales receipt. Anything submitted beyond this ninety-day period will be subject to the publisher's discretion.

If you mail this study guide back for a refund, please include your sales receipt, validated test results,* and a self-addressed, stamped envelope. Requests for refunds should be addressed to Adams Media, Customer Service, 57 Littlefield Street, Avon, MA 02322. Please allow approximately four weeks for processing.

---

* On occasion, exam results are not mailed to the test applicant. Test scores may be posted at either the Corrections Department or the place of examination. If this is the case for you, procure a copy of your test score from the personnel office and be sure your name and address are indicated (Social Security numbers are insufficient to claim a refund).